MOBILITY, MARKETS AND INDIGENOUS SOCIALITIES

Exploring how people from Andean communities seek progress and social mobility by moving to the cities, Cecilie Vindal Ødegaard demonstrates the changing significance of kinship, reciprocity and ritual in an urban context. Through a focus on people's involvement in land occupations and local associations, labour and trade, Ødegaard examines the dialectics between popular practices and neoliberal state policies in processes of urbanization. The making and un-making of notions of the indigenous, communal work, and gender is central in this analysis, and is discussed against the historical backdrop of the land occupations in Peruvian cities since the 1930s.

Through its close ethnographic description of everyday life in a new urban neighbourhood, this book reveals how social and spatial categories and boundaries are continually negotiated in people's quest for mobility and progress. Ødegaard argues that conventional meanings of prosperity and progress are significantly altered in interaction with Andean understandings of reciprocity. By combining a unique ethnographic account with original theoretical arguments, the book provides new insight into the cultural, cosmological and political dimensions of mobility, progress and market participation.

AF695778

VITALITY OF INDIGENOUS RELIGIONS

Series Editors

Graham Harvey, Open University, UK
Afeosemime Adogame, University of Edinburgh, UK
Ines Talamantez, University of California, USA

Ashgate's *Vitality of Indigenous Religions* series offers an exciting new cluster of research monographs, drawing together volumes from leading international scholars across a wide range of disciplinary perspectives. Indigenous religions are vital and empowering for many thousands of indigenous peoples globally, and dialogue with, and consideration of, these diverse religious life-ways promises to challenge and refine the methodologies of a number of academic disciplines, whilst greatly enhancing understandings of the world.

This series explores the development of contemporary indigenous religions from traditional, ancestral precursors, but the characteristic contribution of the series is its focus on their living and current manifestations. Devoted to the contemporary expression, experience and understanding of particular indigenous peoples and their religions, books address key issues which include: the sacredness of land, exile from lands, diasporic survival and diversification, the indigenization of Christianity and other missionary religions, sacred language, and re-vitalization movements. Proving of particular value to academics, graduates, postgraduates and higher level undergraduate readers worldwide, this series holds obvious attraction to scholars of Native American studies, Maori studies, African studies and offers invaluable contributions to religious studies, sociology, anthropology, geography and other related subject areas.

OTHER TITLES IN THE SERIES

Indigenous Symbols and Practices in the Catholic Church
Visual Culture, Missionization and Appropriation
Kathleen J. Martin
ISBN 978 0 7546 6631 8

Aboriginal Environmental Knowledge
Rational Reverence
Catherine Laudine
ISBN 978 0 7546 6430 7

Native Christians
Modes and Effects of Christianity among Indigenous Peoples of the Americas
Edited by Aparecida Vilaça and Robin M. Wright
ISBN 978 0 7546 6355 3

Mobility, Markets and Indigenous Socialities

Contemporary Migration in the Peruvian Andes

CECILIE VINDAL ØDEGAARD
University of Bergen, Norway

Routledge
Taylor & Francis Group
LONDON AND NEW YORK

First published 2010 by Ashgate Publishing

Published 2016 by Routledge
2 Park Square, Milton Park, Abingdon, Oxon OX14 4RN
605 Third Avenue, New York, NY 10017

First issued in paperback 2021

Routledge is an imprint of the Taylor & Francis Group, an informa business

Copyright © Cecilie Vindal Ødegaard 2010

Cecilie Vindal Ødegaard has asserted her right under the Copyright, Designs and Patents Act, 1988, to be identified as the author of this work.

All rights reserved. No part of this book may be reprinted or reproduced or utilised in any form or by any electronic, mechanical, or other means, now known or hereafter invented, including photocopying and recording, or in any information storage or retrieval system, without permission in writing form the publishers.

Notice:
Product or corporate names may be trademarks or registered trademarks, and are used only for identification and explanation without intent to infringe.

Publisher's Note
The publisher has gone to great lengths to ensure the quality of this reprint but points out that some imperfections in the original copies may be apparent.

British Library Cataloguing in Publication Data
Ødegaard, Cecilie Vindal.
Mobility, markets and indigenous socialities: contemporary migration in the Peruvian Andes. – (Vitality of indigenous religions)
1. Rural–urban migration – Peru. 2. Indians of South America – Andes Region – Land tenure – Peru. 3. Indians of South America – Andes Region – Urban residence – Peru. 4. Indians of South America – Andes Region – Ethnic identity. 5. Internal migrants – Peru – Social conditions. 6. Internal migrants – Peru – Economic conditions.
I. Title II. Series
307.2'4'08998323'085–dc22

Library of Congress Cataloging-in-Publication Data
Ødegaard, Cecilie Vindal.
Mobility, markets, and indigenous socialities: contemporary migration in the Peruvian Andes / Cecilie Vindal Ødegaard.
p. cm. – (Vitality of indigenous religions)
Includes bibliographical references and index.
ISBN 978-1-4094-0454-5 (hardcover: alk. paper) 1. Quechua Indians – Land tenure – Peru – Arequipa. 2. Quechua Indians – Peru – Arequipa – Ethnic identity. 3. Quechua Indians – Peru – Arequipa – Economic conditions. 4. Rural-urban migration – Peru – Arequipa. 5. Marketplaces – Peru – Arequipa. 6. Arequipa (Peru) – Economic conditions. 7. Arequipa (Peru) – Social life and customs. 8. Arequipa (Peru) – Religious life and customs. I. Title.
F2230.2.K4O38 2010
307.2'40899832308532–dc22

2010014645

ISBN 13: 978-1-03-209932-3 (pbk)
ISBN 13: 978-1-4094-0454-5 (hbk)

For Candelaria and Fabia Elena

Contents

Acknowledgements

In Peru my warmest thanks to people in Jerusalén who were so kind and helpful to let me follow them in their daily lives and who shared with me their experiences and points of view. In particular I would like to thank all the participants in the women's organization in Jerusalén for patiently responding to all my questions and letting me accompany them during their work and meetings and enjoy their lively company. Many thanks also to people at the market La Feria Altiplano who took time to speak with me during their work and share with me their stories and perspectives. Especially I would like to thank Angelina, María, Juana, Eugenia, Juan, Paulina, Victor, Clara, Teofilo, Carla, Bea, Carola and Jorge for the many conversations we have had, for sharing their experiences with me and letting me accompany them in their everyday lives, on journeys and festive occasions. I am particularly grateful to my dear friends Candelaria and Fabia Elena for their friendship and care for me during fieldwork, and for their insights that have taught me so much. This book is dedicated to them.

The book has benefited from many people's comments on my work at various stages of the process. First I would like to thank John McNeish for his helpful support and advice both ethnographically and analytically during the process of finalizing my PhD and in my later work, and Penelope Harvey for her clear thought and inspiring comments along the way. Thank you also to Sarah Lund for her encouragements and fruitful supervision during an early phase of my work. My warmest thanks to people at the Department of Social Anthropology at the University of Bergen for a stimulating academic and social environment, especially to Bruce Kapferer and the group of postgraduate students from whom my work has benefited through fruitful debates and exchanges. In particular I would like to thank Annelin Eriksen, Anette Fagertun, Christine Jacobsen, Marit Brendbekken, Hege Toje and Lars Gjelstad. Thank you also to my colleagues in the Social Reading group for many inspiring discussions.

I would like to express my gratitude to the staff at Section for Gender and Development Studies at the University of Bergen and the generous academic environment they represent, and especially Haldis Haukanes and Marit Tjomsland for their support and advice. Thank you also to my colleagues in the research group Multicultural Venues and Gro Therese Lie, whose comments and support I always appreciate. I would like to thank Norma Fuller, Juan Ossio, Pablo de la Vera and Oscar Ugarteche for inspiring discussions and support in different phases of my work. I am particularly grateful to Sian Lazar, Karsten Paerregaard, Stephen Gudeman, John Gledhill, Eldar Bråten, Olaf Smedal and Anh Nga Longva for suggestions and encouragement. Thank you to Graham Harvey for his inspiring feedback on my work, and to Sarah Lloyd and Lianne Sherlock for their kind and patient assistance in finalizing this book. I would also like to thank Dianna Downing for her great help and patience with the language editing. I am especially grateful to Olivia Harris for her inspiring work and for her encouraging comments. It is a great loss for social anthropology that she is no longer with us. My warmest thoughts also to my supervisor Reidar Grønhaug who assisted me with his helpful suggestions and perspectives until he so suddenly left us in September 2005.

The errors or omissions that may remain are my responsibility alone.

Funding for field research and writing during my work with the PhD (2000–2006) was provided by the Norwegian Research Council. My later field research and writing has been funded by The University of Bergen and the research group Multicultural Venues. A different version of Chapter 7 has previously been published as 'Informal Trade, *Contrabando* and Prosperous Socialities in Arequipa, Peru', *Ethnos: Journal of Anthropology*, vol.73:2 (June, 2008): 241–66. The questions that I explore in Chapter 3 are also discussed in a forthcoming article 'Sources of Danger and Prosperity: Powerful Surroundings in Processes of Mobility in the Andes', *Journal of the Royal Anthropological Institute (Incorporating Man)*.

Finally, I would like to thank my mother Tone for supporting me in all different imaginable ways all the time since this work began – her faith in me has helped enormously. I would also like to express my great gratitude to my husband Øystein for emotional, technical and logistical support during all the different phases that this work has brought me through. Thank you to Johannes and Oline for being so joyful and sweet, for accompanying me to Peru and for your eagerness that we all go back to visit people. Thank you also to my mother-in-law Synnøve for accompanying us to Peru and assisting us in taking care of the children during fieldwork. To my father Sjur, I will always be grateful for his faith in me until he so suddenly died in 1998.

Cecilie Vindal Ødegaard

List of Abbreviations

APRA	Alianza Popular Revolucionario de América
ASOMA	Asociación de Organizaciónes de Mujeres en Arequipa
COFOPRI	Comisión de Formalización de la Propiedad Informal
FEPUMUVES	Federación Popular de Mujeres de Villa el Salvador
PROMUDEH	Ministerio de Promoción de la Mujer y el Desarollo Humano
PRONAA	Programa Nacional de Asistencia Alimentaria
SINAMOS	Sistema Nacional de Movilización Social

Glossary

(From Spanish/Quechua to English)

aguantar: to endure, tolerate
ahijado/-a: godchild
alcalde: mayor
altiplano: Andean highlands
ambulante: walking trader
ánimo: a dimension of the self or soul, associated with spirit, courage, will, intention
apu: mountain gods
asentamiento humano: officially introduced term for new urban neighbourhoods
ayllu: an Andean system of social and spatial organization, in the form of corporate descent groups for the ownership of land and work exchange
ayni: relationship of balanced reciprocity, for instance in work exchange
brujería: harmful acts
capacitación: training
casera: home-maker or customer, but here used to refer both to customers and traders as a way of expressing a special attentiveness
ch'alla: offering
chanaca (Quechua: **sullquay**): the youngest among siblings
chicha: maize beer, and the name for music from the Andes combined with Caribbean rhythms. Also used to refer to a whole set of different practices associated with the migration of people from the highlands
cholo/-a: person from the Andean highlands who have migrated or changed lifestyle
cillar: volcanic stone
club de madre: mother's club
comedo: kitchen, here communal kitchen
compadrazgo: ritual or spiritual kinship or co-parenthood, referring to the relation established between parents and co-parents (compadres or comadres)
contrabandista/contrabando: smuggler/smuggled goods
corte-del-pelo (Quechua: **rutuchi/-kui**): ritual for the first hair-cutting of children
criollo/-a: people of Hispanic origin, originally a colonial term referring to Europeans born in the colonies
curandero: shaman, or healer
diablada: dance practiced especially in Bolivia and in the district of Puno, for occasions like carnival etc

duendes: small, evil, bearded and human-like creatures living in the ground that may harm people
faena: communal work party
feria: outdoor market
fundador/-a: founder
gamonalismo: the relationship between landowner and peasants or workers, similar to caudillismo but a term specific for Peru, reflecting ethnic differences and associated with exploitation
gente qala: naked or stripped people, a mixture of Spanish and Quechua language and used to refer to *mestizo* property owners (referred to also as gente criollo, grande or decente)
gentil: ancestors who have gone to hide under the ground with all their wealth and who will return one day
hacer daño: do harm through powerful acts
hacienda/hacendado: landed estate/owner of landed estate
huayno: music characterized by a specific Andean way of singing and accompanied by organ and guitars
humilde: humble, poor
indigena: used to refer to a person identified as of Andean or Indian origins
indio/-a: used to refer to a person identified as of Andean origins, often with negative connotations
machismo (machista): the cult of the male in Latin America, or the dominant behaviours and positions of men vis-à-vis the : subordination of women
mal viento: bad wind, especially related to spiritual forces
manta: colourful rug or carpet made of wool and used for a variety of purposes, to carry babies, food or stones for construction
marianismo: the submissive and sacrificial position of women in Latin America, as a complementary to the machismo complex
mestizaje: the mixture of Hispanic and indigenous, or the process of cultural accommodation and assimilation from : indigenous to becoming *mestizo*
mestizo/-a: person with both Hispanic and indigenous origins
minka: hierarchical exchange of work
misti: Quechua for mestizo or powerful other
mita: compulsory work for the state
obra: construction work, and particularly used to refer to the material and technical assistance of official institutions
pachamama: mother earth
padrinazgo: the link between godparents (padrino and madrina) and child (ahijado/-a) established through ritual kinship
paisano/-a: person from the same place, village, region or country
parillada: grill party
pollera: manifolded, colourful skirt worn by women in the Andes
progreso (progresar, also **avanzar, adelantarse):** progress, improvement, mobility

pueblo jóven: term used to refer to new urban neighbourhoods
quinoa: grain-type produced in the Andes
redondillo: the gathering of money to make object of a lottery
runa: Quechua for people and a self-descriptive term used by Quechua-speaking people
serrano/-a: used to refer to a person from the Andean highlands
sierra: highlands
techamiento: work party for roofing
tesorero/-a: treasurer
tierra: earth, land
tinku: ritual battle or competition between equal and oppositional groups or individuals, associated with blood sacrifice to the powers of the landscape
trabajador-/a: worker
tributarios (indigenous tributarios): (indigenous) people obligated to do work for the state (mita) on the basis of fiscal categories
vaso-de-leche: glass or milk, here referring to a state programme for the distribution of milk
waipi: textile materials to undo for the washing of cars

Introduction

People in the Andes were increasingly involved in processes of mobility and migration during the twentieth century, and the migration to cities increased significantly during the latter part of the century. The Andean population took part in processes of mobility also before this, for example in relation to ritual journeys, forced labour and commerce during the colonial period (see Sallnow 1987, Stolcke 1990, Larson and Harris 1995, Saignes 1995). In Peru, the movement towards the cities increased especially from the 1940s and 1950s, as an effect of the mechanization of the hacienda economy, the drop in agricultural exports due to the Great Depression and later the industrializing endeavours around the cities. The movements towards the cities were not reduced by the agricultural reform that was introduced in 1969 under the military regime of Juan Velasco (1968–1975). The intention of this reform was to reorganize the *haciendas* (landed estates) and transform them into cooperatives in which the peasants would take over the responsibility for work and distribution of products. However, the reform did not unambiguously bring about improvements for peasants in the highlands, due to continued land shortages and internal negotiations (see Lund Skar 1994). During the war between the Maoist guerrilla movement Sendero Luminoso and the military in the 1980s and the early 1990s, the peasant population suffered most from the violence and terror. Finding themselves in a vulnerable position between Sendero Luminoso and the military, people in rural parts of the country were made the objects of recruitment as well as suspicion by both parties. The forced displacement of whole villages and the destruction of the rural economy further contributed to the flight of thousands of people from rural areas to the cities. In addition to the 20,000 who lost their lives during this time, more than 600,000 people were forced to leave their homes (Starn, Degregori and Kirk 1995).

To illustrate the extent of the migration to the cities, it is worth noting that in 1940, 64.6 per cent of the Peruvian population lived in the countryside, compared to 72.6 per cent who were living in cities by 2005 (INEI 2005). The growth of Peruvian cities has been characterized by unauthorized occupations of land[1] at the outskirts of metropolitan areas, where occupants have worked together for the construction of new neighbourhoods. As has been demonstrated in the literature (see Matos Mar 1977, 1985, Lloyd 1980, Lobo 1982, Blondet 1990, Lund Skar 1994), a first period of occupation has generally been followed by longer or shorter periods of conflict or negotiation with the authorities for formalization, as well as a common effort by inhabitants to establish streets and infrastructural facilities. Most of this has thus

1 In Lima the first occupations of land took place as early as the 1930s and in Arequipa from the 1940s (Paerregaard 1997a).

been performed through the collective work of inhabitants and the organization of neighbourhood associations. In 1984, Matos Mar used the term *desborde popular* (popular overflow) to address the cultural, political and aesthetic transformations of Peruvian cities that these occupations involved. He saw the land occupations as signalling the start of a new era of contestations that brought about an 'upsurge of the masses', challenging the legal and institutional apparatus and producing what is often referred to as a 'culture of informality'. Despite the impression made by these land occupations as chaotic, spontaneous and violent, however, Matos Mar (1977) demonstrated that they were often carefully planned in advance, with plots set aside for future schools and churches. He argued that through these essentially transgressive forms of action, people had found a response to their disenfranchisement, an alternative to conventional forms of political activism. According to Gandolfo (2009), this 'culture of informality', which Matos Mar believed caused a unique process of modernization, is characterized by economic activities that blur the line between what is simply furtive and what is illegal, and the significance of transactions that are driven by family and personal, rather than institutional, relations. These practices have reconfigured most sectors of the economy, from manufacturing to the building and service industries, and impacted commerce and retail, transportation and public utilities, health services, public safety and justice (ibid:9). From the first occupations in the 1930s and 1940s, these practices were at first highly controversial and often followed by violent conflicts between occupants and authorities. With time, however, this kind of occupation increasingly seems to have been established as more or less common practice, and incorporated into the approaches and policies of the authorities. Indeed, land occupations seem to have become the object of different strategies from the standpoint of inhabitants as well as authorities.

While Lima is the destination for many of those who migrate, others leave their villages for cities located in the region, or to a regional capital, such as the city of Arequipa about which this book is concerned. Arequipa[2] is located in Southern Peru, in the lowest part of a great valley surrounded by long hillsides, volcanoes and mountains. The city is the second largest in Peru with approximately 1.1 million inhabitants, about 24.7 per cent of whom are considered migrants (INEI 2002). Arequipa is the capital of the department of Arequipa and is located at 2325 metres above sea level in an area where the Andean Highlands meet the dry land towards the Pacific coast. The River Chili that flows through the city is said to mark its division into one upper Andean and one lower, coastal part. The upper part is characterized by its dry landscape, while the lower part is green and used for agricultural purposes, producing such crops as potatoes, maize, corn, garlic and peppers. *Vis-à-vis* the capital Lima, Arequipa has a history of struggles for independence, and is still well-known for the somewhat rebellious attitude of its inhabitants. What is more, the city also used to be economically well-situated

[2] The name of the city is said to have originated when the Incas first came to the area and decided to stay: *Ari, quipay*, which is Quechua for 'yes, we stay here'.

due to the textile industry, and although textiles are still important, the industry in Arequipa is no longer booming. Arequipa is furthermore said to be the most conservative Catholic city in the country, and is well-known for its many churches. The city is often called '*la ciudad blanca*', or the white city. This is a reference to the white volcanic stones (*sillar*) that most of the older houses and buildings are made of, but I have also heard it in reference to the light skin colour seen to characterize the Spanish descendants in this city, *los criollos*, many of whom belonged to the oligarchic classes. The city has in many ways changed since increasing numbers of people from the highlands started to arrive in Arequipa from the surrounding departments, often establishing new neighbourhoods in the outskirts. From previously being regarded as a dominantly *criollo* or *mestizo* city, Arequipa has increasingly become influenced by new forms of organization and ways of life. In addition to its geography, situated where the Andean highlands meet the coast of the Pacific, the city is therefore ambiguously positioned in the racialized spatial dichotomies that characterize the relationships between rural and urban, indigenous and *mestizo*.

This book is concerned with one of the new neighbourhoods in Arequipa, Jerusalén, which is located on the hillsides of the volcano Misti, in the upper parts of the district of Mariano Melgar. The area where Jerusalén is located was occupied in 1964, and the neighbourhood is therefore only relatively new[3] and actually represents one of the older occupied neighbourhoods in Arequipa. From previously being a desolate area at the very outskirts of the city, Jerusalén has gradually become a rather established neighbourhood with a population of approximately 4,000 people (INEI 1994). The area was occupied by a group that formed a neighbourhood association to coordinate the construction of infrastructure and the formalization of land ownership. In addition to the coordination of collective work, the neighbourhood association has also been responsible for claiming *obras* from the authorities, that is, material or technical assistance for the construction of the area. In these projects, officials sometimes come to provide materials and technical assistance to the inhabitants who in turn perform the work themselves, coordinated by the neighbourhood association as well as the women's groups.

The people who participated in the occupation of the area were primarily people from rural communities in the Andean highlands. To this day, most of the inhabitants in Jerusalén are people from the highlands or their descendants, mainly from the departments of Cuzco and Puno, but also some from Apurímac and rural parts of the Arequipa department. Many speak Quechua as their mother tongue, while a few speak Aymara. Some have first gone to work in the nearest

[3] Among the many terms for this kind of neighbourhood was *barriada* in the 1960s, later *pueblo jóven* since 1968 and the presidency of Velasco (see Lobo 1982:65). The neighbourhoods established during the 1990s and onwards are called *asentamineto humanos*. Despite these changes in official terms, it is *pueblo jóven* that seems to be most commonly used in everyday discourse.

village or urban centre, and from there worked their way to Arequipa, while others have gone directly to Arequipa. From Arequipa, among the younger generations in particular, people sometimes have a further orientation towards moving to Lima or to leave the country, in order to try out the opportunities in places with a higher wage level than in Arequipa. Some go to Lima or neighbouring countries only for a short period of time, to work and save money and later return.

There are now several well-constructed houses and infrastructure in Jerusalén, the main road is asphalted and there are installations for water and electricity, as well as communal buildings such as a school, a health centre and Catholic and Evangelical churches. The buses from the centre of the city constantly climb the main road of Jerusalén leading further up to the cemetery and the more newly established neighbourhoods above Jerusalén. Other roads consist mainly of sand and the dust clouds rise each time the buses enter. There are few cars in the neighbourhood, except for occasional taxis (*ticos*) owned by local people. The number of grocery shops in the neighbourhood constantly seems to increase, and considering the size of the neighbourhood, the number of soccer fields is impressive. Representing the centre of the neighbourhood is a small park that struggles to survive the dry climate, surrounded by a primary school and a Catholic church, as well as communal buildings for organizational and cultural activities, owned by the neighbourhood committee and the local women's group, that is, the women's organization Asociación de Organizaciónes de Mujeres en Arequipa (ASOMA). In the lower part of Jerusalén there is a small marketplace open for vending activities on Saturdays. In the area around and above Jerusalén there are also more newly established neighbourhoods that are still under construction. As Jerusalén has become part of the housing market – some properties were for instance already up for sale shortly after the occupation – and due to improved building standards, the value of properties in this neighbourhood has risen significantly during the last decade. Despite these changes, the area is still conceptualized as a poor urban neighbourhood, or a *pueblo jóven* (a young town) in the discourses of many of its inhabitants and more generally amongst people in Arequipa.

Like Jerusalén, most of the new neighbourhoods in Arequipa are located on the hills and sides of the mountains and volcanoes that surround the city, and are visible from some parts of the central city. In this manner, the previously desolate hillsides surrounding Arequipa have gradually become settled as people have invaded new land. Some areas of occupation are regarded as more attractive than others, and there is greater pressure on places along central roads or around other important infrastructure and services. Even some of the most fertile land in the lower plains of the valley around Arequipa is becoming urbanized, despite the efforts of the landowning farmers to let this land lie fallow. In the case of Jerusalén and most other neighbourhoods, however, the land that has been occupied was owned by the authorities and generally deserted due to its extremely dry, mountainous and not particularly friendly surroundings on the very outskirts of the city. In other cases, invasions have taken place on more centrally located land for which the authorities have had other plans, sometimes with the result that occupants have been thrown off the land or that disagreements have escalated into lengthy negotiations and long-term legal battles.

Mobility, Sociality and the Animated Surroundings

The spatial surroundings through which these processes of mobility take place are vested with meaning, not only due to the hierarchization of spatial categories in a sociological sense, but also since the natural surroundings are ascribed significant power and potency in Andean thought. While there is widespread interest within current anthropology concerning the significance of mobility in a globalized world, less interest can be observed in the cosmological and ontological dimensions that processes of mobility may involve. My aim in this book is to explore processes of migration and urban settlement and how ideas about mobility and progress are negotiated in terms of Andean notions of sociality. I seek to uncover how people's quest for mobility and progress are informed by Andean practices of reciprocity and exchange between human beings and with the animated surroundings. These ideas about reciprocity and circulation reveal a different understanding of prosperity as well as mobility, and I am particularly concerned with the significance of sociality and ritual at the margins of the formal economy. The book describes people's involvement in occupations of land and economic endeavours, that is, through trade, *contrabando* (smuggling) and often undocumented ways of earning an income. In so doing, I seek to explore the occult economies with which these processes of mobility are often entangled.

While the notion of *progreso* in official discourses historically has been related to *mestizaje* or cultural assimilation, this book demonstrates how notions of progress are re-contextualized in local discourses and given new meanings. In so doing, I seek to compensate for the lack of an encompassing ethnographic account of the particular understanding of progress in contemporary Andean contexts, and to promote further the understanding more generally when it comes to cultural, spiritual and cosmological dimensions of movement and market participation. Through an emphasis on the hierarchization of places (Lund 2008) and indigenous people's relationship to land and the animated surroundings as sources of danger and prosperity, I will demonstrate how mobility is concerned with notions of progress and prosperity not only in a sociological sense, but also in a ritual and cosmological sense. I therefore seek to develop further the comprehension of how indigenous understandings of the animated surroundings are reproduced in new contexts, that is, in processes of physical and social mobility and in relation to economic activities.

Among the central concerns in anthropological studies of the rural Andes are practices of reciprocity and ideas about sociality. Several studies have described how relational understandings of personhood are revealed in relation to work and communal obligation, ritual practices and the reciprocal relationship to the natural surroundings. Practices of communal work are regarded as important for agricultural production, and ritual payments and exchange seen as elements of a sense of communality that includes the supernatural (Mayer 1977, Ossio 1984, Allen 1988, Weismantel 1988, Urton 1992, Gose 1994, Lund Skar 1994, Abercrombie 1998, Harris 2000, Harvey 2001). Ritual payments have thus been seen as connected to notions of fertility in the Andes, for which the ritualized relationship between people and surroundings is considered essential (Harris 1995b, 2000). In this respect, Harris has argued that the responses of people in the Andes to the introduction of markets are characterized by the reproduction and re-conceptualization of their particular understandings of fertility. This does not imply that Andean collectivism can be understood as a type of sociality characterized by a relative absence of individual interest and agency, since Andean socialities are rather characterized by a constant tension between collective and individual values and interests (see Albó 1975, Bradby 1982, Urton 1992, Gose 1994, Harris 1995, 2000, Abercrombie 1998, Lazar 2002, McNeish 2002). This is reflected in what may appear as the somewhat contradictory dynamics also of people's responses to new situations, such as when settling in the city. What is more, Andean collectivism is not to be understood as separated from, or necessarily in opposition to state bureaucracy and rationality, since collective work from pre-colonial times and onwards has been central to state administration. Of particular importance in this book is therefore the cultural and political significance of work, community and communal work in processes of mobility.

By focusing on arrangements with respect to land and labour in the urban context, I will explore some of the spatial and relational dimensions involved and negotiated in processes of urbanization. I discuss people's practices of occupation and collective work in relation to official policies for development and formalization, and analyze the dialectics[4] between popular practices and state policies. Central to the involvement of the authorities in the development of new urban neighbourhoods is gender and women in particular. I wish to explore the background and implications of this focus on gender in official programmes and to illuminate the general significance of gender relationships and imageries in processes of mobility and urbanization. By describing the authorities' involvement in these new urban settlements and the development of policies, the book further reveals how the significance of notions like 'indigenous', communal work and gender is made and un-made through social mobilization as well as policy making.

People generally ascribed a moral value to work and economic activities – often regardless of their more or less informal or un-documented character. This ethic of work and sociality, exchange and circulation apparently conflict with the bureaucratic rationality of the Peruvian state, and the book sees this ethic in relation to questions of legitimacy and authority, such as that of state regulations and involvement. In this regard, I find the practices connected to trade and markets in the Andean context to be particularly interesting with respect

[4] Using the term in an open-ended sense.

to the social and cultural *embeddedness* (Polyani 1977) of economic activities. This is because these markets are characterized by an often intense cultivation of social relationships, and because they are dominated by people primarily from the rural Andes, who are sometimes represented as 'outside' modernity in dominant discourses, but who in fact often act as the most innovative and flexible entrepreneurs. Important for the understanding of these economic activities is the intense cultivation of social relationships through practices of reciprocity and ritual payments, as well as questions of trust, distrust and the use of *brujería* (acts to do harm).

It has increasingly been stressed in economic anthropology that material action may be constructed through religious, social, or other 'non-economic' practices from which they cannot be separated (see Gudeman 2001, Gudeman and Rivera 1990, Hart 2001, Wilk 1996). Indeed, it is argued that there is no underlying, 'true' model of economic action, but multiple, meaningful formulations within particular cultural contexts (Gudeman 2001:4, see also Harris 1995). There has also been an increasing emphasis in anthropological literature on what is seen as the global proliferation of 'occult economies', in relation to which global capitalism is seen to (re-)produce or even lead to an increase in ritual killings, witchcraft, sorcery, zombie conjuring and other 'occult' activities. In their accounts of the global proliferation of occult economies – or messianic, millennial capitalism – Comaroff and Comaroff (2005:183) refer to what appears as the increased significance of magical practices in the everyday production of value. They use the term millennial capitalism to refer to both capitalism at the millennium, and capitalism in its messianic, salvific, even magical manifestations. According to Comaroff and Comaroff, the significance of such practices in relation to economic life have one thing in common, that is, the attempt to create wealth out of nothing, often gaining significance among people who lack fiscal or cultural capital. In their view, these practices represent alchemic techniques that defy reason by promising unnaturally large profits – to yield wealth without production, value without effort (2005:184). In Cameroon, Geschiere (1997) has similarly noted how sorcery, magic and zombie conjuring have become a central aspect of mundane survival strategies and an integral element of what he sees as alternative modernities. Sorcery, according to Geschiere, is an attempt to stop the flow of globalization, in line with previous arguments that such practices[5] work to counter the commercialization of social relations, or individualization (Taussig 1980). The continued significance of magic and witchcraft in modern societies has in this regard been seen as a response to the competition, individualism and alienation initiated by processes of modernization and economic globalization (Moore and Sanders 2001, see also Taussig 1980). As noted by Friedman and Ekholm (2008), however, it is often unclear in many of these accounts what exactly is meant by the idea of 'alternative modernities'. They criticize the stress placed on discontinuity in the understanding of magic and witchcraft by noting that it is often unclear what actually remains the same and

[5] It is worth noting that this lumping together of different sorts of 'magical' or 'occult' practices can indeed be problematic.

what is different in the way people use magic to acquire money or modern goods. While being used to acquire money and commodities, the significance of magic may remain tied to previous logics of sociality in local society, a dynamic that Friedman and Ekholm conceptualize as an example of endo-sociality. This refers to socialities that transform all that enters into the local logic[6] (2008:141).

They further argue that it may therefore be problematic to use the term 'alternative modernities' in reference to the continued significance of magic and witchcraft, since there is often a significant aspect of continuity in these practices, at the same time as involving 'modern' prestigious goods. In this book, I see the continued significance of ritual payments and *brujería* in light of a general understanding of sociality in the Andean context. Instead of separating these practices from the general significance of social relationships in processes of change and mobility therefore, I seek to understand them as interconnected and therefore avoid the reduction of complex processes of sociality to simple notions of 'the occult' or 'the resistance to globalization'. Instead of interpreting such practices as attempts to stop or counter the flow of globalization therefore, I see them as a way in which people seek to influence or redirect such flows. In this manner, I explore how the flow of money and commodities is understood in terms of local understandings of sociality and prosperity.

Migration, Communal Work and Citizenship

While the war between Sendero Luminoso and the military caused thousands of people to leave their rural villages, most of the people referred to in this book left the highlands for reasons other than the war. They have migrated mainly with the motivation to improve their opportunities and standard of living, that is, to find work and, as many of them said, seek progress in the city. Nonetheless, although I pay particular attention to work, I do not conceptualize this movement as a process of labour migration. Instead, I see it as a movement motivated by people's attempts to improve their life conditions on general terms, by seeking *progreso* and an urban way of living – often conceptualized in contrast to what my informants have experienced as a poor and marginalized life in the highlands. These processes of mobility therefore have to do with life conditions and identity as much as they have to do with work or material prospects.

6 This kind of endo-sociality is defined in contrast to exo-sociality, the latter being understood as a strategy of appropriation of the world which is strongly other-directed and consisting of the identification of the foreign as life-force to be appropriated. This is a practice that defines social selfhood as part of a larger whole whose source of power is external to the local society, that is, as the definition of well-being, power, wealth and health. In both endo- and exo-sociality, there may be assimilation of the global to local systems of practice, but taking place in significantly different ways (Friedman and Ekholm 2007:141).

The movement from rural areas to cities – and processes of urbanization – can be seen to alter the relationship between the rural and the urban demographically, culturally and economically in many parts of the world. In response to such changes, the previous perspectives on urbanization in terms of a polarization between rural and urban have also been increasingly criticized for their dualism – in the Andes and elsewhere (Paerregaard 1997, Ferguson 1999, Signorelli 1999, Lazar 2002, Salman and Zoomers 2003). In the notion of rural-urban migration, there appears to be an inherent idea of – and opposition between – periphery and centre, a divide that has been criticized for under-communicating the relationship of exchange, influence and inter-dependence between rural and urban areas. During the last two decades, research on migration and urbanization in the Andes has therefore moved from a concern with oppositional categories between the rural and urban, the indigenous and *mestizo*, to a stress on the interrelationship between people in rural and urban areas and the fragmentation of spatial and social categories. Social categories are destabilized and blurred in processes of migration and mobility, and people do not necessarily identify as Andean or indigenous at all, but often seek to redefine their positions in relation to social categories. At the same time as we thus need to acknowledge both the interrelationship between highland and city and the destabilization of spatial and social categories, however, it is important not to forget that processes of mobility and urbanization may also involve a re-creation of peripheries and centres, or new dynamics of marginalization.

In Peru, the way in which the urban and the rural have been conceptualized and experienced can be seen to reflect some important differences in institutional practices and degrees of state presence, as well as the image of people as differently located in the space of the nation-state (see Nugent 1997, de la Cadena 2000, Stepputat 2005). Since the colonial period, indigenous people have been associated with the highlands, while the *criollo* or *mestizo* population has been associated with urban centres closer to the Pacific coast. Indeed, the relationship between the rural and the urban reflects some important differences when it comes to citizenship, or different conditions for citizenship. In the rural highlands, people in indigenous communities continue to be marginalized when it comes to the access to public services, as well as the often weak infrastructural and communicational standards. People's migration from rural to urban areas can in this regard be seen as an attempt to redefine their life conditions and seek social mobility, or an attempt to acquire rights as citizens. In the city, however, many people from the highlands struggle to make a living. Many also live without the personal documents that are required to formalize land ownership, housing as well as economic activities.

Although almost two centuries have passed since independence, the opposition between rural and urban, indigenous and *mestizo* has in many ways been reproduced from that of the colonial period when the indigenous and *criollo* were conceptualized in terms of two different nations, or Republics: *La república de Indios* and *La república de Españoles* (Harris and Larson 1995, Thurner 1997). During the colonial period and onward, the relationship between the Hispanic and the indigenous was characterized by the recruiting of indigenous people to work as servants and peons, as well as their recruitment for communal work. The separation of two different nations, or Republics, involved the separation into two categories of citizens, which were also fiscal categories, by identifying people as landlords versus *indios tributarios* (Indian people with work duty vis-à-vis the state). The use of communal work by the colonial authorities was built on pre-colonial structures for recruiting work in the Inca administration, and indicates how communal work has a long history at different levels of organization in the Andes, from local community to state. Indigenous peoples were obliged to perform communal work (*mita*) for the colonial administration, often far away from their own villages, either in the mines, in agriculture or in other forms of production (Lund Skar 1994:304). *Mita* thus refers to the payment of tribute to the state in the form of a workforce. This served as an alternative for or addition to their payment of taxes, where labour tribute was meant as a guarantee for the recognition of communal land for those classified as *indios tributarios.* As noted by Lund Skar, the labour tribute was officially dropped in 1810, only to be reinstated and then dropped again in a bewildering succession of legal reforms.

From the time of independence in 1824, the Peruvian Republic was built on Enlightenment values set up in the name of new liberal principles of democracy, citizenship, private property, individual rights and protections (Nugent 2001:263). Since the Constitution of the liberated and independent Peru turned indigenous people into Peruvians, however, the rights they were promised have been slow in coming and people have been placed in what has been seen as a postcolonial limbo between tributary subjects and citizen taxpayers (see Thurner 1997). According to Lund Skar, the construction of infrastructure in the highlands continued to be handled by obliging indigenous inhabitants to contribute with their labour and fining the drop-outs (1994:304). The roads created in the southern part of the country in the period from 1935 to 1942 were for instance built by the recruitment of tributary workers (ibid:59). During its Republican history, Peru's legal development has reflected the paradox of a nation-building project based on a liberal ideology that upholds individual rights to private property ownership while at the same time providing special legal status for an enormous indigenous population with no traditions of private ownership (Lund Skar 1994:187). Stepputat (2005) explores this postcolonial limbo of the nineteenth century, when indigenous peoples became included in the new nation-state and yet remained disenfranchised at its margins. He shows how the internal exclusion of indigenous people received a spatial expression through the bifurcation (Mamdani 1996) of the rural and the urban and the institutionalization of 'indigenous communities'. In this manner, there was a bifurcation of the state made by the distinction between citizens who were subjected to and participated in direct government, and the subjects who were incorporated by means of indirect rule, for example through forced labour recruitment as well as communal rights to land.

Peru is therefore an example of how many postcolonial states have been unable to do away with their existing bifurcation (ibid:65). Similarly, according to Gose

(1992:59), the arrangement of labour tribute for indigenous people has never disappeared in practice (1992:59). He sees a clear parallel between the colonial system of tribute and contemporary ways of recruiting communal work in the sense that the principle remains the same: the state offers material and technical knowledge while local officials recruit the workforce among indigenous people through the organization of communal work. In this respect, Gose claims that the patron-client relations with the colonists that the indigenous population was involved in must still be seen to characterize their position *vis-à-vis* the state and dominant society. He argues that contemporarily, this relationship is reflected in the state's more 'civilized' attempt to 'modernize' the Andean region through official work projects accomplished by the workforce of the indigenous (1992:58).

Several ethnographies from the Andes have stressed the significance of work for the conceptualization of personhood and understandings of indigenous communities. According to Lund Skar (1994), the Quechua word for people, *runa*, is also used to refer to worker. 'For both men and women, to be described as someone who knows how to work really well is tantamount to being described as a really good person, an ideal *runa*' (1994:95). In the Andean town of Huaquirca, Peru, Gose (1994) has illustrated how working hard and working together entail people's mutual recognition of each other as responsible and equal. Similarly it has been noted that in Bolivia, people in the highlands take pride in their ability to work, and that work is thus intrinsic to Aymara or Andean self-identity (Harris 2000, Canessa 1998). A central debate in the literature on processes of migration and urbanization has been whether people's values and orientations become more individualistic once they move to the city. Some authors have stressed a more individualistic and less collective orientation among those who move to the city (Altamirano 1988, deSoto 1989, Blondet 1990, Roberts 1995, Rivera Cusicanqui et al. 1996, Gill 1997, Canessa 1998, Llanos Layme 1998), while others have underlined the significance, for instance, of collective organization among those who migrate, arguing that migrants actively seek out collective allegiance after arrival in the city (Albó, Greaves et al. 1983, Matos Mar 1985, Sandoval and Sostres 1989, Perlman 1976, Calderón and Szmukler 2000, Paerregaard 1997a, b, Lazar 2002). It has also been argued that work remains significant for people's understandings of personhood in processes of migration. Among migrants in Lima, for instance, Lobo (1992) has described how hard work is regarded as the only right and moral way to take part in society (1992:82). Similarly among people who have migrated to La Paz, Lazar (2002) has noted how many people identified highland Bolivians by their hard-working nature, a characteristic that was often associated with the hardships of growing produce in the high altitude of the Altiplano (ibid:199–200). The chewing of coca is in this respect often related to the necessity of coping with the hard work that people from the Andes do (see Allen 1988). The value ascribed to work in the Andes can thus not simply be seen as a response to poverty, as it also has cultural and historical roots (Lazar 2002:199). Indeed, the understandings of work among people in the Andes must also be seen as related to state processes.

Regarding the complementarity that is seen to characterize gender relationships in the Andes, some attention has been given to the significance of gender in processes of migration and the extent to which the gender complementarity is changed or reproduced (Lobo 1992, de la Cadena 1995, Lazar 2002, Widmark 2003, Ødegaard 2006). Through their role especially as market traders, indigenous women have been seen to function as mediators in the relations between urban centres and the rural highlands, *indio* and *mestizo*, and in a way that often serves to resist dominant *mestizo* imageries (Paerregaard 1997a, Stephenson 1999, Babb 2001, Weismantel 2001, Seligman 2004). For instance, Weismantel underlines the importance of women as market traders, as they:

> ... occupy a unique economic niche as low-level, small-scale merchants, usually operating in the rotating markets of the small town that serves large rural hinterlands. They are brokers who mediate between 'Indian' and 'white', between rural and urban, between integration into the cash economy, which provides their inadequate livelihood, and an unbreakable dependence on pre-capitalist economic activities such as creating fictive kinships, as a buffer between themselves and always impending financial disaster (1988:34).

Women in the Andes have played an important role in trade and barter not only as an effect of contemporary migration, but also historically in the region (Harris 1978, Allen 1988, Silverblatt 1990, de la Cadena 1996, Weismantel 2001, Seligman 2004). In this respect, Lazar (2002) argues that the high level of involvement of women in trade cannot be entirely attributed to increased numbers of female-headed households, or to the economic crisis of the late twentieth century, which are the factors usually underlined in the feminist literature (see Berger and Buvinic 1989). These factors have played a major part, Lazar argues, but are also related to the way in which urban indigenous draw on cultural codes about female-male complementarity in labour and a long history of female responsibility for commerce in the Andes (2002:218, see also Zulawski 1990).

From Stigma to Celebration: The Ideology of *Mestizaje*

The idea of *mestizaje* is important in relation to processes of migration and mobility since it represents an ideological notion for the unity of a common Peruvian nationhood. *Mestizaje* refers to what is seen as the cultural or racial 'mixture' between the indigenous and Hispanic, or to cultural accommodation and assimilation in processes when indigenous people increasingly seek to redefine themselves as *mestizos*. In the Peruvian context, *mestizaje* can therefore be seen both as an ideology of the nation-state, and as referring to the processes through which indigenous peoples redefine their 'Indianness' and become *mestizos*. In post-colonial Peru, the notion of *mestizaje* became central to the construction of a national identity as it did in other Latin-American countries, in the attempt by both politicians and academics to create a common basis for national identification and unity (see Safa 1998, Hale 1999, de Grandis and Bernd 2000, de la Cadena 2000). The use of such terms to express national heterogeneity in unitary terms have often turned out, however, to have somewhat problematic and paradoxical effects.

While currently understood in relation to the ideological unification of a culturally heterogeneous nation, the notion of *mestizaje* originated in discourses on biology and race (de la Cadena 2000, de Grandis and Bernd 2000). These ideas gained significance in Latin America during the eighteenth and nineteenth centuries, and were informed by the idea of *the hybrid* in natural science and the cross between what was considered two different races (see Young 1995:18). With the introduction of social Darwinist ideas in Latin America, notions of *mestizaje* were made relevant in scientific research as well as in political discourse, and mixtures between indigenous and Spanish were for a long time expected to prove both biologically and socially damaging, and were suspected of causing bad health, economic disability and moral decadence. In this manner, so-called *mestizo* or hybrid societies and nations were seen not to be organized or to function satisfactorily (Young 1997, Poupeney-Hart 2000). Initially, the *mestizaje* category was neither preconceived nor imposed by law. According to Poupeney-Hart, it was an identity that emerged from a legal gap due to the initial recognition only of two basic categories in official law: the Spanish and the Indian. The purpose of subsequent legislation was to restrain the rights of *mestizos*, since they were viewed as the product of an illegitimate union often caused by rape (Stolcke 1990:8, see also Melhuus 1996). During colonization and the colonial period, rape was often the cause for an increasing number of children in a so-called *mestizo* category, and thus reinforcing the view of *mestizaje* as a hindrance for progress and development. According to Poupeney-Hart (2000), *the mestizo* appeared as a threat to an order that clearly differentiated between conquerors and conquered, masters, servants and slaves.

With the nationalist liberation movements in Latin America during the nineteenth century, the idea of *mestizaje* was given new meanings and increasingly ascribed a positive potential for national change and linked to ideas of development and modernization (de Grandis and Bernd 2000). This was also related to the increasing significance in the region of classical liberalism and a political philosophy that made way for new aspirations about national unity and progress. De la Cadena (2000) claims that in Peru this produced a challenge to the ways in which *mestizaje* had been conceptualized in terms of biology and race, by a turn of emphasis to the importance and heterogeneity of culture. After the Peruvian Republic had been founded in the 1820s on liberal principles such as democracy and citizenship, private property and individual rights, the notion of *mestizaje* became important both as an analytical device and as a tool for nation building in order to promote a common ground for identity. The idea of *mestizaje* was thus transformed in the same way as notions of hybridity more generally (see Werbner 1997), from a discourse loaded with dangerous racial contamination, into one of cultural creativity.

During the military regime of Juan Velasco (1968–1975), there was an effort to replace the terms *indio* or *indígena* (Indian or indigenous) in official discourses by the term *campesino* (peasant). In the promotion of a 'modernized' Peru, it was one of the attempts in this period to underline class rather than race or culture, and served to reinforce the emphasis of a common *mestizo* identity. Also amongst Peruvian intellectuals, there has been a tendency to deny the existence of racism in the country, for example in reference to the idea of *mestizaje* or the celebration of '*todas las sangres*' (all the bloods).[7] Many Peruvians would insist that they are a nation of mixed descent, primarily of *mestizos*. During the presidential campaigns in 2001, before Alejandro Toledo became president, he was careful to underline his own experience of poverty and racism, and identified himself as an Indian or *cholo*[8] in order to appeal to the Andean population. As the debate was getting more polarized, one of the other candidates, Alan García, considered a 'white' or *mestizo* middle-class Peruvian, claimed that all this talk of Toledo being a real *cholo* was just nonsense. All Peruvians are *cholos*, he stated. In this manner, García tried to define *cholo* as a common category for all citizens, in a way that at the same time involved a denial of the existence of inequality and polarized racial categories in the country.

This indicates how ideas about *mestizaje* have been applied also as a device for assimilation of the indigenous population, and have served to deprive them of more specific cultural and territorial rights (see also Hale 1999). With reference to Guatemala, Hale has noted how dominant groups have come to use such ideas about *mestizaje* or hybridity to challenge and de-legitimate Maya Indians' demands for cultural rights. Similarly in Peru, the idea of a *mestizo* or 'hybrid' society[9] has represented an apparently inclusive form of hegemony that has involved a large degree of cultural accommodation and assimilation. This is related to the way in which *mestizaje* involves an idea about modernity, that is, modernity as defined by the dominant *mestizo* society.

---

7 A notion forwarded by the author José María Arguedas (1964), although his original use of this term was meant as anything but unproblematic or un-politicizing.

8 Often used to refer to people from the highlands who have moved to the cities.

9 Safa (1998) outlines the contrasts between the inclusionary notions of *mestizaje* or hybridity in Latin America versus the rigid bipolar racial construction in the United States. Her argument is that this model has made ideas about 'race' a fundamental distinction in U.S. society and encouraged the formation among African Americans of a separate racial identity that is often lacking in Latin America and the Caribbean. The hegemonic form of Latin American and Caribbean societies can thus be seen to interpret and incorporate contestatory elements, while the dominant U.S. society represses and excludes them (ibid:6).

Notions of Progress and Modernity

Like the term *mestizaje*, the notion of progress that I intend to discuss in this book is in many ways problematic for its connotations to a liberal, teleological way of thinking. This does not mean that we should avoid these kinds of terms altogether, however, since it is important not to take their meaning for granted but instead to explore the 'social life' of such terms. While a focus on 'progress' can be seen as somewhat politically incorrect from what has been called an 'anti-development' critique (Peet and Watts 1995, Coronil 1997, Escobar 2005), I nonetheless find it important to reflect upon the different effects that such powerful notions may have. It is worth noting Ferguson's (1999) point in this regard – that although certain terms (that is, the modern, in his account) may be empirically (and analytically) inaccurate – we may nonetheless need to examine such ideas in regard to their strategic effects. He suggests we must follow Foucault when exploring concepts by asking not simply 'What does this concept mean; what does it really refer to?' but: 'How and to what effect is this concept being deployed, what does it do?'(ibid:205). In relation to notions of modernity in Zambia and the African Copperbelt, Ferguson argues that an exploration of such terms may help us to understand how the idea of modernity itself has been implicated in larger configurations of power and resistance, thus affecting processes of change (ibid:206). While acknowledging that the term modernity is notoriously vague, Ferguson insists on the term for two reasons: first, since the dismantling of linear teleologies of emergence and development remain an unfinished task, and second, to suggest that debates on modernism and postmodernism need to be explored in relation to different regional experiences. This is to say that we need to turn an ethnographic eye toward the conceptions (scholarly and popular alike) of the modern (ibid:17). He describes how the overdramatic and exaggerated narration of the rise of industrialism and urbanism in Zambia involves not simply a movement in space but an epochal leap in evolutionary time, and reflects people's ambition to participate on equal terms in some kind of 'first-class' modernity. An urbanizing Africa has been seen as a modernizing one, a view that has often been related to exaggerated dualisms, for instance between rural and urban, traditional and modern. This dualist understanding of urbanization has entailed that urban migrants are seen as entering the mainstream of history, and urbanization has come to appear as a movement toward a known end, a Western-style industrial modernity (ibid:5).

Rather than presupposing the political and normative dimensions of ideas about progress, it is therefore important to explore such terms according to their often multiple and complex meanings and implications in social life. This is particularly so when such notions are explicitly referred to and given importance in people's lives, such as among the people with whom I have worked, where ideas about progress were often addressed. In the literature from the Andes, however, people's ideas about progress in processes of mobility have not been sufficiently explored, although briefly mentioned by Lobo (1982), Lund Skar (1994) and Paerregaard

(1997a). In the way my informants used the term, progress appears to be associated with some kind of moving forward, improving or developing, and refers to the moving forward of persons as well as society. Progress appears to be closely associated with ideas about modernity, and can be seen as related to people's search for progress in the form of social mobility on the one hand, and the state of society as more or less 'modern', or modernity, on the other. In particular, the idea of progress among people in Jerusalén seemed to be related to notions and expectations of urban life. The reference to progress may therefore say a great deal about people's expectations for their future and for the city, and thus for how they manage and conceptualize a situation of change. Notions of progress are referred to by a variety of different actors and sometimes by giving different meanings to the term. State and NGO agencies involved in the neighbourhood used the term in reference to the improvement of the neighbourhood, and the betterment of infrastructure and conditions of living. Work is central for such appeals to create progress in the neighbourhood, and work is similarly made relevant for understandings of progress in the many Evangelical churches in the area. Progress is in other contexts seen to depend also on the quality of social relationships and practices of reciprocity, for instance among people involved in trade.

People's concern with modernity and progress often involves an attempt to redefine their position in society, of re-conceptualizing self and identity in the attempt to become somebody different from who they were before. This entails a consciousness about climbing the social ladder that can be seen as in itself representing a modern discourse, at the same time as it involves often nostalgic attitudes towards the past. Notions of authenticity or tradition can in this manner be seen as a product of modernity (Latour 1996). In a conventional sense, the notion of modernity is related to a particular organization of society and way of thinking connected to the initiation of industrialism and rise of a capitalist economic system, and the rationalization, secularization and individuation that it has entailed. Modernity can thus refer to a specific organization of society related to a specific way of conceptualizing the individual in relation to the collective, society and nation. For instance, modernity has been related to a valuation of the person on its own terms, in contrast to the conceptualization of the person in terms of collective or communal entities, and thus involving an increasing significance of individuality and self-reflexivity (Giddens 1991). In many ways, people's concern with and search for progress can be seen as a characteristic of modernity as such, due to the pre-supposition involved in such a notion that the self and identity are not ascribed but achieved, developed, constructed, and possibly made the subject of re-creation and change – a pre-supposition that nonetheless suggests change in a specific direction, or change in a specific way. Modernity thus involves a linear understanding of time and society and the differentiation of society as accompanied by the possibility of upward mobility. As noted by Friedman and Ekholm (2008:7), modernity is in many ways a future-oriented cosmology that becomes generalized to all domains of life.

While modernity can be associated with liberal ideas of individual rights, flexibility and reflexivity, it is at the same time related to a dualist way of thinking and particularly to a dualist understanding of difference, not only in terms of cultures or civilizations, but also in terms of gendered differences. This is illustrated by the organization and conceptualization of gender ideals and relationships in terms of dualist oppositions, by the association of the female and male to oppositions between nature and culture, primitive and civilized, private and public, Indian and *mestizo*. In the Peruvian context, notions of progress have implied ideas about 'race' as well as culture (Altamirano 1996), in a way that is reflected by the binary contrast between rural and urban and the conceptualization of the urban *mestizo* as modern – in contrast to the traditional indigenous.

From primarily serving as a fiscal category during the colonial period, the term Indian underwent change during the mid-nineteenth century. In this period, Harris (1995a) notes that the contrast between tribute-paying Indians and those who enjoyed access to their labour and resources as intermediaries of the state was increasingly seen as an ethnic difference (ibid:361). During the period between 1880 and 1930, the designation 'Indian' underwent further social, economic and ethnic transformations when liberal and positivist discourses recast the Indian as 'an impoverished, hapless, illiterate, and uncivilized subject ... who remained on the margins of the market economy, neither interested in nor capable of mercantile initiative or productive enterprise' (Larson 1995:29). This was related to a shift in economic and ideological discourses as the historical era when *mestizos* defined the Indian as being politically and economically situated at the periphery of the culture of modernity (ibid:29–30). In this manner, notions of modernity have become closely connected to the *mestizo* in Peruvian society. The movement of people from highland communities towards the cities can in this regard be seen to involve an attempt to redefine their position at the periphery of modernity, in line with the definition of centre as future. This may involve an accommodation to and reproduction of dominant categories and discourses on the one hand, while also destabilizing or re-conceptualizing the oppositional categories of identity on the other. These dynamics may represent an example of what is sometimes conceptualized as new, multiple or alternative modernities, that is, as practices of identity that re-conceptualize or add new meanings to dominant categories, although to a certain degree building upon some of the same categories and ideas (Calderón 1988, Geschiere 1997, Ferguson 1999, Comaroff and Comaroff 1993, Moore and Sanders 2001). Similarly in the literature on social movements, notions of alternative or multiple modernities have been applied with reference to how people often use dominant terms of identity and values of citizenship to promote popular and cultural demands (Calderón 1988, Warren 1998, see also Nugent 1998, Starn 1999). In this book, I will illustrate how people's understandings of mobility and progress involve associations to dominant notions of *mestizaje*, modernity or development on the one hand, but also how such notions are informed by an Andean understanding of prosperity and the fertile force of exchange and circulation on the other (Harris 1995b, 2000). In this manner, I seek to explore how indigenous notions of sociality and ritual payments are made relevant for people's quest for and understandings of progress.

State Processes

While the processes of movement and migration described in this book are based on people's own decisions to migrate – or that of close relatives – it is also important to understand this mobility in relation to state processes. People are imagined as differently located within the space of the Peruvian nation-state in a way that must be seen as closely related to state processes, as reflected for instance in the two republics and the bifurcation of the state as previously mentioned. Such a spatial organization of social categories illustrates how space/territories and social or fiscal categories become related. The work duty to the state at the same time required indigenous people to move in many cases, often across great distances and thus illustrating how the state also canalized certain physical mobility. Some people further tried to manipulate or change their position in relation to these fiscal categories, for instance by moving away from their village either to neighbouring villages or to the cities (Silverblatt 1990, Larson and Harris 1995). Mobility and migration may in this manner be implicated in state processes in different and sometimes contradictory ways.

States work to produce social personhood and categories, and serve to canalize a certain social and physical mobility through, for instance, bureaucracy, education or work duties. Physical mobility and migration may at the same time be subject to control and regulation in a way that is closely connected to the creation and maintenance of states, in the sense that sovereignty and the control over territory involve control over the movement of people and products, as well as property rights. According to Scott (1998), techniques for sedentarization, that is, to make people permanently settle down, is a central dimension of states, for purposes of taxation, the prevention of rebellion and the like. In a study from Ecuador, Radcliffe (2001) has discussed how the state works as a spatial matrix into which subjects are slotted. One effect of this spatialization is the establishment of territory as self-evidently sovereign and made up of varied component elements of regions, cities and natural resources into an integrated whole, which is made evident in the imageries of people as differently located in the space of the nation-state (ibid:123). She underlines how the establishment of that spatial outreach, and the techniques of control that work through the territory, relate to how a state responds to the challenges of territorial integration and internal contestations of power. Drawing on de Certeau (1984), Stepputat (1999) similarly argues that we should be concerned not only with the creation of abstract space, but also the practices through which space is consumed and its organization disrupted. In this regard, migration within the nation-state can be seen to challenge the territorial constitution of the state and its projection of itself through spatial territories, arrangements and borders.

Anthropological studies of state processes often aim to see states as products of specific historical processes, and to recognize the significance of cultural differences in the development of and processes connected to states. This is in many ways a response to the tendency in (neo-) Marxist and (neo-) Weberian perspectives to see culture as produced by states, often underestimating the extent to which state processes can also be seen as effects of specific cultural processes (Steinmetz 1999). In particular, it is important to understand state processes as effects of specific cultural practices and understandings of difference, that is, majority and minority relations and the way in which they may be organized and conceptualized in culturally specific ways. While state institutions and practices are generally produced through the cultural, political and economic interests of a dominant group, this does not mean that minority groups are insignificant to the understanding of state processes. Central for anthropological perspectives of states is the criticism of the understanding of the state as a territorially based and centrally coordinated unity, or as an 'autonomous actor' (see Mitchell 1999, Trouillot 2001). Das and Poole (2004) have suggested the significance of 'margins' as an alternative point of departure for the study of states. Society's margins play a significant and necessary role in state processes, due to what is often seen as the need to create and maintain order and control at the spatial and social margins of society. Such a creation of order can entail for example state projects of civilization and modernization, a bureaucracy of documentation and statistics as means for control and taxation, and bio-politics for the production of bodies.

People who move can be seen to represent a kind of margin, especially those who move without economic resources and documentation and beyond the system or control of the bureaucracy. Nation-states often seek to control, or at least survey, processes of migration at the same time as migration is a phenomenon that often escapes control. In order to understand this state-society interaction in processes of mobility, we need to follow the everyday tracks of rule through dispersed institutional and social networks through which rule is coordinated, consolidated and sometimes contested (see Gupta and Sharma 2006). State-society interaction has often been understood in terms of the state as somehow separate from 'society' or something more 'local' and less rigid, and of the state as seeking the control of people. Such an oppositional way of thinking about state and society – and especially what has been called civil society – has deep historical and epistemological roots. This is reflected in Marxist and neo-Marxist theories that consider the state as separate from society, and of civil society in particular as (ideally) in opposition to the state. In contrast, such a divide between state and society has also been considered the result of a projection, that is, through the projection of a divide that in itself is made central for governance – despite a close interrelationship (see Mitchell 1999). Hence the relationship between state and society is not to be taken as in any way a given,[10] but rather as a hegemonic field for the exercise, contestation and concealment of power in a Gramscian sense (see also Trouillot). In this book, such dynamics will be discussed by a focus on the dialectics between popular practices and state policies through the exchange and appropriation of language forms, practices and techniques for administration.

Notions and practices of citizenship are central for the understanding of state-society interaction, and anthropological perspectives often question the understanding of citizenship as a fixed set of rights and obligations. As argued by Sieder (2001:203) citizenship is best understood as a cultural dynamic process rather than a static juridical construct in the relationship of citizens to the nation-state. As a contract between state and individual citizens, or groups of citizens, citizenship is contested and constantly negotiated. With reference to people's involvement in social and neighbourhood organizations in El Alto, Bolivia, Lazar (2002, 2008) argues that citizenship can be understood as a set of practices that are defined by people's participation in social organizations and associations, many of them collectivist in nature. By exploring the cultural constitution of citizenship in the Bolivian context, Lazar thus questions Western liberal notions of the citizen by suggesting that citizenship is not only individual and national but in many ways communitarian and distinctly local, constituted through different kinds of affiliations. Although my concern in this book is not primarily that of citizenship, I will nonetheless reflect on how the responses of Peruvian authorities to people's participation in collective work and organization involve the re-creation of specific conditions for citizenship.

Liberal understandings of citizenship concern the relationship of individual citizens to the market, based on an idea of the apparently equally distributed opportunities and access to manners and means of market participation. In this regard, there is often a link made between the involvement in markets, individual responsibility and what is seen as the moral 'good' of work in relation to the nation-state (see McNeish 2003). From the perspective of state authorities, the involvement in markets requires a system of formalization through which individuals can register their presence as well as economic contribution. One of my intentions in this book is to explore how market participation is negotiated and understood in contexts where the involvement in markets is not always registered or formalized. In particular, I am concerned with the ways in which people use land and markets – often informally so – to make claims for citizenship and progress.

10 This can be related to the critique of the tendency to reduce questions of power to simple oppositions between domination and resistance (Roseberry 1994, Ortner 1995, Starn 1999, Nugent 2001). For instance with reference to the *rondas campesinas* (peasant vigilant groups) in Peru, Starn demonstrates how people may rework influences from national society into their own special idioms, and criticizes the tendency among theorists to present anything less than total antagonism toward the state as a failure of political ideals.

Periods of Fieldwork, Use of Methods and Structure of the Book

This book is based on participant observation and qualitative interviews during several periods of fieldwork over ten years (1997–2007). The time span for my fieldwork represents an interesting context to explore the situation of people in a process of mobility and the significance of political changes, that is, in relation to Alberto Fujimori's (1990–2000) combat of terrorism and a certain optimism in the beginning of his term, to his dramatic exit and the entrance of the county's first president with an indigenous background, Alejandro Toledo (2001–2006), and later the return of the current president Alan García. My two principal periods of fieldwork were over six months in 1997 and seven months in 2001, with shorter periods in 2003 (from December and through January) and 2007 (from April through May). I have primarily conducted my fieldwork through participant observation in the neighbourhood of Jerusalén, in arenas and through social networks where my informants are involved, especially in the local women's organization ASOMA and a market association for traders called La Feria Altiplano. In this manner, I have often worked by following key informants in their everyday lives, and this book has therefore taken the form of person-centred ethnography. Most of my key informants are women, a result of practical concerns on the one hand, since it is easier to make contact with other women, being a woman myself. On the other hand, my stress primarily on female informants is also due to my interest in the role of women in the construction of new urban neighbourhoods, and their involvement in trade at the margins of the formal economy. Attempting to address questions of gender in a relational sense, I have also spoken a lot with men, particularly the partners or male relatives and colleagues of my key informants. By living in the neighbourhood for long periods during my fieldwork, and renting a room in the house of some of my informants, I have been able to form a significant impression of household relationships, as well as of everyday life and routines. While some conversations and interviews were recorded, most of the material in this book is based on field-notes written down during conversations or immediately after. Most people said they were intimidated by the recorder, and many conversations took place in rather noisy environments.

During my first fieldwork in 1997, I spent most of my time in the women's organization ASOMA in Jerusalén, where women came together to participate in different kinds of work: to cook, to contribute in the improvement of infrastructure in the neighbourhood, or to establish different forms of production or business. Several of these activities were supported by state, municipal or NGO agencies, contributing with food rations or training in return for the women's work. Many people in the neighbourhood had supported Fujimori in the elections, thus reflecting what has often been used to explain his somewhat surprising rise to presidency, namely the wide support of people from the highlands. Despite what had become the increasingly authoritarian regime of Fujimori, the period of my first fieldwork was characterized by optimism among the people I got to know. The leader of Sendero Luminoso had been caught and the violent period was finally over, and the economy was stabilizing after the hyper-inflation in the 1980s.

Fujimori initiated economic reforms in response to IMF's demands for structural readjustment, involving the privatization of national assets as well as a reduction of the public sector. Despite the problems of unemployment, people in Jerusalén and in the women's organization nonetheless seemed optimistic and hopeful about their situation and future prospects, and were experiencing an increase in the external support to improve the neighbourhood. Part of this support they received through state programmes and institutions established or maintained by Fujimori.

For my second fieldwork in 2001, I followed up this focus on work and organization among people who have migrated by including a merchant association in my different arenas of fieldwork. I started to follow some of the people from Jerusalén to the markets where they work, primarily to a market called La Feria Altiplano, located closer to the centre of Arequipa. I accompanied people during their work days and got to know their colleagues from other neighbourhoods, thus expanding my network of informants. As in the women's organization, most of the traders at the Feria Altiplano are people from the highlands, who make a living by selling different kinds of goods, some by working grand-scale and having a stable pitch at the market, others by selling on foot with a tray or a small blanket on the ground. There is a majority of female traders at this market, and some of them bring their small children with them, and when the children grow up they come along to help out with the work. Some of the women also try to combine this work with participation in local women's organizations. This second period of fieldwork in 2001, that is, the period following the end of Fujimori's presidency, was characterized by political uncertainty and the scandal revealed in connection with the Fujimori government. It had been discovered that Fujimori had been involved in corruption as well as human right violations. Among the official institutions implicated in Fujimori's corrupt regime was also one of the state agencies that he had initiated to provide support for women's organizations in new urban neighbourhoods, that is, Programa Nacional de Asistencia Alimentaria (PRONAA), among them ASOMA. The political uncertainty of this period was also related to the arrangement of new elections in 2001, after the election round in 2000 was disapproved due to the suspicion of corruption and fraud. Several state institutions were in crisis after the authoritarian regime and the scandal that followed, and the new Toledo government largely replaced the state institution staff, such as that of PRONAA. Especially among members in the women's organization, but also elsewhere, I experienced people to be less optimistic regarding their future prospects at this time. People were frustrated by the political scandal and often criticized politicians in the country for generally being corrupt. There was a down-turn in official support for the women's organization as well as in people's opportunities for employment, especially in construction. At the market, traders were complaining about increasing competition since larger numbers of people seemed to be turning towards trade to earn a living.

During my subsequent fieldwork, I have followed up my contacts with people in Jerusalén to explore how their situations have changed, and also to follow up on the social organizations they are involved in and to explore further more specific questions of interest. Over the years, I have followed closely the changing circumstances of eight different families in particular, by regularly coming to visit, accompanying them in their everyday lives as well as by travelling with some of them to their villages of origin. My position as a light-skinned and apparently well-situated foreigner has to some extent probably influenced the things that people have said and wanted to speak to me about. On the one hand, my somewhat 'exotic' presence in the neighbourhood made people interested in getting to know me, while on the other, my different background also made some people careful about giving me too much information, especially concerning things they suspected I might frown upon. There was also a dilemma of loyalty in my relationship with my informants, in the sense that I tried to act the same toward all, but at the same time, those who I knew best and included me most also expected more loyalty in terms of my attention and time. This concern was also related to the fear of gossip and envy – and with *brujería*, or harmful magic, as a possible result.

To inform my arguments, I have used a combination of methods, that is, not only by following the everyday lives and work arenas of people in the neighbourhood, but also exploring the involvement of the authorities and how people are affected by official policies and legislation. During my fieldwork, I have therefore spoken not only with inhabitants and workers in this neighbourhood, but also with representatives of the authorities and NGOs. One of my informants is also a *curandero* (shaman, healer), and in addition to always using the opportunity to talk with the other *curanderos* who sometimes came to the house where I lived, I thus had the opportunity to speak with a few ritual 'experts' to supplement the information about ritual practices that I otherwise gathered among non-expert practitioners.

Chapter 1 explores the negotiation of space and spatial boundaries in the urban context. In this chapter, I focus on the establishment of new urban neighbourhoods and practices of land occupation, communal work and the process of formalizing land ownership. I explore these processes in relation to how the authorities have responded to practices of land occupation through the creation of new policies, and how the city is thus changing through a dialectics between popular practices and state policies. The chapter briefly outlines the practices of work among people in a process of mobility, and argues that the cultural understandings of work in this context must be seen in light of the colonial and postcolonial history. While the claims to land are not made within a discourse of indigenous identities, the policies created in response to these new urban practices are nonetheless made specific to migrant or indigenous groups, although not limited to them. A new category for the use of urban space is thus created, one based on a collective and informal use and organization of land as well as workforce. In this manner, the chapter explores how the process from collective construction of neighbourhoods to formalization, bureaucratization and commodification of land is not unambiguous, unilinear or unproblematic, and how practices of land speculation are created in response to policies of formalization.

Chapter 2 is concerned with how people from the highlands often seek to reposition themselves in relation to social categories and redefine their Andean background in a quest for social mobility. It illustrates how people do not simply seek to become *mestizos*, however, nor do they necessarily revitalize their Andean background. Categories such as *indio*, *cholo* and *mestizo* rather become blurred, contested *and* reproduced in a highly complex and contradictory way. People's understandings and use of the term progress (*progreso*) represent a particular focus in this chapter, and are seen in light of their experiences of migration and the hierarchization of spatial and social categories. By relating this to the ideology of *mestizaje* in the Peruvian context, this chapter illustrates how this ideology involves the concealment of inequality, at the same time as it produces a fundamental ambiguity in relation to people's identification with an Andean background. In particular, the chapter is concerned with the use of Spanish and Quechua among people in a process of mobility, and relates this to the ambiguity of identification and the interchange between subject positions.

Chapter 3 follows up on the focus on mobility and progress, but from a ritual and cosmological point of view by describing how the powerful surroundings are negotiated as people move and accommodate to life in the city. The chapter is concerned with understandings of movement and mobility in light of cosmological ideas of origin and the significance of a reciprocal relationship to the animated surroundings. It explores how people re-create a reciprocal relationship to landscape in the urban context, and how understandings of spatial situatedness are important for notions of prosperity and progress. Migration to the city does not entail a one-sided process of, for example, bureaucratization or commercialization, since space is simultaneously understood on spiritual terms, as animated and powerful. As sources of danger and prosperity, the powerful surroundings are appealed to as mediators in making hostile space into places of identification and possible prosperity. The chapter argues that notions of mobility and progress are thus concerned here with prosperity not only in a sociological sense, but also in a ritual and cosmological sense.

The focus of Chapter 4 is sociality in a process of mobility and the significance of practices of reciprocity for how people seek to redefine their social position and negotiate the Andean stigma, that is, through the recreation of kinship and relations of *compadrazgo* (ritual co-parenthood). In this chapter, I discuss the dynamics of power and inequality in relations of reciprocity in a way that reveals the subtle forms of power that are reproduced as well as negotiated through these relationships. An important concern here is the negotiation of trust and distrust and how practices of reciprocity work to confirm notions of 'community' and communal obligation on the one hand, and serve as a means of personal progress or prestige on the other. In this manner, I explore how practices and values of reciprocity articulate with notions of progress and prosperity. I argue that the quest for mobility and progress does not necessarily entail a dynamic of increasing individualization, but encompasses an intensification of the cultivation of ritual and social relationships.

The focus of Chapter 5 is how gender relationships and ideals are made the object of reproduction or change in processes of mobility. It illuminates how gender as a difference articulates with other differences such as class and ethnicity, and how contrasting discourses on gender – such as the gender complementarity of the rural Andes and the Latin American *machismo* – are negotiated and (re-)created in a process of mobility. The chapter is concerned with the negotiation of same- and opposite-sex relationships especially in relation to work, within the household and between the generations. I reflect on the significance of gender in the negotiation of personhood and sociality, and relate this to the understanding of progress and practices of *brujería.* Following up the discussion of spatial boundaries from previous chapters, the chapter discusses why the trading activities of women – in the Peruvian context as elsewhere – are often associated with and considered an extension of the household, and explores what kind of ideological construction this is, in light of its gendered connotations and considering that most traders are women.

Chapter 6 is concerned with local organizations and especially the women's organization in the neighbourhood. I explore how inhabitants relate to NGO, local and state authorities through these associations and the sometimes unexpected or contradictory outcomes of official involvement. The chapter outlines the reference to ideas about progress within the women's organization, and how such notions are negotiated in terms of collective obligations and personal achievements. By exploring the significance of trust, mistrust and accusations of corruption, the chapter discusses the negotiation of leadership and mobility in social organizations. It explores the changing relationship between social organizations and the state in the Peruvian context during the last couple of decades, and the significance of gender for the (re-)creation of ambiguous spaces for citizenship. In particular, this chapter is concerned with how notions of 'the indigenous', communal work and gender are made and un-made through social mobilization and policy making.

My focus in Chapter 7 is people's involvement in trade and practices of *contrabando* at the margins of the formal economy. I explore how these practices of trade involve an often intense cultivation of social relationships, and how the participation in 'markets' is negotiated in terms of moralities[11] in a context where trade is of a more or less informal kind. This chapter illuminates how local ideas of market and prosperity are informed by Andean notions of reciprocity and circulation, and sees this in relation to the approach taken by the authorities, varying between silent acceptance and occasional moves to abolish these practices. By describing a merchant association in a process of formalization, the chapter is particularly concerned with the negotiation of trust and distrust between traders and in relation to leaders and authorities. I explore the significance of ritual payments and *brujería* in the market context, and thus continue the analysis of relational and ritual practices from previous chapters. In so doing, I illustrate how

[11] For a discussion of the notion of morality, see Signe Howell (1997) and Zigon (2007).

these practices should not be seen in terms of resistance as is often asserted, but in terms of Andean notions of reciprocity and circulation as significant for the establishment and maintenance of prosperity.

Chapter 1
Ambiguous Spaces for Citizenship

This chapter is concerned with people's access to land in an urban context, and discusses some of the spatial dimensions involved and negotiated in processes of urbanization. It outlines the way in which the differentiation and hierarchization of space in the Peruvian context seem to be reproduced in processes of urbanization, and how spatial categories inform people's ideas about mobility and progress. In particular, the chapter focuses on the history of occupation and construction in the neighbourhood Jerusalén, with a particular emphasis on the significance of kin and collective work for practices of settlement. I will argue that such practices of communal work on the one hand can be seen as an important cultural value and basis for mobilization among the inhabitants themselves, while also representing a device for policy making on the other. I thus relate these often collective occupations of land on the outskirts of urban centres to the development of state policies in response to the growth of new urban neighbourhoods, and demonstrate how the authorities have created different policies and institutions to facilitate the formalization of land ownership and to coordinate popular organizational efforts. In this manner, I illustrate how the approach of the state toward these practices has involved the co-optation of the initiatives of local movements into official policies, for example by making compulsory the collective construction of infrastructure in these neighbourhoods. By discussing how the dialectics between popular practices and state policies thus often shape the expansion of cities, the chapter reflects on the relationship between the city as concept and the city as practice (de Certeau 1984).

The significance of collective work[1] is further seen in relation to the increasing significance of individual land titles and loans in the city, and one of my aims is to explore how the co-existence between collective work and individual entitlements to land leads to what can be seen as the recreation of often vaguely defined, ambiguous spaces for citizenship. These ambiguous spaces for citizenship seem to leave a certain room for manoeuvre for politicians as well as citizens in a way that often serves to reproduce informal arrangements.

---

1 I have discussed a related issue in an article published by *Forum for Development Studies* (Ødegaard 2010).

The New Neighbourhood

The area where Jerusalén is located was occupied[2] in 1964 by a group of people who needed a new settlement due to the high costs of houses and rents in the city. In their claim for territory in Jerusalén, the occupants established neighbourhood associations[3] (*comités vecinales*) and the initiative-takers took position as leaders, represented in the Central Neighbourhood Association (*Junta Directiva Central)*. Infrastructure in the area was then gradually constructed through the collective efforts of inhabitants to provide materials and perform the construction work. The responsibility for these constructions was thus taken by inhabitants in the neighbourhood committees themselves, sometimes by acquiring support from governmental and NGO agencies for material and in technical advisory capacities. There were also constant collections of money from the participating families in order to cover the expenses for materials, legal advice and formalization fees. In this process of becoming recognized as a *pueblo jóven*, the negotiation between the government and lawyers became a significant expense for occupants, since each household was required to pay its share. In this and similar cases of negotiation over occupied land, occupants claimed their right to a place to live and referred to a law[4] stating that land unused for habitation or other purposes can be claimed for the purpose of housing. Due to their efforts, this claim to the land was later recognized, and their ownership formalized. The land was formally divided into separate plots for housing, and the neighbourhood association was organized into ten smaller work groups – or committees – ordered by neighbourhood quarters[5] and expected to take joint care of smaller tasks in their immediate neighbourhood. The original inhabitants often recalled how they thus used to form groups in order to dig ditches and carry stones for construction purposes. In their recollections, it

---

[2] Invasion or occupation is the term also generally used by the inhabitants themselves.

[3] The neighbourhood associations are led by an elected committee or central assembly (*asemblea central*) supposed to meet every two weeks to a month. Once or twice each year they hold a General Assembly of all the residents. Their primary responsibility is to obtain and realize *obras* (public works, electricity, street lighting, sewage system and parks).

[4] Ley 13517, from 1961 (see Riofrío 1988).

[5] As noted by Lund Skar (1994), there is an arrangement that binds the individual blocks and streets of a *pueblo jóven* with the national office for all *pueblos jóvenes*. This was a prerequisite for being officially recognized as a *pueblo jóven* and a result of the law passed by the Velasco government in 1968 seeking to create a nationwide network of block organizations. In one such settlement, each square block or street (approximately 30 families) was meant to choose three members to represent them on the Committee for Promotion and Development of the entire *pueblo jóven*, in turn choosing representatives for the Central Directive board in the area, which again elected six of its members to participate in the Central Office of the city. In this manner, the reform of Velasco was based on the idea that physical improvements in the *pueblos jóvenes* required group effort and that the state should serve as coordinator (ibid:185).

took many months before streets were cleared and formed in the area, and even longer to have them covered with asphalt. During these first years people walked miles to collect water from a river further down in Mariano Melgar. After a couple of years, a few water basins were installed for communal use, and in the late 1980s these were connected to individual water basins for separate households. It took about ten years to get electricity in the area, and there are still some households lacking connection to the network.

Most people in the neighbourhood have low-skill jobs, as day workers in the fields around Arequipa, as servants, traders, or in transport, factories, mining or construction. The adult population in the area has generally had a limited number of years in school, while the new generations growing up in Arequipa generally attend primary as well as secondary school, and some also begin university education. People often talked about the ability to work hard – and especially to do communal work – as an important and necessary quality that people from the rural Andes have in common in contrast to '*gente qala*' (referring to white, or naked people). Indeed, for many the only way to gain access to land is through collective work and effort, such as through the establishment of neighbourhood committees to work out infrastructure and acquire rights to land.[6] In the highlands, agricultural activities are often organized through communal work, and people in Jerusalén often talked about communal work as a quality of Andean community life. Communal work in the urban context is thus conceptualized as a cultural or traditional quality that people associate with their rural background, as well as to their common poverty. As I will illustrate, practices of communal work are made relevant not only by the inhabitants themselves though, but also by the official institutions and NGOs involved in the area to provide technical advice, economic support or practical training. This emphasis on collective work in official programmes represents in many ways an invention or reinvention of tradition (see Hobsbawn and Rangers 1983) in the sense that traditions, rituals and/or identities that are regarded as 'ancient' are reintroduced 'from above' in order to legitimize a specific political objective (McNeish 2002:257). In the literature, there has been a discussion about whether the neighbourhood organizations serve elitist aspirations for urban integration (Jongkind 1974), or whether they are an urban form of an essentially highland organizational practice (Doughty 1970). While this appears as a somehow unavoidable question, I am more interested in understanding the relationship and dialectics[7] between these different dimensions, that is, between official strategy and local identities or practices.

Due to the improvement of housing standards and infrastructure, Jerusalén is increasingly referred to as an *urbanización* instead of *pueblo jóven*.[8] Some of the inhabitants in Jerusalén are also involved in the occupation and construction of

---

6 In order to formalize rights to land that has been occupied, it is required that it be organized into neighbourhood committees.

7 Using the term in an open-ended sense.

8 *Urbanicazión* refers to a neighbourhood that is more established.

other new neighbourhoods that have grown up in the area around Jerusalén: Señor de Huanca, Cenepa, Cerrito Belén and El Mirador. It is interesting to note the choice of names for these neighbourhoods, as they are often biblical, or refer to a heroic Incan past, thus indicating people's hopes for future well-being. In addition to the work organized by the committees, there is also organization of collective work through official programmes for women such as the *clubes de madre* (women's groups), *comedores* (soup kitchens) and *vaso-de-leche* (the glass of milk programme), such as in the local neighbourhood organization Asociación de Organizaciónes de Mujeres en Arequipa (ASOMA).[9] This women's organization receives support from state agencies as well as NGOs, but has experienced a decrease in interest and numbers of participants in the last decade. Such women's groups are intended to function as self-help groups among women in a situation of poverty and marginalization, but as I will discuss further in Chapter 6, they also represent a significant instrument of political power.

Housing

In Jerusalén, there has been a significant improvement in the standards of most houses during recent years, but several houses are still made of simple material, and the contrasts in housing standards are therefore considerable. Indeed, housing in Jerusalén bears witness to the time-dimension in the development of housing, as well as people's different degrees of success in their quest for the living conditions associated with the urban middle class. The way in which people in the neighbourhood construct their houses and organize space and relationships within the household tends to go through a gradual process of change. This is related to a general improvement of standards, as well as the gradual reorganization of houses and households. In their first period of settlement, many people start by constructing and organizing their housing in a manner informed by rural household forms, and from there they gradually adopt what are considered more modern and urban forms. The contrasts between these different forms of house construction are particularly evident when it comes to the use of materials. Initially, houses are generally built in the cheapest way possible, and often with materials and construction forms similar to those in the highlands. These first dwellings often consist of a series of several small square-formed houses, rather than one big one, without windows and framed with stones, *sillar* (volcanic stones) or adobe bricks (mud and straw) and roofed

[9] Through the *comedor*, the women in ASOMA receive food from a state agency that they prepare together and sell at low prices to the members as well as other inhabitants of the neighbourhood. *Vaso-de-leche* involves the distribution of milk to families with children, a distribution for which women in local organizations are responsible. Women in ASOMA have also taken on other tasks for the local authorities in the form of light construction work and maintenance in the neighbourhood, performed in return for food rations or small sums of money.

with corrugated iron. They often have a carpet or the like at the entrance. With time, however, these buildings are often replaced by bigger and more complex constructions of cement, with grids and glass windows, as well as a door at the entrance. These newer houses are often constructed with two floors or with iron rod preparations for a second floor to be constructed later, thus illustrating people's visions of what their house will be like in the future – and the construction of houses as a gradual process. Such changes of construction forms are often notable because of the differences between the first and oldest buildings – which are generally kept, but for other purposes – and those more recently constructed. On the same plot of land, most people thus have several small buildings that have been constructed during different periods in the owner's history.

In the first period of construction, a household often consists of one building or room in which whole families live and perform domestic activities such as eating, relaxing and sleeping. At first all family members thus often sleep together in one small room and cooking tends to be done outside, or under a provisional roof. In part, this is due to necessity, as it takes time to construct what is considered a 'proper' house, particularly so when economic resources are scarce. It is also related to the fact that people are generally used to living and sleeping in less space. With time, however, more buildings are constructed – unless they are replaced by one big house – and separated from each other in terms of location and function, so that there is one building for sleeping (or several, in the case of extended families living together as they often do), one for cooking and everyday meals, unless this is still done under a provisional roof as it commonly is, and with a separate building for the reception of guests and parties. In this manner, there is a gradual transformation in the construction and organization of housing, from one small building to several – or otherwise into one big house – and thus from little to more space defined as 'inside'.

One can ask whether these changes may entail at the same time a change of sociality and the meanings ascribed to spatial boundaries or physical distance. According to Gose (1994), there are significant differences between *runa*[10] and *mestizo* regarding how they understand domestic space. People from the highlands are for instance not used to the material and symbolic boundaries between inside and outside, *casa* (house) and *calle* (street) that are made significant in the city where the use of space is also more individualized. As people accommodate to the city, they increasingly seem to give significance to such a separation between inside and outside, something which is illustrated by the demarcation between inside/house and outside/streets through such things as doors and high fences. As I will discuss later, the increasing significance of such a separation is also made relevant to gender imageries and ideals. What is more, while ritual payments in rural areas are generally performed outside, in the urban context they are increasingly realized within the household (see also Allen 1988).

10 *Runa* is Quechua for people, and is used to refer to people from the highlands.

As people construct more buildings and rooms, the newest or nicest room is often kept for the reception of guests. This is also often the most spacious room, and the room which displays all the pretty and expensive things. In comparison, the other rooms are often small and simply equipped, and although there may only be one room for sleeping and cooking, the living room is generally still left unused and kept exclusively for parties or visitors. This priority given to the reception of guests is significant and may indicate not only the importance of a festive sociality, a topic I will come back to, but also the importance of housing standards for the presentation of self. This last point is also reflected in the great hesitation I often noted among people in the neighbourhood with respect to inviting new people to their homes. Indeed, I was often surprised by the way in which people seemed to have second-thoughts about asking people to visit, particularly less familiar people or people of middle-class status. People were often concerned that others should realize how their house really looked inside, and thus feel pity or lose respect for them because they live in poor conditions.

There are also great contrasts between the front and back of most houses, in the sense that the tallest wall of a building complex is often the one in the front, and also the only one which is painted, thus making the house look more modern and completed than it really is. This illustrates the importance of signalling success and progress through housing standards and material achievement, and indicates how the house is often understood as an extension of the person (see Carsten and Hugh-Jones 1995). This significance of the materiality and spatiality of housing – the house as image and boundary – may further indicate how spatial organization and practices more generally seem to be made objects of reflection and change among people who migrate. As I will expand upon later, it indicates how spatial practices are informed by social categories and differentiation, for example how they relate to the conceptual opposition between highland and city, *indio* and *mestizo*.

Kinship and Settlement

Like many of her neighbours in Jerusalén, one of my informants, Angelina,[11] settled in the neighbourhood after living a couple of years in Arequipa in the house of employers and in rented rooms. She heard from her sister, who was already settled in Jerusalén, that a plot of land close to her own was advertised for sale not long after the occupation of the area. As individual plots had recently been divided and organized for construction, Angelina and her husband Juan bought a plot that had not yet been cleared nor formalized, for a price corresponding to the value of a couple of hundred soles.[12] There was therefore a lot to be done with this plot, but this was the only way Angelina could realize her dream of having a house of her own. The plot is located in the upper part of Jerusalén, just above the principal

[11] The real names of my informants have been replaced.

[12] The currency at that point was Inti.

football field which is in the centre of the neighbourhood dividing the upper and the lower part. Just below the football field are the school, the Catholic Church and the health station, surrounding the only park in the neighbourhood and the location also of the estate of the women's organization ASOMA. Since Angelina's sister lived nearby, they asked her and her husband for advice and help to clear the plot and construct the house. In general in Jerusalén, people organize work parties (*faenas*) for the clearing of land and construction of houses on individual plots, asking kin and neighbours for work help in return for food.

The above indicates the significance of kinship for the process of settlement in the city. Family and kin tend to cluster together, by living in extended households or settling down in the same or nearby neighbourhood. Indeed, settlement composition tends to be defined not only by kin, but also by people's different department, district, or village of origin. Several inhabitants in Jerusalén were barely in their teens when they left their villages, often in order to look for a job or to stay with relatives already living in the city. In this manner, the significance of kinship ties and relationships are often reproduced in the city. It has also been noted elsewhere that the great majority of migrants in the Andean context are young people, most often between 15 and 24 years of age, who are just about to enter the labour force (RED-ADA 1998). People's participation in the occupation of new neighbouring areas further reflects the importance of kinship for settlement composition. For instance, after Angelina established her own house in Jerusalén, she later acquired a second piece of land by participating in the occupation of new land just above Jerusalén, in El Mirador. She acquired this plot with her oldest daughter María in mind, so that María would have her own place to live and therefore hopefully stay in the area.

In the accounts of most people I talked with, the relationship to family and kin is significant not only for settling and accommodating in the city, but also for why or how they left their highland village. Many left in the company of some relative, while those who left on their own often had some relatives in the city to go and live with, or at least from whom to seek help and advice. In Jerusalén, many households continue to receive young relatives from their home village who come at an early age to study or work while living with their older kin in the city. In return, these newcomers are often expected to contribute to the family and household by assisting in the house or at the workplace. This is the case for Juana and Javier, a couple from the department of Cuzco living in the lower part of Jerusalén, just below the park that marks the centre of the neighbourhood. In their house, they often have visits from one or more young relatives who come to stay with them for shorter or longer periods to study or work. Among them is Juana's niece Victoria who lives with them while studying at the University, as well as working as a servant in a house closer to the centre of the city. Victoria's parents have also left their village in Chumbivilcas to live in Camaná, where they have found employment on one of the farms. In order to be able to study, Victoria instead went to Arequipa to live in her aunt's house. In the same period, one of Javier's nephews, Carlos, also came to live with them for shorter periods when not living in the house of his employers. This illustrates how many households become extended households as people receive younger relatives who come to Arequipa needing a place to stay.

Among young people who grow up in Arequipa, it is common that they continue living with their parents after finding a partner and having their own children. This is until they have established an income and/or found a plot of land for themselves. For instance, in the case of Juana's close neighbours, Eugenia and Antonio, their household has gradually expanded as their children have grown older. First one of their daughters, Carola, became pregnant, and since she and her boyfriend had nowhere to live, it was decided that they would live with them. Because there were only two rooms in the house but a lot of free space on the roof, they built a little house on the top of the old house. On some occasions, the young couple also go to live in the house of his parents, but generally they stay in Carola's parents' house. A couple of years after Carola's baby was born, Eugenia's first son José and his girlfriend were also going to have a child. In order to arrange some extra space, the little building that used to serve as the kitchen was changed into a sleeping and/or living room, and the kitchen was moved into the open air under a provisional roof.

With respect to the extension of urban households, Lund Skar (1994) has underlined that there is an emphasis on male bonds of uncle/nephew and brothers, such as in the inclusion of newly arriving migrants (1994:105–6). My impression is, however, that female bonds are not given any less importance than male ones in this binding of newly arriving relatives to the household. In fact, female bonds across the generations also seem to be strong, as previously illustrated in the case of Juana and her niece who has come to live in her house more or less permanently. This significance of female bonds is similarly reflected by the extension of households not only through patrilocal but also uxorilocal practices, by the settlement of young couples not necessarily in the household of the boy's parents, but also in the house of the girl's parents such as in Eugenia's case. In my experience, there does not appear to be any clear tendency toward uxorilocality nor patrilocality in Jerusalén, since these arrangements seem to depend more on convenience than principle. In many of the cases I know of, priority in these matters is given to age rather than gender, in the sense that it is often the oldest among siblings who is given a new place to live on the land of the parents or nearby in the neighbourhood. In the case of Angelina as well as Juana, for instance, it is for their oldest daughters that they have acquired new land by participating in the more recent occupations of land surrounding Jerusalén. Similarly, with respect to young relatives living in the highlands, it is generally the oldest who are invited to come and stay in the household of relatives living in the city.

In relation to the access to land, it is furthermore worth noting the significance of inheritance practices in processes of migration. In the rural highlands, all siblings are given a piece of their parents' land, so that the land owned by a couple is divided according to number of siblings,[13] who subsequently are given a piece more or less of equal size and value. These inheritance practices appear to reinforce, however, the demand in many rural areas for cultivable land and over time they may produce an acute scarcity of land. As the division of land for every generation gradually reduces the size of properties, it produces a situation which may require alternative solutions to make a living. From a rural perspective then, the principles of land inheritance may reinforce both the individual urge, as well as the general necessity for migration. The scarcity of land may indeed form part of people's motive to migrate, a motivation that is further strengthened in many cases by the possibilities and practices of land occupation in the city. Ironically then, land in the city may appear more achievable and expandable than in many rural areas.

In rural contexts, the access to specific parts of inherited land may furthermore depend on a person's position within the sibling group, in the sense that it is generally the youngest sibling who is expected to take over the house of the parents. This is in contrast to older siblings who are expected to construct their own house on a different piece of land. This inheritance by minor siblings seems to have a certain influence with respect to who chooses to migrate and who does not. As the youngest among siblings – the *menor* or *chanaca* (*sullqay* in Quechua) – is supposed to take over the land and house of the parents, he or she is simultaneously expected to be the one to take care of them when they get older and thus stay in the community. Although the other siblings may choose to leave, the youngest is expected to stay and eventually take over the parent's house. Based on the accounts of different people in Jerusalén, I got the impression that these expectations concerning the youngest among siblings are often respected, and most of my informants seemed to have at least one younger sibling who has stayed in the village. This tendency for the youngest to stay behind further seems to be reinforced in cases when there are older relatives already living in the city and, as described above, these relatives tend to give priority to the oldest in a sibling group when they want to bring young relatives to the city, and/or arrange a new plot of land for them. In the city it is thus often the oldest among siblings or younger relatives who is given their own piece of land. These are generally new plots of land that their parents or older relatives have worked to get hold of through occupation. In rural contexts, land inheritance is often bound up with specific expectations and traditions as well as limited opportunities for expansion. In the city, in contrast, there is the possibility of invading new land, although the effort it requires in terms of communal work and payments is too demandings to be managed for all siblings.

---

[13] In some cases, girls inherit land through their mothers and boys through their fathers, although it is not uncommon to inherit from both (Urton 1992:234).

The Hierarchization of Space

In accounts from rural Andean contexts, much has been written about the spatial organization conceptualized as *ayllu*. The *ayllu* system has been interpreted to characterize spatial organization and the formation of social groups (Gose 1994, Lund Skar 1994, Harris 2000) by emphasizing the opposition between equal segments of a larger territorial whole (Sallnow 1987). *Ayllu* relationships particularly define the formation of work groups for the local *faenas* (communal work), and are often characterized by intense competition (Lund Skar 1994: 110) and reciprocal exchange (Platt 1976). Gose (1994) sees the *ayllu* as a flexible social institution, and underlines how it primarily works as a land-holding group that comes to be equivalent to a work group (see also Allen 1988). The *ayllu* can thus be viewed as drawing together the significance of kin, land, and the spiritual bonds between them (Lund Skar 1994).

Although people in Jerusalén do not refer to the organization of their neighbourhood in terms of *ayllu*, similar oppositions are nonetheless made relevant. For instance, there is a similar organization in terms of different neighbourhood groups (and committees or teams) that co-operates and competes in relation to work parties, football matches, festivals and dancing competitions (*concursos*). Among people who have moved to Lima, Lund Skar (1994: 105–6) notes that the arrangement of such neighbourhood-based competitions may illustrate the reproduction in the urban context of the close relationship between kinship and land. In Jerusalén, the central neighbourhood association is divided into ten small committees, each intended to function as the local unit for the most immediate neighbourhood and having representation in the main committee. These local committees are generally the basic work units for the realization of communal work in the neighbourhood, and are often composed of people who are related to one another or come from similar districts. Inhabitants also speak about their neighbourhood as divided into an upper and a lower part, in a way that seems to be informed by the fact that there is a majority of people from Puno (*puneños*) in the upper part and a majority of people from Cuzco (*cusqueños*) in the lower part. Each Sunday, there are big football matches in the neighbourhood, arranged either on the biggest field along the main road or on one of the many other small fields on the periphery of the neighbourhood. In these matches, teams are organized according to membership in neighbourhood committees, or otherwise by more informal relations based on neighbourhood, kinship and *compadrazgo* relationships (ritual kinship). In the realization of festivals and anniversaries there is an arrangement of competitions (*concursos)* along similar lines. These festivities generally take the form of competitions in which each committee or neighbourhood presents its own groups of dancers and singers.

In Peru, the image of people as differently located in the space of the nation state has been informed by the differentiation of space in terms of rural highlands (*sierra*), Amazonia (*selva*) and urban lowlands (*costa*). Such a differentiation has been influenced by geographic characteristics like an extremely mountainous and inaccessible terrain versus the modernized cities closer to the coast, and related to an idea of centre and periphery as associated with social categories such as indigenous and *mestizo*. This differentiation also relates to standards of infrastructure, means of communication and other ways in which the physical distance to urban centres corresponds with less access to matters of national interest and concern.

In the course of migration and processes of urbanization, this differentiation between highlands and lowlands is in many ways also reflected in discourses about the city. For instance, the high urban hillsides of new migrant settlements tend to be associated with the Andean highlands, with poverty and *indios* or *cholos*, whereas low parts of the city continue to be associated with a more modern form of urbanity, with wealth and *mestizos* or *gente criolla*. These categories are often informed by symbolic oppositions such as high versus low, dirty versus clean, dangerous versus safe, violent versus non-violent, chaotic versus structured, and backward versus modern. These associations connected to the urban landscape can be understood as an expression of how the urban condition to some extent reflects and reproduces the oppositions often connected to urban lowlands *vis-à-vis* rural highlands. Since I was living in Jerusalén during most of my fieldwork, I several times experienced that people from the centre of the city worried about me due to the perceived problem of crime in the area, and taxi-drivers were sometimes reluctant to take me there. Other people I got to know were curious since they had never visited such a neighbourhood themselves, and therefore wanted me to bring them along. Indeed, ideas about rural and urban, periphery and centre seem to be continually made relevant with respect to the new neighbourhoods *vis-à-vis* the more established parts of the city. In this regard, the differentiation of space in the urban context reflects the way in which city and countryside continue to be constituted as places of difference, at the same time as the boundaries between them are increasingly unsettled.

Among people in Jerusalén, this oppositional categorization of highland and city, centre and margin is often reproduced through their own use of such images, for example in considerations about their own or other people's degrees of success or progress. If they should acquire the economic capacity, people said, they would move downhill by buying a new house closer to the centre, or send their children off to schools in the centre. Being able to answer '*en el centro*' when somebody asks where your children attend school or where you have your job, may signal a betterment of status and prestige that many people aspire to. Also within the neighbourhood of Jerusalén, some areas or plots of land (especially the lower parts) are also regarded as more attractive than others, due to standards of infrastructure and relative proximity to means of communication and the centre of the city.

On the plot of land that Angelina acquired for her daughter María in El Mirador, María and her husband soon managed to construct a house where they went to live. After several burglaries in the house, however, she and her husband decided to move back into Angelina's house. María actually suspected that her neighbours were the burglars, and said that the area in which she had constructed her house is inhabited by thieves. This illustrates how more recent neighbourhoods often have a bad reputation also among inhabitants in Jerusalén, and in addition to being associated with low morals and the presence of thieves, these areas are often said to be dirty and consist of '*puro tierra*' (only dirt, sand), due to the lack of asphalt on the roads.

In this manner, the low status of new and not so new urban neighbourhoods tends to be confirmed, in spite of the gradual, but often great improvement of infrastructure, housing and service standards. It indicates how the practices of migrants concerning land and space in the urban context should be understood in terms of the ways in which they are structurally as well as symbolically differentiated. It also illustrates how the dominant views of these new neighbourhoods are to a certain extent reproduced by the inhabitants themselves.

Documents of Identity

When Angelina, still a girl, first left her village for Arequipa all on her own,[14] the only personal documentation she had with her was her birth certificate. Just before leaving Arapa where she was born – and without telling her parents who were still unaware of her plans – she asked her teacher to give her the document. Except for the birth certificate, Angelina lived for a long time in Arequipa with none of the other documents that are required by official institutions. She gave birth to her first child at home, and it was not until she was to formalize her property in Jerusalén and had her second child that she went to solicit the other documents, both for herself and her newborn child. In this regard, it is worth noting Lund's (2001) point that the requirement of documents can be regarded as a way in which the state creates people as subjects and regulates the social making of meaning in an essentially material and textual way. She notes that the creation of administrative spaces of modern municipal life in Peru is part of the state's goal of creating islands of civilization through which citizens must move in order to process their documents. People's movement in these bureaucratic spaces becomes an embodied experience of the state, creating citizens through the sequence of bureaucratic identification and at the same time making the state evident through the identification process (2001:2).

Until recently,[15] a range of different documents were obligatory for all Peruvians and thus required in citizens' interaction with state or official institutions, particularly so in the city. These were the documents of birth and baptism, as well as electoral and military documents. Personal papers of this kind used to be requested on a range of occasions, such as when entering the education system or

[14] In the next chapter I will describe in more detail the background of how and why Angelina left her village for Arequipa.

[15] The arrangements and demands of personal documentation in Peru have been subject to a range of changes. The last one I know of took place during the first part of year 2004, and stipulated that only one document would be obligatory for personal identification instead of the previous demand for several.

formal employment, to own property or receive an inheritance, to acquire loans, health services or insurance, or take any form of legal action. During the period of terrorism, Peruvians also needed such documents to protect themselves from false accusation. People therefore had to carry the appropriate documentation in order to have freedom of movement without fear of being accused of subversive activity (Lund 2001:1). People may still experience difficulties due to a lack of identity papers, and among those who have moved from the highlands, there are many who have no such documentation (see also Lund 2001). Some people have not been baptized or otherwise officially registered in their home communities, either due to geographic isolation, inaccessibility or inability to make the payments, and others have lost their papers during the conflict between Sendero Luminoso and the authorities related to the burning of archives. Upon arriving in the city for the first time without such documentation, contact with official institutions may be problematic, such as getting access to services and making claims of different kinds. As a result, people may be excluded from certain forms of participation – the school and health systems, ownership of land and formal employment – which may sometimes be a condition for other rights and services. This lack may thus evolve into a vicious circle in which it is impossible to get, for example, formal employment without personal documents, at the same time as the acquisition of such documents represents a significant expense and effort.

The acquisition of such documentation may also require that people return to the district capital of their place of origin, at the same time as there are both photos to be paid for and an administrative fee, and the procedures involved are often difficult to understand. It may thus represent a significant effort to acquire this personal documentation, and while most people gradually do so, there are some who spend long periods in Arequipa – and sometimes their entire lives – without documentation. These people will not be able to enter formal employment, and self-employment is therefore the only way to gain a living for many. Among those who have their personal documentation it is also common to work at the margins of the formal economy, due to general unemployment and difficulties in entering the formal job market.

The City as Concept and Practice

In the settlement and livelihood practices of new urban inhabitants, urban spaces are made objects of occupation, new use and re-conceptualization through a reliance on social networks and collective work. Conventional uses of space in the urban context are in different ways negotiated and changed, such as through the organization of new neighbourhoods. These practices can be seen as the responses of people to different forms of marginality and exclusion in the urban context.

Taking place beyond any strategic form of official urban planning, the establishment of many new urban neighbourhoods is characterized by the lack of an overall vision or administration. In this manner, the practices of land occupation in Peruvian cities – as well as the more or less informal character of economic activities – have in many ways disrupted what is often the attempt of urban planners to create an orderly, secular and homogenized urban landscape (de Certeau 1984). De Certeau discusses the liberal modernist desire to control the development of cities, and how the administration of a city entails an expectation of planned development. Such planning in Peruvian cities has in different ways been disrupted by the high number of land occupations. It is interesting to relate this to de Certeau's argument that the city and the concept of it cannot be seen as identical, but as forming a progressive symbiosis (1984:94). As the creation of cities is both to think about the plurality of the real and to make this thinking about the plural effective, de Certeau argues that the transformation of the urban fact into the concept of a city depends on a mythification of the city in dominant discourse.

In Peru, the migration to the cities from the countryside since the 1940s and 1950s is often seen to have transformed many of the *criollo* or *mestizo*-dominated cities closer to the coast, by encompassing and reproducing the cultural and economic differences between the *mestizo* middle and upper classes and previously rural indigenous populations. Due to the great numbers of urban migrants as well as numerous occupations of land, cities have expanded rapidly and produced a conflict between the concept of the city (as *criollo* or *mestizo*) and the city itself (as heterogenous and increasingly indigenous too). In many ways, the city has been de-mythified. In this process, new and somewhat competing concepts of the city are created in relation to what has become an urban fact.

While located in an area where the Andean highlands meet the dry Pacific coast, the city of Arequipa used to be inhabited primarily by people categorized as *criollos*. What thus used to be regarded as a dominantly *criollo* or *mestizo* city has increasingly become a city influenced by rural forms of organization and use of land, practices of occupation and extended networks of kinship. Gandolfo notes that this steady growth along the urban periphery has kept alive and in many ways made real the fantasies and anxieties of an 'Indian' invasion (2009:1). From the perspective of the dominant classes, this can serve to illustrate de Certeau's point that the city may produce effects that are contrary to its aims, in the sense that there may be a re-emergence of elements that the urban project at first excluded. In de Certeau's terms, an effect of this re-emergence is that the development of the city is made prey to contradictory movements, due to the multiple local practices that the urban system was meant to administer and suppress. While urban spaces are made the object of a certain transformation through practices of occupation and collective construction, there is at the same time a re-appropriation of these spaces and practices by the state. In the last part of this chapter, I will therefore discuss the ways in which the multiple social and spatial practices of inhabitants are nonetheless made the subject of administration and policy making.

The Appropriation of Popular Practices

In response to the occupation and collective construction of new urban neighbourhoods, the authorities have tried to appropriate and co-opt many of these practices as a way by which to make the city and its inhabitants subject to administration. It is therefore important to explore to what extent this readjustment of state policies has resulted in a re-structuring or re-bureaucratization of these practices/spaces, such as through policies of formalization or the appropriation of popular initiatives into official policy.

The occupations of land on the outskirts of urban areas, as well as the informal establishment of housing on this land, represent a kind of practice that at first, during the increasing waves of migration in the 1940s and 1950s, the state sought to abolish. Later, the government reforms in the 1960s represented a first step toward the state's recognition of these claims and even a co-optation and institutionalization of these practices by the state. Such a co-optation took place with the government of Velasco's (1968–1975) creation of an official system for neighbourhood organizations (SINAMOS: Sistema National de Movilizacion Social) in 1968, and the requirement that all newly invaded urban areas should be organized through the coordination of neighbourhood committees. So while other military governments in Latin America during the 1960s and 1970s tried to oppress the working classes by violent means, Velasco's reforms involved an attempt to incorporate marginal groups in organizations coordinated by the state (Burt 2006:226). In Lima in 1971, the military was nonetheless ordered to expel occupants from the then newly established neighbourhood Villa el Salvador, and several occupants were killed in the process. After strong protests on behalf of the occupants, the authorities finally decided to accept their claims for land. This incident was followed by similar acceptances, and marked the beginning of a general practice that later was adopted by succeeding governments (Castañeda 1993:219, Rudolph 1992). Today, when land claims in the outskirts of a city are to be recognized by the authorites, inhabitants are expected to work together and form organizations in order to construct a new neighbourhood.[16] As I will discuss later, the establishment of official support to women's groups and the creation of state institutions to coordinate these arrangements were similarly the results of popular initiatives that have been co-opted by the state. Also after Velasco's reforms, later governments have similarly worked to coordinate popular efforts, such as the government of Fujimori in particular: (see Rousseau 2009). He followed a similar line with the initiation of state institutions such as Programa Nacional de Asistencia Alimentaria (PRONAA) aimed at co-ordinating many of the existing state programmes in new urban neighbourhoods, for instance the *comedores* (soup kitchens) and school breakfasts.

The authorities have in this manner integrated some of the initiatives and projects that at first represented the 'multiple responses of citizens' (de Certeau

[16] Similarly in Bolivia, there is a law about popular participation that was introduced in 1995 (Lazar 2002, 2008).

1984). The occupation of land on the outskirts of urban areas has in many ways become well established, not only through the practices of citizens, but also in how the authorities approach these matters. The 'unrestricted' response of citizens thus seems to be made subject to a co-optation or institutionalization by the authorities, so that the destructuring of space seems to have been accompanied by a re-structuring. What is interesting in this regard is the way in which bureaucratic institutions and functions have thus been altered in response to the responses of inhabitants, so to speak. This is not to say that the authorities responds to all the efforts and demands of citizens, which is of course not the case, but that this inclusion and co-optation can be seen as a way in which the urban authorities work – through a dialectics between popular practice and policy, or the city as practice and the city as concept (de Certeau 1984). Indeed, the issue of land occupations and popular organization has become increasingly important for the social and development policies of the authorities as well as the programmes of political parties. The access to land and the recognition of ownership has for instance been made a central issue for politicians seeking votes and political support in the new – or relatively new – urban areas such as Jerusalén, as they represent a great number of potential votes. Just before the presidential elections in 2000, Fujimori recognized the claims to land made by a group of occupants on the outskirts of Lima. About a year later, with the ascendance of Toledo to the presidency, these inhabitants were violently thrown off this land, and the houses they had constructed were destroyed. The reason for this somewhat late intervention was that the land already had a private owner who had apparently never agreed to the transaction, nor received compensation from the Fujimori government. This and similar cases illustrate the political significance of these land occupations and the informal arrangements they entail, in a way that is reflected in the political programmes and involvement of authorities and politicians.

The practices of occupation and collective construction of neighbourhoods in urban contexts have given rise not only to thousands of neighbourhood associations all across the country, but also to grand-scale organizations such as the Asociación de Organizaciónes Populares en Arequipa (AUPA), that include several hundred neighbourhood associations in Arequipa. By counting on numerous members, this organization has during the last decade even come to represent an important political faction. What is more, AUPA has become important also for its promotion and strengthening of so-called popular cultures (*culturas populares*) in Arequipa, for instance by providing support for the arrangements of Andean festivals and anniversaries, as well as a radio station.

According to Lund Skar, the co-optation by Peruvian authorities of these practices can be seen to relate directly to the strong populist political tradition in Peru in which self-help is promoted as a central value, and in a way that frees the state from the responsibility of providing basic services to a growing urban population (1994:181, see also Collier 1976, Lobo 1982). Several governments in Peru have underlined the necessity and value of inhabitants coming together in local organizational projects to construct or develop *el pueblo* (the community, nation) in order to *progresar*, *avanzar*, or *adelantarse* (progress, develop or move forward). For instance, while relatively new and unknown in the political domain, Fujimori gained much of his popularity through his emphasis on technology, hard work and honesty. Various authors have noted that this was an ideology that strongly resonated with Andean practices of communal work (see for example Starn, Degregori and Kirk 1995:420). By appealing to Andean traditions for communal work, governments and state institutions have in this manner come to rely on the initiatives and accomplishments of local organizations for the improvement of marginalized urban neighbourhoods.

Historical Background

It is important to underline that many of the organizational projects in these neighbourhoods involve the recruiting of participants to construct infrastructure and perform physically hard community work, in a way that simultaneously serves to save costs and responsibilities for local or state authorities. According to Gose (1994), these arrangements can in many ways be seen as a modernization of the colonial system of tribute – that is, indigenous people's payment to the state in the form of labour as previously described. The reference to Andean traditions of communal work in official projects can illustrate Gledhill's (1994) point that the production and inner logic of discursive constructions must be considered as closely related to historical processes, at the same time as the selection of particular constructions over others must be understood in terms of its relevance to people's everyday life. Indeed, the obligatory social organization of new urban neighbourhoods can be understood in relation to the way in which, during the colonial period, indigenous and *mestizo* were not only social categories, but fiscal categories reflected in the arrangement of *mita*.

Considering that these structures are further reproduced as people move to the cities, Lund Skar (1994) argues that the claims for land in urban occupations are similar to those of indigenous communities. They reflect how there is a category of people within the nation that has special constitutional status, particularly in terms of rights to land. The occupations of land by indigenous people in the city can therefore be seen as an extension of this kind of arrangement into an urban context (ibid:188). At the same time, it is important to note that the claims to land made by occupants for instance in Jerusalén have not been made by reference to an indigenous identity or belonging, or that they as indigenous people have a right to land. Among the inhabitants who were or had been involved in the neighbourhood committees, I never heard anyone mention their identity as indigenous people when referring to their claims to land or other rights. Nor did I hear such claims during my work in the local women's organization or the association for traders, where they instead stressed their position as poor people who should have the opportunity to work in order to improve their situation. Similarly in the literature, there does not seem to be any references to claims being made in this way. The absence of an emphasis on an 'indigenous identity' in their claims can be understood in terms of their general aspirations for social mobility and urge to escape the Andean stigma. But although the claims to land among Andean migrants in the city are not made with reference to their indigenous background, the policies of land/citizenship that are created in response to their practices are nonetheless in many ways specific for indigenous or migrant groups – although not limited to them. A new category for urban space and citizenship is thus created through these urban policies. Indeed, these are spaces based upon collective organization required by the state, and gradually changing into formalized and individual ownership of land. By being based on a collective organization of neighbourhoods that is increasingly combined with the formalization of individual ownership of land, these spaces – and the kind of citizenship that is created – are in many ways ambiguous, or 'hybrid'. These ambiguous spaces open up new possibilities for negotiation between inhabitants, community leaders and state representatives, but also relations of clientelism and increasing distrust towards local leaders, a point I will come back to. In many ways, the coordination of collective effort enables the authorities to relate to groups of people instead of individual citizens. In this manner, some kind of indirect rule seems to be maintained through the necessity of collective organization and the ambiguous spaces for citizenship that are created.

State Policies

During the presidency of Fujimori, a new state institution was created to take care of the registration and formalization of previously occupied land as well as non-formalized housing and economic activity, the Comisión de Formalización de la Propiedad Informal (COFOPRI). Previously, these formalization processes had been extremely difficult and time-consuming, particularly so for the migrant population. The initiation of COFOPRI can be interpreted as a response to a particular notion of development related to the formalization of ownership and economic activity. It corresponds to an argument put forward by the Peruvian economist de Soto (1989), who advocates formalization and ownership titles as a means to include marginalized groups. What may be problematic with this kind of approach, however, is that it is based on a neo-liberal economic principle[17] that emphasizes the transformation of poor and marginalized people primarily into economic agents through the means primarily of ownership and formalization. As occupied land becomes formalized, people may indeed take out loans and construct higher quality houses – and increasingly become consumers. What is more problematic though is that people may also have trouble matching the terms of the loan with their often low levels of income, and are bound to work continuously harder in order not to lose their properties and become increasingly marginalized. Ironically, people often continue to invest their work efforts in more or less informal ways of earning an

[17] See also Riofrío (1988) for a critique of de Soto's approach.

income, since it remains the only way for many to gain a living. It is furthermore important to acknowledge how the simplification of the formalization of occupied land or informal economic activity can accommodate other kinds of interests as well, that is, not only or necessarily the interests of citizens, but also those of economic agents interested in offering funding or loans for the construction of new properties or economic activity. Since neither funding nor loans can be given/obtained as long as the ownership of land is not formalized, policies of formalization partly serve to accommodate this kind of interest. In the areas around outdoor markets in Arequipa, the interest among loan agents is illustrated by the great number of micro-finance institutions that have been established during the last decade. Loan agents here are extremely aggressive in their campaigns towards the traders..

Among the initiatives during the presidency of Fujimori was the creation of the *Banco de Materiales* (The Bank of Materials). This bank involved a scheme for allowing inhabitants in new urban areas to borrow materials – instead of money – for the construction of lots and houses. In contrast to other loan arrangements, these loans were given without a guarantee of formal employment. Such an arrangement created good opportunities for some people in Jerusalén, although the high interest rates charged became problematic for many who could not count on a stable income. When I first visited Angelina in 1997, she had one room (or small house) that was constructed of cement, while the other room still consisted of stones and corrugated iron for the roof. By my second visit in 2001, in contrast, she had constructed a new big building made of cement and nicely painted, due to the new loan programme of the Fujimori government. The interest for this loan is quite high, however, and she often fears that the house will be taken away from her if she cannot meet the loan requirements.[18] Nonetheless, Angelina now manages several bank loans and seems to be used to the procedures and requirements that are involved, although she still needs some assistance from her daughter to help her with documents that need to be read. Sometimes she also gets loans from kin and neighbours as she did before. Other people fear taking out loans from the bank, however, due to the instability of employment and since '*el banco no perdona*' (the bank does not forgive). Instead, they prefer to ask for loans among kin or neighbours or participate in collective saving groups. This may indicate some dimensions that de Soto's approach does not take into account, such as the complexity in the dynamics of marginalization, related for instance to unemployment and the lack of formal education that serve to reinforce marginalization despite a certain economic agency. What is more, the policies of formalization also have opened up new kinds of speculation in land, a dimension I will expand upon later.

---

[18] In relation to the presidential elections in 2000, inhabitants in Jerusalén and other neighbourhoods mobilized in order to protest against the high interest on these loans. The project was led by a lawyer who would run as a candidate for the local elections. Among those who participated from Jerusalén, it was continuously underlined that as long as this bank was apparently intended to help the poor, they should not need to pay such high interest rates.

Ambiguous Spaces for Citizenship

It has been noted that the policies for collective organization and formalization may serve as a way of making legible what is already informally there (Lazar 2002). According to Scott (1998), the efforts made for the permanent location of inhabitants are part of a state's attempt to make society legible, or to arrange the population in a way that simplifies the state functions of taxation, conscription and the prevention of rebellion. This entails the creation of overviews or maps of a state's terrain and people, and the translation of this knowledge into a common standard. In this manner, the inhabitants' complex, illegible local social practices are used to make a simplified standard grid whereby practices can be centrally recorded, monitored and manipulated. The policies of formalization in Peru can in this regard represent a form of mapping, or of making legible, for purposes of administration, taxation, consumption and so on. As underlined by Li (2001), however, there are often divergent interests at work in this and other forms of mapping. For instance, she notes how the World Bank has been involved in land titling projects in different countries that are intended to free up land for capitalist investment which could also have the effect – conveniently enough – of fulfilling the World Bank's more recent commitment to recognizing and protecting indigenous land rights. In this regard, Li notes that there is at the same time a disadvantage to detailed maps, even from a government perspective. Detailed maps may diminish the power of officials to assign vast concessions to capitalist interests on the basis of vague land classifications, or to resolve conflicts according to their own priorities. In the context of Indonesia's forest zone, she thus argues that the continued illegibility of forest spaces, the lack of official data about the numbers and location of people living there and the inadequacy of official forest maps may give the forest authorities room to manoeuvre. Indeed, Li argues – contra Scott (1998) – that illegibility has an ongoing role in modern systems of rule (Li 2001:665). In this regard, it is worth asking whether citizens' practices in the often vaguely defined, or ambiguous spaces for citizenship as described above, are perhaps also only partly made legible. This is due to the possible advantages of such vaguely defined spaces from the perspective of the authorities as suggested by Li.

On the one hand, the policies for collective organization and formalization in new urban neighbourhoods in Peru could be considered a way to administer people in a process of mobility. By entailing the production of an overview, a knowledge and language for governance in new urban neighbourhoods, the policies for and involvement of official agencies in popular organization can – to a certain extent – make these popular practices more 'legible'. As I will describe later, state agencies' arrangement of practical training or so-called *capacitación*, such as through the women's groups, can for instance be regarded as central in the attempt to make inhabitants into 'proper' urban citizens. This involvement may also serve to increase the authorities' knowledge about the subject group, a knowledge that may serve to create and uphold a certain overview of these new urban neighbourhoods. At the same time, the effects of the state policies and involvement in these neighbourhoods do at the same time appear to be somewhat contradictory. On the one hand, the demand to formalize ownership works to individualize inhabitants (for example by involving a demand for documents of identity that many people often lack), while on the other hand the demand for collective effort is often reproduced due to limited official investments. The coordination of collective effort also enables the authorities to relate to groups of people – that is, through organizational leaders – instead of individual participants. The state is in this manner ambiguously present in these spaces, and official policies can therefore not unambiguously or necessarily be seen as serving to make legible the practices of citizens. Indeed, a certain degree of illegibility seems to be maintained through the necessity of collective organization and the 'hybrid' spaces for citizenship that are thus created. In these ambitiously defined spaces, administrative projects of regulation are mixed with strategic political pragmatism in times of elections, in a way that adds to the diffuseness of interests invested in the making of illegible spaces of manoeuvre.

Central for the maintenance of a certain level of illegibility in these spaces is the role of women in many projects of communal work and organization. Indeed, there is an explicit focus on gender, and women in particular, in many of the official institutions involved in new neighbourhoods. By being 'women' and not expected to be providers for their households, their workforce has gained particular significance in these hybrid and partly illegible spaces of citizenship created between popular organization and state.

During my first period of fieldwork in 1997, the participants in these local organizations often talked about their participation as a way of improving the situation of their families as well as of the neighbourhood, and as part of their attempt to seek progress (*progreso*). It is important in this respect to note how participants conceptualized this kind of work and whether they saw it as performed for the community or for the state, something which again depends on the degree to which the state is seen as external to the people. While people's perspectives on these projects seemed to vary according to the tasks they were performing, there was often a certain tension as participants on the one hand saw the work as something they did for themselves and their neighbourhood, while on the other hand phrasing the relationship with state institutions as exploitative. In particular, the leaders of local organizations have a significant position in this regard, not only for the realization of work projects but also for how they are conceptualized, since they are the ones who mediate the relationship between individual citizen and the state by standing at an interface (see Lazar 2002:69). In relation to similar organizations in Bolivia, Lazar (2002, 2008) has made an important argument. One of her points is that the collective nature of cholo citizenship is (re-)created by the way in which the state creates the community as an administrative entity, first by requiring the inhabitants to develop the zone without the state's help; and later by administering local development through local leaders (2002:69).

Communal Work and Leadership

Due to their efforts in establishing the neighbourhood, the original occupants in Jerusalén are still looked upon with certain respect among more recent inhabitants. They are often referred to as the *fundadores* (the founders) due to the time and effort they have contributed to construct the neighbourhood. One of the original occupants, Eugenia's husband Antonio, often spoke of his experience as a founder of the neighbourhood, and underlined the effort that he made in contributing to its development and making it into what it has become today. At the same time, he also complained about what he experienced as a lack of gratitude and respect among fellow neighbours for the work he once did for their communal benefit. This is particularly as he has been accused of corruption in the aftermath of his position as a leader. In this manner, histories of the construction of the neighbourhood are sometimes ambiguously recollected by inhabitants, particularly due to suspicion that leaders misuse their positions. As I discuss later, the existence of this kind of 'corruption talk' is in fact often prevalent in this and other local organizations. It illustrates the tension between collective and individual arrangements, values or interests as noted above, and the fear that leaders misuse their position and people's trust for personal purposes. What is more, it may be related to people's experience of insecurity regarding such things as land titles and the collective payment of fees. The prevalence of 'corruption talk' in local organizations can therefore be related to the maintenance of a degree of illegibility in these 'hybrid' spaces. This is similarly reflected in the re-creation of practices of occupation that I describe below.

I have already mentioned how, in the areas above and around Jerusalén, new occupations took place during the 1990s with the subsequent creation of several new neighbourhoods. Although these areas had already been occupied when I first came to Jerusalén in 1997, the process of constructing and getting recognition for this land had just started when I arrived for my second period of fieldwork in 2003, and was not completed in 2007. In these more recent neighbourhoods, some of the inhabitants in Jerusalén continue – together with first-time settlers – to participate in communal work, to pay the regular fees (or *cuotas*) and contribute to the establishment of infrastructure and housing. Some inhabitants from Jerusalén thus participate in the establishment of new neighbourhoods just as they did in Jerusalén. The intention is to get hold of new plots of land and thus expand their property through communal participation. In most cases, people do this to acquire some new land for their children to take over when old enough. Others get involved in these new neighbourhoods for the sake not only of their own children, but for other relatives such as those in the highlands who are planning to leave for the city, or for young relatives who stay in their house as a temporary solution. For instance, in the occupation of the area now called Cenepa, there were several people from Jerusalén who went along to this hillside to participate, and among them were my informants Juana and her husband Javier. At that point their own house was more or less completed, well built with cement walls and glass windows, with two stories, water and electricity.

As previously mentioned, they used to share their house with a nephew and niece from Chumbivilcas who had come to the city to study and work. During the occupations of Cenepa, Juana and Javier got hold not just of one, but two pieces of land, one that was intended for Clara, their oldest daughter, and another that was intended for Javier's nephew Carlos. Although the neighbourhood was still without roads, water and electricity, Carlos immediately moved up to live on his new lot in Cenepa. He built a simple house of stones and started to participate in the work parties himself. As representatives for Clara's lot, Juana and Javier, but most often Juana, continued to join the work parties in her place, as Clara was still young and with no extra time since she had just started studying at University. Clara's parents wanted her to take over this piece of land when she got older, so that she would have a place of her own and at the same time stay in the area. This illustrates how kinship is made relevant not only in the first process of settlement, but also in the arrangement of new occupations. From Clara's perspective, however, this new lot did not correspond with her own plans for the future and was not somewhere that she would like to live at all, since '*alla es puro tierra*' (there, it is only sand/dirt). Rather, she would like to rent something further down towards the centre of the city, probably because of the simple standard and relatively low status of this new neighbourhood. This indicates how people may ascribe different meanings to the idea about progress, and how these meanings are made object of negotiation, for instance between the generations.

There are also people who participate in occupations of new land in the city in order to sell[19] their old house and plot of land, and move to the new piece of land that they have just obtained. This is a way to accumulate capital of course, as the price they can get for the old plot of land is generally much better than the price for the new one, by representing a better standard, being located in a more established neighbourhood, and with the conditions of ownership more formalized. Over time, these plots are therefore likely to increase substantially in value. With this in mind, some people even make these practices of occupation and neighbourhood construction into a business.[20] They participate in the occupation and construction of different areas, get access to a piece of land and pay their part of the expenses in order to sell when the value rises without ever having lived in the place. It is said that some such people who speculate in occupations even

[19] As invaded lots are formalized and recognized as private property, they can also be bought and sold. As previously illustrated, there are also many cases in which lots have been sold before formalization.

[20] This making of land occupations into a business involves not only or necessarily migrants or people with low-skill employment, and may include also people with professional occupations.

become leaders of neighbourhood associations. From this position,[21] they may not only obtain several pieces of land that they soon sell, but also get access to cash from the collection of money among participants – money that they are often accused of stealing. In this manner, the collective occupation of land can also represent an opportunity for some people to make a living, by participating in a range of different occupations. This is a practice that most inhabitants criticize quite strongly for being immoral and a bad way in which to misuse the efforts and trust of other occupants. It illustrates how the complex co-existence between collective arrangements and individual land titles may open up new possibilities for marginalized urban citizens, while at the same time creating problems of distrust, speculation and misuse.

The authorities have also formulated a law intended to prevent the same person from occupying and owning more than one plot of land in this way, stating that one person can only have one such piece of land (acquired through occupation) registered in her name.[22] It is not difficult to see the necessity of such a law in light of the previously mentioned practices of speculation, but it is nonetheless interesting to note that land ownership laws concerning other land deeds do not entail this kind of restriction. It illustrates how this particular arrangement for occupied and collectively achieved land seems to imply a notion of special arrangement or aid, and a kind of arrangement from which nobody is supposed to prosper. Such an arrangement does not seem to prevent people from expanding their properties though, as people inscribe the new plot of land either in the name of their partners – as many couples live together without being married – or in the name of their children or some more distant relative. In many ways, the speculation in collective occupations of land can also be understood as a response to the authorities' policies of formalization, and thus reflect Mitchell's point (2002) that policies of formalization can result in new practices of land speculation. While some individuals may of course prosper from these new practices of speculation, he argues that they may also serve to make already marginalized people even more impoverished.

As previously occupied areas turn into more established neighbourhoods and land ownership becomes increasingly formalized – and thus individualized and personal loans are taken up – there is also a tendency for people to gradually participate less in communal work and increasingly rely on their own personal efforts (see also Blondet 1990, Lazar 2002). In Jerusalén there is still work that should be done, such as maintenance and roads that need preparation, but the neighbourhood committees have been unable to complete it. Although there is a fee imposed upon people who are absent, it has become increasingly difficult to realize such works. Many people say they do not have time, that nobody else

21 There is sometimes also a degree of spatial ranking in these organizations in that the originators of the invasion acquire the most favourable sites (Lund Skar 1994:193).

22 See Comisión de Formalización de la Propiedad Informal N 009-99-MTC, Lima 1999.

attends these work parties either, and that the leaders of the committees tend to be corrupted anyway. As I will explain later, there was also a significant drop in the number of members in the women's groups in Jerusalén from my first fieldwork in 1997 to my latest in 2007. These changes may of course be a result of the general improvements that the neighbourhood has seen, but must also be considered in relation to more general changes of attitude that may have to do with the relationship between local organizations and official programmes.

Conclusions

In this chapter, I have discussed how urban spaces are in many ways transformed through practices of occupation and the collective construction of new neighbourhoods, and how these practices at the same time are appropriated by the authorities. I have been concerned with collective occupations and labour in the outskirts of urban centres, and related this to the development of state policies regarding the growth of new urban neighbourhoods. Among the reactions of the authorities to the popular practices of land occupation and collective construction are the initiation of policies and institutions to accommodate the formalization of land ownership and to coordinate popular organizational efforts. Indeed, the collective organization of inhabitants in these urban areas into neighbourhood committees has become a requirement by the authorities in order to formalize people's land ownership. It involves a space initiated by collective organization, and a space in which the tension between collective and individual organization of, entitlements to, and responsibility for land is maintained. So while the inhabitants' claims to land are not made with reference to their indigenous background, the arrangements created in response to these new urban practices are nonetheless specific to migrant indigenous or marginalized groups. A new category for the use of urban space (and citizenship) is thus created, based on a partly collective and partly formalized use and organization of land as well as work force. This space revolves around a dialectic between 'city as concept' and 'city as practice' (De Certeau 1984), in the sense that 'city as concept' is continually reformulated through the integration in official policies of citizens' practices. The making of what are considered 'Andean traditions of collective work' into a means of administration is an example of this dialectic. The ambiguous spaces for citizenship that are thus created may open up new possibilities for marginalized urban citizens, but may also fuel practices of clientelism and problems of speculation, distrust and misuse. Reflecting upon the effects of these policies, I have argued that they do not necessarily serve to make popular practices more 'legible', but rather that they serve to maintain a certain level of 'illegibility'. I have therefore illustrated how the ambiguously defined, hybrid spaces for citizenship – created through the co-existence between collective and individual organization of land in new urban neighbourhoods – may open up room to manoeuvre that often serves to reproduce a level of illegibility.

Chapter 2
The Negotiation of Identities

While the previous chapter was concerned with spatial differentiation and the negotiation of categories related to space, this chapter focuses on identity and the negotiation of social categories. I will illustrate how movement in space can be related to a reconfiguration of social categories and identities, in the sense that people sometimes attempt to negotiate the way they are positioned in such social categories. I focus on the ways in which identity and personhood are defined and negotiated through social relationships, such as in relations to kin and marriage partners, affinals and colleagues, and how redefinitions of identity have consequences for whether such relationships are negotiated or confirmed, rejected or extended. The chapter illustrates people's experiences of discrimination as well as some of their attempts to avoid this discrimination, and how discrimination is made relevant not only in public encounters but also in the relationship between kin and neighbours.

In a society characterized by inequality and discrimination toward the indigenous, the stigma of people from the highlands has created a fundamentally ambiguous attitude to Andean identities, reinforced by the ideology of *mestizaje* and the complex intersections between ethnicity and class relations. The chapter therefore explores the sometimes contradictory implications of the discourse on *mestizaje* in the Peruvian context, a discourse that can be seen to individualize as well as conceal the persistence of inequality. The ideology of *mestizaje* has not simply resulted in cultural accommodation and assimilation however, since people do not unambiguously seek to become *mestizos*, nor do they necessarily revitalize their Andean background. Categories such as *indio*, *cholo* and *mestizo* rather become blurred, contested *and* reproduced in a highly complex and contradictory way.

The ambiguity of identification in this context is evident also with respect to language, and the last part of the chapter is concerned with people's experiences with and use of the Spanish language, and how they simultaneously relate to Quechua as their mother tongue and associate it with their place of origin. Here I connect people's management of linguistic competence and boundaries to the ambiguity of identification and the interchange between subject or speaking positions (Moore 1994a, Polar 2000), and relate this to the negotiation of categories like *mestizo* and *indio*, rich and poor, city and rural highland. Through people's dialogues and interactions, I explore how these ambiguities of identification take the form of an interchange not only between language codes, but also different ways of viewing the world or 'speaking positions' within different discourses.

First, in order to give the reader an impression of people's experiences of migration and how they have come to settle in Arequipa, I will now expand upon the stories of two of my most important informants. The life experiences and social networks of these women will represent nodal points for my ethnographic descriptions and explorations throughout the book. At this point, I will present a summarized version of central parts of their life histories in order to give an impression of life experiences and situations that are typical of those who have migrated to Arequipa and settled in Jerusalén.

Mobility and Identification

Me Perdí (I Disappeared)

At the age of ten, Angelina came to Arequipa on her own, after secretly leaving her family in the countryside of Arapa,[1] located close to Juliaca in the department of Puno. She will now soon turn 50 and in addition to her husband Juan, she currently lives with her adult daughter and her daughter's husband and son. Looking back, Angelina said she left Arapa because she wanted to earn money, and because she was eager to buy the flowery modern skirts she had seen worn by girls from the city. If her parents had known, they would never have let her go, she said. She was her father's favourite child and the eldest of several much younger siblings. After arriving in Arequipa, Angelina found work on the grand-scale farms in the valley that surround the city by working for the farmers during periods of sowing and harvesting. After a while, she was hired as a servant and moved into a house of *gente qala* (referring to rich or white people),[2] where she learned to clean, cook and speak the Spanish language. As the years went by she got a boyfriend, who came from a neighbouring house in Arapa. On discovering she was pregnant, she left her job as she figured she could not live in her employers' house with both a boyfriend and a baby. Instead, she and her boyfriend hired a room whilst she tried to find work in the fields as she had before. After a few months, however, her boyfriend left her for a good job in the silver mines further north, and she never heard from him again. This was an experience Angelina took long to recover from, both emotionally and economically, as she was still pregnant at the time he left and their daughter María was born soon after. Having only her sister to support her, Angelina had to manage as well as she could, but chose to stay in Arequipa instead of going home.

A few years later, when she met an older man called Juan who asked her to marry him and who seemed like a nice and responsible man, she agreed to throw her lot in with his. Together they acquired a piece of land in Jerusalén, where they began constructing a small house of stone, and later expanded with two somewhat

1 I have changed the names of the places where people come from in order to protect their identities.

2 *Qala* is Quechua for naked or stripped person, referring to people with white skin and particularly those who own much land.

bigger houses made of bricks and cement. While Juan worked in construction, Angelina went back to work in the fields. For a while they both also worked taking out stones from the mines on the hillsides of Misti, as did many of the other inhabitants of Jerusalén. In addition, they participated in the work parties organized by the neighbourhood committees on Sundays in order to establish infrastructure in the area, although it was Angelina who most often took care of these communal obligations. Angelina also took part in the women's groups (*clubes de madre*) that had been organized in the neighbourhood since the 1980s, where she participated in different work projects and from which she could also benefit by receiving rations of food. Angelina gave birth to three more children, all boys, but it was later decided that her two oldest sons should live in the house of her sister nearby, since Angelina and her husband were too poor at the time to take care of them. Angelina's sister earns well through the shop she runs on the ground floor of her home as well as by owning a couple of taxis, so they expected that she would be able to take better care of the boys. As her oldest daughter María and youngest son Pablo were getting older, and after having tried to run a food store from her house for a few years, Angelina decided she would try her luck with trade. She started by selling small amounts of fruits and vegetables in the streets close to one of the big outdoor markets in town, La Feria Altiplano. At first this work did not really bring in much money, but she was nonetheless determined to continue trading. After years of hard work she finally managed to establish her own market stand at La Feria Altiplano. While gradually expanding her business, she also decided to withdraw from the women's organization because of a growing lack of time and motivation.

A few years after finishing secondary school, Angelina's daughter, María, managed to establish her own market pitch in the centre of the city, and her son, Pablo, finally gave up looking for work in Arequipa and went to Argentina to work in construction and mining. Once or sometimes twice a year, Angelina used to travel to Arapa to visit her mother. After the death of Angelina's father, her mother lived on her own, sometimes looking after the children of one of Angelina's sisters who works in Bolivia. Angelina often used to worry about her mother because of her age and because she only had her grandchildren to help her work the fields. Although Angelina managed to convince her mother once to come and live with them in Arequipa, her mother soon went back since she did not really like city life. After years of living in this neighbourhood with migrant neighbours like herself, Angelina often underlined her appreciation that many of them are from the department of Puno like herself. On other occasions though, she complained about what she addressed as the poverty and 'lack of education' of people in the neighbourhood, and stressed that she did not really want any contact with her neighbours. She has not kept much contact with her sister who lives nearby either, except to go over to inform her occasionally when something is wrong.

Me Trajeron Para Trabajar (They Brought Me to Work)

Eugenia is 48 years old and has lived in Jerusalén since she arrived in Arequipa where her husband Antonio had acquired a plot of land during the occupation. Their house is located in the lower part of the neighbourhood, where they live with their four children (one from Eugenia's previous relationship). Two of them are now adults and live there with their partners and children of their own. Eugenia grew up in a sibling group of eight, close to a village called Tarabamba located in the department of Cuzco. When she was 13 years old, one of Eugenia's aunts – who was living in the city of Cuzco – offered her work as a servant there. This turned out to be a difficult period for Eugenia, since her employers did not treat her well. She did not speak Spanish at the time, and her employer (*patrona, señora*) sometimes hit her due to her problems with the language and understanding what her employer wanted her to do. Her employer even cut off Eugenia's braids, since she said they were ugly and dirty. One day her father came from Tarabamba to the employer's house in Cuzco to see her. He understood how much she disliked it there, and brought her back home with him without giving notice to the employers.

At about 15 years of age, Eugenia went to Puerto Maldonado in the Amazon, also in order to work as a servant, and from the money she earned there she used to buy sweets for her younger brothers and sisters back home. In Puerto Maldonado she met a boy and became pregnant, and at first she did not tell her employers out of fear of what they would say. Her boyfriend suddenly drowned, however, and she decided to tell her employers she wanted to go home. The *señora* tried to convince her to stay, but Eugenia left without notice. Back home her mother decided that she would bring up her daughter's newborn baby so that Eugenia could be free to find herself another boyfriend later. Soon after giving birth, Eugenia went back to Cuzco in order to work. Once again she found herself with a *patrona* who was unkind to her, and she went to work as a servant in Lima instead. Again she got pregnant and went back to Tarabamba. Both her children were growing up in Tarabamba when one of the neighbours one day came to ask her father if Eugenia would marry their son who also had children from previous relationships. At first Eugenia hesitated, but as the families had gradually reached an agreement, it was decided that the couple should go to live in Arequipa where Antonio had already lived for some time working as a car mechanic and had appropriated a piece of land during the occupation of Jerusalén. As the years passed, three more children were included among the ones they both had from previous relationships.

Eugenia often underlined that she and her husband have not advanced as much as she had hoped beyond having acquired their own house in the city. They have not been able to give any of their children a professional education, and the earnings brought to the house are barely enough to put food on the table. Whilst Eugenia tries hard to earn money through various forms of trade, her husband has not contributed much since he often spends his earnings from the garage on alcohol. Antonio has withdrawn from his previously active position in the neighbourhood committee, and only occasionally do they participate in work parties. For a while,

Eugenia's participation in the women's organization in the neighbourhood seemed to be a good opportunity to improve their situation somewhat by acquiring rations of food in exchange for work. However, after several years of participation she retired from the organization in order to spend more time working and looking after the family. During my fieldwork Eugenia sometimes said that she still wondered if she should go back to live in Tarabamba, but worried that she and her family would have difficulties fitting in. Most of her siblings except the youngest have now left the village, one for the city of Cuzco and a brother and a sister to neighbouring localities in Arequipa. Her father still lives in Tarabamba though, and sometimes he comes to visit in Arequipa. He always decides to go back home though, since he does not really like it in Arequipa. Eugenia said she understands him, because in the beginning, she did not feel comfortable in Arequipa either, since she did not know people there, could not speak the language and had no work. Since she began to work in different forms of trade she has started to like life in Arequipa better, except that she does not really feel comfortable in her neighbourhood. She claims that people in the neighbourhood do not like her, and that some of them have caused her harm (*daño* or *brujería*, that is, harmful acts) so that she and her family will not progress, but suffer. She underlined that unlike her, most of her neighbours are from Puno, and she often talked about people from Puno as *mala* (bad). As her daughters were growing up, Eugenia said that one of her primary concerns was that they should not have to work as servants, since she does not want them to experience the often bad treatment of servants that she has experienced. Instead, her adult daughters currently work in trade, while her oldest son works as a taxi driver.

The Question of Identity in a Quest for Progress

As the life stories of Angelina and Eugenia illustrate, people have different reasons for coming to Arequipa. By escaping her parents, Angelina came to look for work and earn money on her own initiative, while Eugenia was first brought by a relative to work as a servant in Cuzco and later moved to Arequipa to marry. Both were quite young when leaving their villages, typical of many of the people with whom I spoke. For Angelina as well as Eugenia, and common for people in Jerusalén more generally, work represents a significant factor in why and how they moved to the city.

Many people also said that they left the countryside in order to acquire a better standard of living, one that is associated with the middle class, the 'urban' and 'modern', that is, the city life they had heard about from city-dwellers visiting the countryside. The aspirations for moving to the city are thus often infused by dreams of a better way of living, and contrasted with the hard life and poverty of their villages. This is illustrated in the case of Angelina, for instance, when she refers to her desire as a little girl not to end up like her parents, living poorly and in an old-fashioned way in the countryside. Instead, she wanted to work and earn her own money, be independent and become somebody different from her parents. Many people similarly expressed an urge to change their lives and live more like people in the city. 'We come looking for modernity' (*venimos a buscar la modernidad*), Angelina's son-in-law Eduardo once underlined. Central in many people's accounts of their own and others people's quest for social mobility were thus terms like modernity and progress (*progreso*), terms that are also widely used in official discourses.

In Jerusalén, people seem to associate the notion of progress with the life standard of the middle class, or more generally with modernization, industrialization and economic growth. This reflects an understanding of society as subject to change or development, a kind of change that individuals can also experience through social mobility. Modernity and progress were often talked about as things that can be sought and acquired in a city, thus reflecting an understanding of modernity as intrinsically urban. The stress on modernity and progress in this context therefore relates to the way in which highland and city, *indio* and *mestizo*, are often referred to as oppositional poles or categories. Indeed, the quest for progress appears to involve an attempt to re-define a rural Andean background by seeking to acquire some kind of urban *mestizo*-ness and reflecting how mobility is understood in economic as well as 'ethnic/cultural' or 'racial' terms. The search for mobility and progress may in this regard involve a desire for 'otherness', that is, to become more like the 'other' and less like one's 'origins'. One can see this reflected in Angelina's story and the way in which she expressed a wish to become someone other than her parents. For many, this wish seems to be an attempt to escape what is often characterized as the 'lack of modernity' in the highlands, that is, the isolation, poverty and rural way of life, or what people sometimes conceptualized as backwardness or a lack of civilization (*la barbaridad*). Lobo (1982) has similarly noted that progress was often spoken of by migrants in Lima in contrast to what was perceived as the 'backwardness' and 'under-development' (*atrazado*) of the rural highlands (1982:64). According to her, people spoke about progress in terms of moving away from something negative, such as a hard life in the highlands, scarcity of food, illnesses, a severe climate and hard work, and as a moving towards the positive ideal associated with urban living – plentiful food, good health and productive work (1982:65). When people in Jerusalén referred to the notion of progress, it was often with reference to stable employment, a proper house, and being able to give the children a professional education. Education seems to be particularly important for understandings of mobility and progress, and people often described their villages in the highlands as characterized by a lack of education – *son ignorantes* (they are ignorant). Access to modern goods and commodities may also be important in the quest for progress, in the sense that one has to be a consumer of modern objects in order to be seen as an urban *mestizo*. Goods may thus have a metonymic effect by indicating a person's position in society, in the same way as the standard and location of people's houses may be a sign of progress and success. Money may also increase one's *mestizo*-ness, in the same way as education or urban *mestizo* behavioural codes may socially 'whiten' one's skin, that is, make one whiter in the view of others. This indicates how the use of terms associated with colour and background may be subject to certain flexibility and even redefinition, with the effect that a person can redefine her position as indigenous through the acquisition of cultural or economic capital of a certain kind. In this manner, categories and identifications referring to culture or ethnicity must be seen to inform, as well as be informed by, dimensions of class.

In Jerusalén, people do not necessarily identify themselves as indigenous people, and there was no single term with which they self-identified. They sometimes referred to themselves as *serranos* (people from the highlands), or with reference to their mother tongue, as Quechua or Aymara speakers (*Quechua/ Aymara hablantes*). When speaking Quechua, they mainly referred to themselves as *runa*, which means human being. People also referred to themselves in terms of their department or district of origin, such as *puneños*, *cuzceños*, *chumbivillcanos*, or *ayacuchanos*, and some of those who had lived in Arequipa for a while sometimes referred to themselves as *arequipeños* or *mestizos*. In Peru more generally, people commonly use terms associated with cultural background or colour in order to identify themselves or others, some of which are given rather negative connotations, such as *cholos*, *indios* or *la cultura chicha*.[3] These terms are used with reference to people from the Andean highlands, and people generally do not self-identify through these terms due to the negative connotations. The term *cholo* is used to refer to indigenous people who have migrated and become more urban or *mestizo*, and is thus given connotations of an 'urban *indio*'. *Cultura chicha* is another term used to refer to a whole set of practices similarly associated with the migration of people from the highlands and their accommodation to the city. Although these notions are generally taken as being offensive, they may also be positively understood in familiar situations, and used as a good-humoured reference to an Andean background. When referring to the original population in Arequipa and the well-situated people of the city in particular, people in Jerusalén spoke of *gente decente* or *grande* (decent or grand people), *mestizos*, *criollos* or simply *arequipeños*. They also spoke of *gente qala*, meaning naked, white or stripped people as previously mentioned. There were also cases in which people referred to the class dimension of differences between themselves and the *arequipeño* population by terms such as *la clase alta* (the upper class) or *gente de dinero* (people with money). As already noted, the ability to work was often crucial in these ascriptions of difference and important for how people in Jerusalén differentiated themselves from people born in Arequipa.

The quest for mobility and progress seems to be associated in many respects with becoming more *mestizo*-like also through the acquisition of cultural capital of a certain kind, like education or urban manners of speech, dress and behaviour.

---

3 *Chicha* is the term for corn beer produced in the highlands, and is the name also of a music style associated with the urban indigenous or working classes. The term is often applied when talking negatively about certain kinds of politics, corruption and illegality, or when referring to gossip-prone parts of the press.

When I asked Eugenia about her background, she referred to the presence of Spaniards in the region of her birth, arguing that she, like other people in the Cuzco region, has mostly Spanish blood in her veins. She thus sometimes identifies herself as a *mestiza*, at the same time as her mother tongue is Quechua and she has a Quechua surname. This self-identification as a *mestiza* is not always recognized by others however. Once when I accompanied Eugenia to the city of Cuzco, we went together to the local municipality in order to change her son's identity document. She was on her way to visit her relatives in Tarabamba, and used the opportunity to visit the Cuzco municipality since her son was registered there. Any changes to these documents need to be done at the same district office where they were solicited. For the journey from Arequipa, Eugenia had really dressed up according to urban dress codes, with a skirt and blouse and her hair loose. At the office in Cuzco, she spoke to the bureaucrat in Spanish, but had trouble understanding the formal procedure which had been explained to her. The man behind the desk was annoyed, and started to speak to her in Quechua instead, asking if she was too stupid to understand Spanish. In this case, it was obviously her incomplete knowledge of Spanish, as well as her lack of knowledge about formal procedures, that made Eugenia fail in this attempt to be identified as *mestiza*.

The above does not imply, however, that all people in Jerusalén would necessarily value or aim to become *mestizos* as the term is generally understood, since they may also prefer to maintain and underline their identity as *serranos* (people from the highlands), or as indigenous people in a quest for progress and an urban way of life. It is useful in this regard to note de la Cadena's (2000) insights in how working-class indigenous people in Cuzco have redefined the meaning of *mestizo*. They use *mestizo* to identify literate and economically successful people who share indigenous cultural practices yet do not regard themselves as miserable, a condition that they consider 'Indian'. Instead of equating 'indigenous culture' with 'being Indian' then, they perceive Indianness as a social condition that reflects an individual's failure to achieve such things as educational improvement. People may thus refuse to be called Indian, but proudly celebrate their 'indigenous culture' and call themselves *mestizos*, a process de la Cadena terms 'de-indianization' (2000:6). In this regard, the quest for mobility and progress is not necessarily or unambiguously about seeking otherness, but about new ways of forming one's self-identity. As noted by Calderón (1988:225), such a quest is concerned with how to become modern without necessarily leaving the identity as indigenous (or *serrano*) completely behind. It indicates how people's ideas about mobility and progress are informed by more than the dominant discourses of urban *mestizos*, since these ideas are simultaneously re-created and redefined according to local meanings and identities.

Work and Dependency

As previously mentioned, the relationship to kin in these processes of mobility is often significant, and while Angelina came to buy a plot of land in Jerusalén because her sister already lived there, Eugenia moved to the city because of agreements made by her parents. As in Eugenia's case, several of my informants have left their communities and come to Arequipa because they were requested to do so – either by a relative, a godparent (*madrina* or *padrino*) or some patron – in order to work and assist in a house or family enterprise. This indicates how many young people's wish to leave their rural background may be reinforced by the demand[4] in the cities for cheap, young and inexperienced labour. It illustrates how the Andean region continues to supply the urban centres with a workforce, and partially explains why migration to the cities has not diminished even though formal employment opportunities are scarcer than before.

It is particularly among upper- or middle-class families in the city that there is a demand for young servants or assistants, although it also happens that migrant families similarly seek assistance from young rural relatives to contribute with their labour. In many cases, employers explicitly prefer to hire young migrants who have recently arrived from the highlands, especially girls. This illustrates how young people from the highlands are often considered a convenient workforce, as they are perceived as knowing how to work hard and are likely to accept low payments as well as long working hours. I have also heard people say that the less familiar these young people are with the city the better, since they will not have many friends, and they will not know how to get around in the city or submit to urban temptations. Young people from the highlands who have recently arrived in the city are thus often considered to be more trustworthy and *humilde* (humble or poor; here also inexperienced or innocent). This is in comparison with more experienced city-dwellers who are sometimes considered more likely to cheat or steal from the families for whom they work. For those looking for work, stressing their rural Andean background can represent a certain advantage *vis-à-vis* potential employers (see also Crain 1996). This indicates how people are perceived as not only going through a process of 'civilization' when they grow accustomed to life in the city, but also somehow becoming corrupted, thus revealing a notion of 'the noble savage' – in relation to which 'modernity' causes moral degeneration.

Many scenarios similar to Angelina's and Eugenia's indicate that it is not primarily men who migrate at a young age, but also women, and often before marrying (see also RED-ADA 1998). In Jerusalén most of the women have left their villages as young girls to work as servants in the houses of urban middle-class families or to assist their relatives or godparents living in Arequipa. Sometimes

[4] Regarding the demand for a workforce in the cities, a significant shift took place in the beginning of the 1980s from a great demand in the cities for cheap labour, particularly in construction and the industries, to a dramatic decline in this demand with increasing unemployment.

people bring young girls from the highlands to work for themselves, but they may also bring them as a favour for someone else, for people who have asked them to find a young rural girl with *garantía*, someone whom they can guarantee is trustworthy. In some cases, I have even seen middle-class families come to the marketplace and approach the traders to ask if they know a young girl who has just arrived from the countryside and is perhaps willing to come and work in their house. For instance, well-dressed *mestiza* women have several times approached Angelina at her market pitch to ask if she knows a girl from the highlands who is reliable and works well. In many of these cases, I have been told that employers give promises of good wages and education, a nice house to live in and a whole lot of new, modern clothes. These promises are not always kept, however, and I heard many women say that they had not received wages or the opportunity to finish school.

While Eugenia's neighbour Juana was still attending school in the rural town of Santo Tomás in Chumbivilcas, Juana's teacher asked her to leave the village to come work for her in Cuzco. Since Juana really liked her teacher and was curious about life in the city, she asked her parents for permission to go. Her teacher told her she would receive a salary and at the same time continue school if she wanted. Once in Cuzco though, she could not work in her teacher's house after all, but was moved to the house of some of the teacher's relatives. She was not paid, nor was she given the opportunity to attend any classes. She was miserable and wanted to go home, but at first she did not want to let her parents know. I have heard several women tell similar stories, and there are also cases in which young girls have experienced sexual harassment and exploitation during their work as servants. It is important in this regard to acknowledge how these processes of movement among young people from the highlands are often informed by relations of patronage with middle and upper classes as well as with older kin. Indeed, the dimension of patronage seems to influence at what point in their lives people migrate and the conditions under which they do so. As a result of these often quite specific labour demands in the city, the geographic mobility of young single people becomes a crucial characteristic of the migratory process. Furthermore, it is important to note that these relations of work and patronage also seem to influence the way in which people see and understand themselves. People in Jerusalén, women as well as men, often underlined that they see themselves as workers, as people who know how to work hard and are used to working for others, '*somos trabajadores*' (we are workers). In this manner, they also conceptualized themselves as different from those who do not know how to work hard, that is, people they see as *mestizo* upper- and middle-class.

The Problem of Discrimination

Many people worry about being discriminated against because of their Andean background, and therefore are always careful about how they dress when they go to the centre of the city, particularly before encounters at public offices or the like. Discrimination and racism is a considerable problem in Peruvian society, and many people told me about negative experiences with people and institutions in the city, including medical experts and hospitals. While Angelina has given birth to two of her children at home, she has also given birth at the hospital. On one occasion, there were medical students present during her labour. The birth went well but it was nonetheless decided – after the baby was born – that one of the students should cut her so that he could practice. Nobody asked for her consent, and there were obviously no medical reasons to cut her *after* the baby was born. Indeed, there are reasons to believe that the medical personnel made this decision only because Angelina was considered a poor indigenous woman, thus indicating some of the dynamics that characterize the status of people from the highlands in Peruvian society. After such encounters, I have often heard Angelina and others complain about bad and humiliating treatment, that '*aca en el Perú tratan a la gente como si fueran animales*' (here in Peru they treat people like animals). For this and other reasons, many prefer local *curanderos* (shamans) to treat their illnesses, as well as for spiritual advice and support since they at least treat people with respect.

In interactions more generally between people considered to be *arequipeños* and people from the highlands, it is furthermore worth noting the terms that people use to address each other. For instance, I heard people from the city of Arequipa almost invariably address people from the Andean region in terms of '*tu*' and not '*usted*', even in cases of unfamiliarity and when the other person was older, to which they would have used '*usted*' if the person had been another *arequipeño*. Correspondingly, people from the highlands tend to use the polite and respectful form '*usted*' in all their interaction with *arequipeños*, even to address people younger than themselves. The different uses of these terms illuminate the positioning of people in a hierarchy defined by class, culture and 'race', reflecting the ways in which *arequipeños* and people from the highlands address each other from different positions in this hierarchy. What is more, it illustrates how people from the highlands may also consent to these differences in power and authority.

Similar hierarchical mechanisms are actualized also in relations between kin, in the sense that kin may take or be given different positions in the hierarchy defined by class, culture and 'race', and are related to the different degrees of progress or *mestizo*-ness that people achieve. This is particularly so as a high degree of geographic and economic diffusion may be created as families and kin become localized differently in rural and urban spaces through processes of mobility, producing a multiplicity of class-ethnic identifications in relations between kin. This is illustrated for example in cases when people who have newly arrived in Arequipa come to visit or live with their urban relatives. In August 2001, Juana's neighbour Roxana had her nephew coming to Arequipa to visit for a couple of weeks. When I came to Roxana's house to say hello, I was struck by how very shy and silent her young nephew seemed to be, hardly saying a word during the three or four hours that I was there. Although his shyness could of course have been related to my presence and this being his first time in Arequipa, it seemed that he was first of all bothered by the way in which his aunt and her daughters treated him. In fact, they constantly made fun of him and made jokes at his expense, such as asking him to speak in his very correct Quechua, saying that they thought he sounded so cute that way. They also kept asking how many llamas[5] he has back in Cuzco, and criticized him for not knowing how to speak Spanish well enough, and not even knowing how to greet people properly. The boy was obviously troubled by their teasing, but simultaneously seemed too shy or afraid to respond. In this manner, newcomers in the city may be placed at the bottom of the hierarchy by their kin and experience ridicule even by their own relatives for not knowing how to speak for themselves or get around in the city, and for being 'backward' or 'Indian-like'. Indeed, I saw other newcomers being treated in a similar way. After Angelina had been to visit her old mother in Arapa, she agreed to bring one of her nephews home with her for a couple of months in Arequipa. He was 11 years old at that time and did not speak much Spanish, and when arriving in Arequipa, he seemed to be intimidated by the new people and unfamiliar surroundings. Angelina generally made him stay at home to watch the house most of the day, and before leaving for work in the morning she gave him a range of tasks like cooking and cleaning that he was supposed to finish before the others got home. While it is not unusual that newcomers are made to work like this, I was puzzled by the way in which Angelina never seemed to remember the name of her young nephew. Instead she called him all sorts of incorrect names, and in this manner demonstrated that he was of so little significance that she could not even remember his name. In this relationship, Angelina thus seemed to take the position of the authoritative patron *vis-à-vis* her young nephew by treating him as a servant.

Similar dynamics may be actualized during people's visits to their villages of origin in the relationship between those who return and their relatives in the village. In these situations, those who return are sometimes concerned with presenting their success in the urban context, by underlining their new experiences and knowledge of urban ways. When Juana and I went to visit her relatives in Chumbivilcas, she continually seemed to be making an effort to present herself as knowledgeable in the ways and codes of the city. She kept giving her brothers advice about how to make things better for their families through different suggestions as to how they ought to modernize the farm. She also continually scolded her oldest niece for not yet having learnt Spanish. 'What do you think about your future, when you have not even learnt Spanish?' and 'You will never manage to get out of here' (meaning Chumbivilcas) or the like. In these situations, those who return sometimes underline the knowledge of Spanish as a necessary and important skill, and simultaneously stress their own competence in urban ways compared to that of their rural relatives.

---

5 Llamas are often referred to as symbols of the Andean, and sometimes, as in this case, also of the *stigma* of the Andean.

Marriage, Offspring and 'Racialization'

Since the majority of my informants have left their villages whilst young and single, many of them have found a marriage partner in the city. Most of the people I know have settled down with someone who has a migrant background similar to their own, sometimes even from the same community or a neighbouring district. It seemed to be a widely supported opinion that in this manner, a couple will be able to understand each other better due to the sharing of a similar background. Combined with this concern that people with the same background will understand each other better, people are at the same time concerned that these marriages are likely to produce children with dark skin, which is generally considered a negative attribute. Angelina's husband Juan has a migrant background similar to her own, and also comes from the department of Puno, although from another district. Angelina's daughter María has similarly married a man with a migrant background, Eduardo, who came from Cuzco as a boy. María sometimes said she is glad she married another person from the highlands because they have a similar background and understand each other better that way. After five years of marriage they have one child called Alejandro. He is sometimes just called *cholo*, particularly by his grandmother, because of his dark skin. Both María and Eduardo would have liked to have another child a couple of years after the first, but because of the strained economic situation they doubt that they will take the chance. At one point, María speculated that in case she should have another child and could afford it, she would like to contact a sperm bank to get semen from '*un hombre blanco*' (a white man), perhaps from another country. That way she could improve the family and '*la raza*' (the race), she said. As far as I know however, she had not discussed this with her husband.

On several occasions Angelina told me that she had been against María's marriage with Eduardo from the start. Even though María was already pregnant when planning the marriage, Angelina had tried to convince her not to marry him. Angelina had argued that he would not be any good for her and suggested that she raise the baby on her own with the help of her parents. As far as I know, it is not common for a parent to argue against a marriage in this manner, and especially not when the girl is already pregnant. While the expense of organizing the marriage often prevents young couples from getting married, the pressure on being a couple when bringing a child into the world is, as I will discuss later, nonetheless significant both as a social and cultural value as well as an economic necessity (see also Lazar 2002). Despite this, Angelina wanted to help her daughter take care of the baby without the baby's father. This can be an indication that she and Juan at this point regarded themselves as financially able to help the mother and child with their future needs, a situation that changed when Juan became ill and Angelina was the only one with an income. However, perhaps the most relevant reason for Angelina's reluctance toward this marriage was simply that in her eyes the candidate was not good enough. During my different periods of fieldwork, Angelina often criticized Eduardo, saying that he does not really know how to work, that he mistreats María, and that he is generally ugly and badly behaved. She also called him *indio*, using the term in a negative sense ('*este indio*'). On these occasions, Angelina simultaneously stressed that María was a much harder worker than her husband. When confronted with these negative characterizations of her husband, I never heard María make any protest, and there were also situations in which she said similar things herself. At the same time, there were other occasions when she underlined how clever and hard-working he is, and how much he had suffered as a little boy when he was left on his own with only an old grandmother to look after him in the village where he was born. This suffering has made him a hard worker, she said, but it has also given him a difficult temper.

There are also a few people who have found partners born in the city and with a middle-class background. Some talked about such marriages with *arequipeños* in positive terms and characterized them as a way in which to 'upgrade' the family and 'whiten' the 'race' through marriage to someone with a lighter skin and urban, middle-class status. When comparing her own situation with the situation of her sister Vera who has married a man with a middle-class background from Arequipa, Eugenia stated that her sister has managed to achieve the kind of progress that she has never acquired herself. When her sister has children, she said, they will probably have whiter skin – which she considers beautiful – while her own children are dark-skinned (*morenos*) like herself. In this manner, people are generally very concerned about the colour of skin of newborn babies, and often refer to them by terms referring to phenotype: *negro* or *cholo*, *moreno*, *chino*, *blanco* or *gringo*. This illustrates how differences in appearance are often racialized, also in relations between family and kin. About the children of migrant-*arequipeño* marriages, it is sometimes said that the first-born is likely to have a rather dark skin colour, while those following will be born with whiter skin and fairer hair. Eugenia's daughter Victoria got married to a rather well-situated *arequipeño* a couple of years ago, and moved into the house of her husband and his parents, which is located in the centre of the city. After a while she gave birth to a little boy, a boy that Eugenia adores, always making a fuss about his white skin and bright hair, stressing how beautiful he is and how different from herself. Also more generally, Eugenia seemed to be very proud of her daughter who has done so well and is now living in a big house in the centre of the city, with *gente grande*. One day when I came to visit, however, I found Eugenia worried about her daughter due to problems that she increasingly was experiencing in her marriage. Victoria had recently been to visit and revealed her frustrations about her marriage and her parents-in-law, saying that their attitude towards her gradually had changed. She complained that her parents-in-law are treating her badly, and calling her names such as *chola* and *india* in a way that upsets her. She said they treat her almost as if she was their servant, and that they at times will not even let her eat with them at the table. What is even worse, Victoria had told Eugenia, is that her husband has adopted some of these negative attitudes and started to speak to her in the same humiliating manner. In general, he treats her differently now from the way he did when they first met, saying that after all, she is used to living in '*pura tierra*' (pure dirt), referring to new urban neighbourhoods or the highlands. In the period that followed, I heard that Victoria had started coming to Jerusalén more often, bringing her son with her to stay for a few days with her mother.

After this and in contrast to her previous pride for her daughter's marriage, Eugenia said it might have been a mistake for her daughter to marry a *mestizo* in the first place, as she would have been happier marrying someone from the highlands like herself. This case thus illustrates how people may also experience such marriages with people from Arequipa as problematic, due to the awareness of differences in economic and cultural backgrounds in the relationship between affinals and the conceptualization of these relations in terms of 'race'. Indeed, the above illustrates how people may explicitly refer to notions about 'race' in these relationships, and particularly so in connection to questions regarding marriage and reproduction. It indicates how mobility is referred to in terms of categories related to 'race' as well as economic and cultural background, for example in the sense that people value an 'improvement of the race' in terms of a lighter colour of skin, which is understood as superior to a darker one. This illustrates how notions of 'race' as well as 'culture' are given significance in the negotiation of identities in the urban context. In the case of María, she underlined a positive evaluation of an Andean background or 'culture' with respect to her marriage with a migrant, while she referred to their 'race' as preferably subject to whitening and 'improvement' for her future child. She thus seems to evaluate her marriage differently within a framework of 'race' than she does within a framework of 'culture', thus revealing the ambiguity in the values with which people identify.

The Contradictions of *Mestizaje*

As noted in the introduction, the idea of a *mestizo* nation entails the presupposition of a gradual evolvement from 'primitive Indianness' into a more civilized stage (de la Cadena 2000) or increasing 'whitening' (Safa 1998). As a formula for identity, *mestizaje* seems to entail a common reference for identity and equal possibilities for all, by apparently opening up the opportunity of every person to become a *mestizo*. It gives the impression that all citizens share the same opportunities – but within a specific value system – and if one does not succeed within this system, it is seen as a result of one's own disability, not a product of society. In this manner, as similarly argued by Safa (1998), the ideology of *mestizaje* has an individualizing effect by representing a racial continuum based on individual mobility rather than group solidarity. The *mestizaje* formula therefore represents a liberalistic way of thinking about difference.

While it was long argued that class supersedes ethnicity and 'race' in Latin America (see for instance Wagley 1958, Harris 1964), I agree with Safa (1998) that ethnicity or 'racial' constructions should not be reduced to class difference. It is worth noting a point made by Gose (1994) in this regard, that class must be understood as a cultural category, and that 'economy' in this respect can never be seen as neutral, but informed by understandings of culture as well as 'race'. According to de la Cadena (2000), it is the re-conceptualization of ideas about 'race' into terms of culture and class that has made it possible in the Peruvian context to individually manipulate, change and redefine social categories. Since the early twentieth century, 'race' has been redefined in terms of culture, the soul or the spirit instead of skin colour, and as a result, Peruvians think that their discriminatory practices are not racist, as they do not connote biological differences, but cultural ones (2000:2). In this manner, de la Cadena argues that culture is used to mark social differences and justify discriminatory practices, deriving from a belief in the intellectual and moral superiority of one group of Peruvians over the rest. It is a way of thinking that is not necessarily related to racial terminology, but is a version of what has been identified as new racism or racism without race (ibid:4). While I agree with de la Cadena's argument in most respects, it is nonetheless important to recognize that such a re-definition of 'race' in terms of culture is not necessarily that clear-cut. People do still refer to ideas of phenotype and 'race', and often quite explicitly so, as previously illustrated by the wish to 'improve the race' in relation to marriage and offspring, thus indicating clear biological connotations.

The project of becoming *mestizo* among people from the highlands may involve a re-positioning in relation to social categories that take place within – or even work to reproduce – dominant discourses, by producing an active replacement of 'Indianness' and accommodation to urban *mestizo* forms (de la Cadena 2000). In this manner, the search for progress through *mestizo*-ness can in many ways be seen to involve the consent with dominant forms of discrimination and inequality. Such a dynamic can be understood in terms of the complexity of contradictory consciousness, that is, as the 'co-existence in individual minds of two conceptions of the world' (1971:326). As de la Cadena (2000) argues with respect to the subtle reproduction of racist attitudes for instance, such a contradictory consciousness may lead people into denying the existence of inequality, at the same time as they comply with the legitimacy of social difference (ibid:5). It is a contradiction that can re-confirm the hegemony of dominant principles of inequality and discrimination. De la Cadena notes that the possibility of redefining one's position in relation to social categories can serve to disguise the hierarchical circumstances that for some actually make such a redefinition and mobility impossible. This is particularly so as the limitations as well as the possibilities for this kind of redefinition are understood in individualizing terms. The opportunity to redefine one's position in relation to social categories can thus mask the persistence of these categories, as they are unsettled and blurred but also continually being reproduced.

Despite the ideology and practices of *mestizaje* – and the possibility of redefining the boundaries of social categories – there is still a polarization of indigenous and *mestizo* with connotations to 'race', as well as a reproduction of difference and inequalities. In these processes, some exotic and polarized 'other' is continually being reproduced. So while *mestizaje* has represented a core symbol in nation building, there are processes of 'othering' that also involve a great degree of polarization (see Dumont 1980). In this respect, Latin American representations of the 'Indian' can be compared to the 'Orientalism' in Western discourse (Said 1993), as the 'Indian' in Latin America is conceptualized similarly as the 'Oriental' in the West (Ramos 1998). In the Peruvian context, this reveals an important paradox of identification, as the 'Indian' represents a distant 'other' but at the same time an integrated part of the *mestizo* self and images of the nation. As a political symbol, *mestizaje* can represent a liberal formula for national unity, in a way that apparently entails equality for all, but by being defined in terms of and on the basis of a hierarchy (see Dumont 1980) that creates a desire to become 'the other'. The ideology of *mestizaje* thus creates a necessity of becoming 'the other', in relation to which 'the self' becomes filled with ambiguity and is partially denied. As the 'Indian' is regarded as both inside and outside the '*mestizo* identity', the notion of *mestizaje* has produced some rather contradictory effects. Indeed, there is a fundamental ambiguity in the signals from public society when it comes to the place and evaluation of aspects and degrees of Andean-ness. While the everyday practices and identities of indigenous people are often stigmatized, an essentialized and exotified version of 'the Andean' is at the same time valued and made object of celebration, as we see for instance in the promotion of festivals and cultural practices in tourism. In this manner, the exotic *Indian* – or *the noble savage* – may be highly valued in national imageries and representations, while the urban *Indian* becomes more problematic (see Ramos 1998). The urban Indigenous can in this manner be seen to challenge a dualistic mind set. By redefining the content of these social categories and adding new meanings, people are involved in processes of both unsettling and reproducing some of these categories.[6] The quest for social mobility in processes of migration can thus be seen as a contradictory one, involving accommodation to dominant discourses on the one hand, and redefining the content of these dominant categories on the other.

Spanish and the Written Word

Most of my informants described their first period as a newcomer to the city as rather difficult, often due to their lack of Spanish language skills. In the women's organization there were a couple of women who had very recently arrived in Arequipa. Sabina was one of them, and she was said by the other women in the organization to be extremely shy and described as somewhat stupid (*tonta*). Sabina does not speak any Spanish, and although she always attended the meetings and work, I hardly ever heard her speak other than a few words in Quechua to her neighbouring *compañeras* (companions or colleagues). On the advice of one of her neighbours, Sabina had started to participate in the organization soon after she

6 I have discussed a related issue in the book chapter 'From Stigma to Celebration: The (Re-)Generation of Dilemmas in Discourses on Cultural Hybridity' (Asgharzadeh, Lawson, Oka and Wahan 2007).

arrived in Arequipa. However, she always stayed on the periphery without saying much, even after she had lived some years in the neighbourhood. The other women considered it a bit strange that she has not learnt Spanish yet, and they continued to speculate whether she is stupid or just shy. Before electing new leaders for the different women's groups, they also made jokes about choosing Sabina to be the organization's president, something they obviously found terribly funny. This indicates how, even amongst Quechua-speakers, the lack of competence in Spanish may be criticized and ridiculed.

In general, people in Jerusalén seemed to be extremely self-conscious and ambiguous regarding their own linguistic status and competence. In reference to her first experience in the city after leaving her village in Chumbivilcas, Juana for instance expressed the following thoughts: 'When I first came to the city I did not speak any Spanish. It was terrible; I did not understand when people spoke to me and I was too embarrassed to speak myself. I did not know how to make food either, as my mother had only taught me to walk behind the animals. But little by little I learned, at school and as a servant.' Similarly I heard other people speak of themselves as *perdidas* (lost) in their first period in the city, that is, as lost and confused by the city and the language spoken there. Although they gradually increased their knowledge of Spanish, people said that they often found it embarrassing to speak, as the problems with pronunciation and vocabulary continued to bother them.[7]

While many of the men I spoke with had learnt some Spanish by attending school in their villages, most women had started to learn Spanish after coming to Arequipa and mainly through working as servants in middle-class *arequipeño* homes. It was not until Juana had lived some time in Arequipa that she knew enough Spanish to feel confident, and she still regards herself as less than competent in reading and writing. Each time she wants to have a letter or something written, she has to go to her oldest daughter to have her write it for her. Her daughter Clara only knows Spanish though, so nothing is ever written in Quechua, not even the letters to their kin in Chumbivilcas. Juana herself finds it even more difficult to write something in Quechua than in Spanish, because she has never received any education in her mother tongue. She sometimes said she feels incompetent in both languages, as she has never learned Spanish to perfection, and tends to forget more and more of her Quechua. This indicates how many people feel that they are not fully competent in either of the languages, a situation which is reinforced by a lack of bilingual education in the city. In particular, Juana stressed that she often felt frustrated by her lack of knowledge in order to help or advise her children, particularly concerning school homework or further education.

People's competence in Spanish is made a particular concern during encounters with official institutions. At these encounters, the Quechua-sounding surnames of many migrants may also represent a concern in their fear of being criticized or

7 See Gumperz et al. (1982) about how even accents can be key in the perception of ethnic boundaries.

discriminated against. It is therefore not unusual for people arriving in the city to change their surname into a more Hispanic-sounding one, in an attempt to escape the Andean stigma. As previously noted it was not until Angelina was to formalize her property in Jerusalén and had her second child that she went to solicit the documents of identity that she still lacked. This was an opportunity she also used to change her surname. Angelina's paternal surname was Ccari, a Quechua surname that she thought sounded too Indian. She therefore worried about the future of her children and whether they might suffer discrimination and perhaps have difficulties in finding jobs with this kind of surname. In the end, she chose to take away one c and change their surname into Cari, which is less Quechua-sounding. Hence her children are now named Álvarez from their father and Cari from their mother. By changing a Quechua surname into something more *mestizo*-like in this manner, some people seek to be identified as *mestizos* and not as *cholos* or *serranos*. It indicates how people may seek to re-define their cultural capital in order to enter a process of symbolic 'whitening'.

In such processes of documenting personal identity, Lund (2001) underlines how people must not only go through a series of procedures in different offices and public spaces as previously noted, but also relate to a written, literate and Spanish-speaking paradigm. According to her, dealings with bureaucracy can in this manner be seen as an exchange of words in which their textual rendition is the ultimate goal of the exchange (2001:3). When considering Angelina's case, her decision to change her surname can be regarded as a result of the process of moving through these bureaucratic spaces. In the exchange of words that this bureaucratic space requires – and that is realized in the Spanish language – she experienced her Quechua-sounding surname as inappropriate and decided to change it. In this regard, the question of documentation in the urban context can be viewed as one of many senses in which Peruvian society functions against a dominant background of Spanish. People thus find it necessary to view themselves (and their language): '... in the light of the Spanish word, through the eyes of the Spanish idiom, and theirs was always – as Bakhtin puts it – a word with a sideways glance' (Zavala 1992:146). This aspect has been reinforced by the fact that the realm of literacy has been dominated by Spanish, thus excluding the speakers of indigenous languages from the realm of literacy and non-literates from the realm of Spanish (see Harvey, forthcoming).

As competence in Spanish is often related to a person's level of literacy, those who arrive in the city with limited or no basic education or literacy generally start out with little knowledge of Spanish as well. Less fluency in Spanish is thus often accompanied by illiteracy, which must be viewed in light of how the world of literacy has been dominated by the Spanish language. Since 1993 when the government of Fujimori reinforced previous laws on bilingual education, schools in Andean communities have offered teaching in Spanish, Quechua and Aymara. However, this opportunity for bilingual education is available only in regions in which the majority speak Quechua or Aymara, in a way that limits this arrangement to rural areas of the highlands (except for a few, private schools in the city). As the opportunity for bilingual education is thus defined according to region and the designation of cultural-linguistic areas, it is not offered in areas in which the majority speaks Spanish, such as in cities towards the coast. In effect, the problem of illiteracy among speakers of indigenous languages may be reinforced by this lack of multilingual education in the cities, especially among monolingual speakers of indigenous languages who migrate while still of school age. In this regard, the arrangements for multilingual/cultural policies seem to be based on a notion of 'the indigenous' as contrasted to the 'non-indigenous' in a way that, particularly to Andean people in the cities, may be rather artificial.

Despite good intentions then, the programmes for multilingualism and multiculturalism appear to reproduce the notion that there are a limited number of categories and options that people consistently have to choose between (Harvey, forthcoming). When it comes to the children of those who have migrated, they are generally raised as monolingual Spanish-speakers, and the Quechua they learn at home is often limited to a few words or expressions. Few Quechua-speaking parents in urban areas have the time or the capacity to teach their children to speak Quechua, and they often see it as a language of their rural past and not particularly useful to the future or *progreso* of their children. This is contrasted by a very different attitude towards English, which is regarded as an important way to invest in the children's future. As I will illustrate in the following section, the above does not imply, however, that migrants are muted (Ardener 1975) or necessarily excluded from important manners of expression. On the contrary, they seem to develop a voice and form of expression of their own.

Quechua and Playful Interchange

Some people under-communicate their knowledge of Quechua due to the stigma of the Andean, sometimes by pretending that they have no knowledge of Quechua at all. There are for instance people who choose to answer in Spanish when they are spoken to in Quechua, thus obviously understanding Quechua but refusing to speak it. Different authors have described how Quechua-speakers in urban contexts choose to under-communicate their language, and how many migrants speak Quechua mainly when travelling to the highlands and their villages of origin (see, for instance, Paerregaard 1997a). Paerregaard notes how migrants from Tapay (in the rural part of the department of Arequipa) seldom used their native language in the city of Arequipa or outside the village due to the prejudice against Andean culture in urban parts of Peru (ibid:71). This does not imply, however, that Quechua in urban contexts is always under-communicated. In fact, the knowledge of Quechua may also be related to a certain pride, and in some contexts regarded as an important way of expressing the identification with and valuation of an Andean background. In Jerusalén, women seem to use Quechua to a greater extent than men, which is probably a result of the way in which women more often work in contexts with a majority of migrants,[8] such as at the market and in local organizations. Being dominated by migrants and bilingual Quechua- (or Aymara) speakers, these contexts create situations in which Quechua (or Aymara) is spoken more frequently than in other more formal work situations.

People may prefer Spanish on some occasions and Quechua on others, and there are situations and relationships that are regarded as a meeting between people from the highlands (*serranos*) and not people from the city (*arequipeños*), something that may be achieved or underlined by the use of Quechua instead of Spanish. In this regard, many people stressed the importance of confidence in a relationship if one were to choose Quechua instead of Spanish. The interchange between Quechua and Spanish is particularly evident in people's interaction at the marketplace.[9] In this context, people constantly switch between Quechua and Spanish, in an interchange between languages that is also characterized by certain playfulness. There is a general making of jokes in this context – mostly in Quechua or Aymara, but also in Spanish – many of which refer to linguistic differences or peculiarities. It is a kind of play that seems to be ascribed an important value in itself, and much of it is done with reference to cultural, 'racial' or sexual matters.

Like most of her colleagues at the market, Angelina is a bilingual Quechua and Spanish speaker. Although she and her colleagues use Spanish in much of their work and everyday life, jokes tend to be made in Quechua or Aymara. When I asked her why this is so, she explained it by referring to her own and her colleagues' limited knowledge of Spanish. Making jokes, therefore, is better done in Quechua, she said, although they otherwise use Spanish just as much as Quechua. This opinion is widespread, and it is even said that Quechua or Aymara are better languages for making jokes.[10] Angelina has also learned a bit of Aymara from the other traders, particularly some really bad words and expressions that she sometimes uses to make jokes or insults, especially in front of Spanish-speakers who will not understand. Often, when Angelina was by her stand at the market, some of the Aymara-speaking traders came over in order to play or make jokes. Sometimes they stole things from her and teased her by saying stupid expressions in Aymara – which she knows how to respond to in a witty manner, either in Spanish or Quechua or in the phrases of Aymara that she has learnt from the same traders.

It is especially the Aymara-speaking *puneñas* (women from Puno) who have a reputation for their constant joke-making – often quite crude and sexually explicit – about customers and other traders. They also make their Quechua- or Spanish-speaking colleagues say things in Aymara, have a great laugh among themselves,

---

[8] That is, except when working as servants.

[9] The same is true for interaction between participants in local organizations such as ASOMA, but I will here focus on interaction at the marketplace.

[10] By being semantically structured by suffixes that are added one after the other at the end of a word, Quechua may actually give room to semantic play and jokes that a language such as Spanish does not accommodate to the same extent.

and afterwards reveal to people that what they have just said is something very rude, bad or insulting, such as the Aymara name for male and female genitals or more personal insults. In this manner, people play with semantic differences and make jokes out of language peculiarities. The knowledge of two languages is in this regard often underlined as an advantage, as it enables people to speak in the presence of others without their knowledge of what is being said. It makes people curious, it is said, or anxious about not knowing whether the joke is referring to them or not. The intention of this open joke-making, while at the same time hiding its contents, could also be a way of embarrassing or excluding the non-speakers of Quechua or Aymara. People's appreciation of this form of communication seems to be related to the way in which it also serves to mark the differences between traders from the highlands and middle-class customers, particularly so since this way of speaking would be regarded as improper for most urban middle-class women. This is related to the middle-class values of decency and chastity for what is regarded as a 'good' woman in the context of Arequipa.

There was a period in which Angelina and her colleagues used to direct many of their jokes towards one of their few male companions at the marketplace. This companion is called Toledo among the other traders, due to his physical similarity to the president at that time as well as his explicit political support for this candidate during the electoral campaigns in 2000 and 2001. The 'Toledo' at the market tended to underline very strongly the fineness of his Spanish surname and his identity as a *mestizo* and that he was not an Indian like the other traders. He stressed this despite the fact that everyone else knew very well that he is poor and comes from a small rural village close to Chivay and that Quechua is his mother tongue. They thus teased him for pretending to be something he is not, while he teased them for being ignorant *cholas* and *indias*. Toledo was single and has been so all his life, having passed 40 years of age. His female companions made much fun of him for this, even to his face. Sometimes they asked him if he is a virgin, or a woman or perhaps homosexual. Toledo generally just smiled, and said he has fallen in love with one of their companions, one of those who prepares and sells meals to the other traders. This woman is already married, although Toledo did not take much notice of this and asked the other women to give him advice on how to attract her attention. The women happily gave him one piece of advice after another, and even tried to talk to this woman in his favour. At the same time they used the opportunity to tease him, and said for instance that they intended to come along on his honeymoon. They would like to check whether he is a virgin, they claimed, and while laughing loudly they suggested that they may even assist him with the way to do things in bed.

The above indicates the importance of play in social interaction and in the interchange between languages. Indeed, the switching between languages in itself seems to be essential to some of this playfulness, as well as ideas about cultural and sexual identity and difference. The playful dimension of interaction in the market context is also expressed in the ways in which people often play physically, by hitting each other, stealing things from the stands of other traders, or playing different tricks on each other (see also McNeish 2001). These are important ways of communicating and relating to other people, not only when making friends or confirming social relationships, but also when flirting or finding a partner.

The above illustrates how the stigma of indigenous languages does not necessarily result in under-communication, particularly not in contexts dominated by migrants. In these contexts, the stigma rather seems to be handled in a variety of creative and sometimes playful ways, and Quechua is used to define social situations and interaction in a specific way, to signal intimacy and confidence, or to make fun of and exclude those who do not understand. The use of Quechua may thus represent a linguistic device of exclusion in the same manner as Quechua-speakers experienced linguistic exclusion when they first came to Arequipa, but this time Quechua is used to exclude Spanish-speakers. The jokes made in Quechua and Aymara are given importance in this manner not only for relating to other migrants, but also to relate to linguistic and cultural 'others'. These forms of play can therefore be understood as a way of negotiating identities and to contest dominant ideas about behavioural codes and norms of categorization. The making of jokes in Quechua or Aymara seems to rest in this manner on a negotiation of social and linguistic categories, at the same time as it represents a way of joking with and contesting the relations of dominance and inequality.[11] In this respect, the importance of linguistic play may work as a device to comment on a specific situation, to underline or undermine distance, and deal with it by creatively referring to it in exaggerated or ironic ways through combinations of semantic and cultural differences.

The choice of a particular language to a particular utterance, word or meaning is not necessarily random, but may also be related to the world of practice and experience that it is associated with or acquired. I several times heard Angelina discuss prices or talk more generally about her business with other traders. In one of these conversations she discussed a down-turn in her earnings with one of her colleagues, a conversation that took place in Quechua, except for a couple of words of Spanish. Interestingly, these words in Spanish were expressions related particularly to the context and activity of trading, like numbers, prices and terms to refer to quantity or money values. This indicates the way in which certain spheres of experience can be related to the use of a particular language, thus indicating that the switch between languages is not necessarily random. Such a dynamic can also be an example of what Bakhtin (1981, 1984) has conceptualized as the political dimension in the use of words, and hence the relationship between linguistic practice and its ideological dimensions. Such ideological dimensions in the use of words indicate the significance of language for the negotiation of social categories, and for how people may take different positions from which to speak, for example as highlander or city-dweller. As I will illustrate, the indexical values of Quechua and Spanish may in this manner be reproduced through the different

[11] At times it may even be the switching in itself, rather than the specific code choice, that is most important in this kind of interaction (see Urciuoli 1995:528).

speaking positions in relation to which people constantly position and re-position themselves. This interchange between speaking positions can also be practised as a statement of identity, playfulness or contestation, in a way that reflects the situation of migrants as continually negotiating their place within linguistic and social categories.

The Voice of the Other

Bakhtin (1981, 1984) has stressed the need to grasp the instability and playfulness of language, particularly by the way in which language always brings with it the voice of an 'other'. This perspective opens up a discussion of the categories and boundaries of language, as well as the socio-cultural references to which it is associated. In the approach to language in general and bi- or multilingualism in particular, I thus find it useful to draw on a Bakhtinian perspective on dialogism. He sees language as entailing a continual re-contextualization of sign and meaning, as constituted by a dialogical nature that also reflects the dialogic constitution of self and person (Slaattelid 1993:57).

Such a perspective implies that the most important aspect of an utterance is its relation to other utterances – as part of a chain of utterances. An utterance can in this respect be seen as limited by a shift in the speaking subject – or a shift of person – and must hence be understood as a response to other utterances. In this sense, all understanding is in itself a response and hence forms new parts in a chain of utterances (Bakhtin 1979:246–7). It is this responsive relationship between utterances that Bakhtin means by dialogic (Slaattelid 1993:64–8). There are thus no neutral words as underlined by Bakhtin, since words are bearers of voices that have belonged to previous users of the word and accompany the word every time it is used again. In a broad sense, dialogue is thus a characteristic of all linguistic activity, speech acts and utterances, although the degree of dialogization may vary (Bakhtin 1981:358).[12] The idea of the 'voice of the other' relates to syntactical forms in language that are used to refer to another person's utterances, and incorporates these as the 'utterances of the other' in a new utterance (Slaattelid 1993:72). We thus speak with many voices or a choir of languages, making every one of us a 'we' and not an 'I', and constituting the polyphony or dialogical nature of the self. A voice is a semantic position, a view of the world, and an utterance responds both to others outside and to others that are embedded in the self. This can be related to the way in which people sometimes use Spanish in order to speak from the perspective of a *mestizo* – or otherwise confirming the perspective of the dominant, for instance in the relationship between city dwellers and younger

[12] 'A hybrid construction is an utterance that belongs, by its grammatical (syntactic) and compositional markers, to a single speaker, but that actually contains mixed within it two utterances, two speech manners, two styles, two "languages", two semantic and axiological belief systems' (Bakhtin 1981:304–5).

kin who recently have arrived in Arequipa. People may sometimes accommodate in this manner not only to the dominant language, but also to a point of view by taking the position of the dominant. In this regard, the dominant position of Spanish in a multilingual context creates a situation in which Spanish – or 'the voice of the other' as Bakhtin would put it – is more or less ever-present in people's consciousness and presentations of self. It is a situation in which 'the voice of the other' is made use of in reflections and dialogues between self and other.

In Peru, the same person may be considered a *mestizo* in the highlands and a *serrano* in the city, thus illustrating the situational and contextual dimension of identification. What is more, the same people may seek to define themselves as *mestizos* in one context and *serranos* in another, or denying their Andean background in one relationship and praising their rural origins in another relationship. Even in the course of the same conversation, people may switch positions from which to speak, interchangeably taking the view of both indigenous and urban middle class, speaking both from the Andean countryside and the city. In the framework of Bakhtin, this switching can take the shape of a constant dialogue, both within and between subjects. It can be seen as a switching between different speaking positions (Polar 2000), in which the 'voice of the other' is constantly referred to, integrated and made use of. Indeed, it is as if the more people strive to become urban *mestizos*, the more they simultaneously long for their origins and a more rural way of life. This interchange can be understood not only in terms of language and the crossing of linguistic boundaries, but also as an interchange between speaking positions or ways of viewing the world.

This speaking from different positions can be regarded as part of the creative constitution of self and other, involving positions from which to accommodate or rebel against the identity and affiliations granted within relations of power (Zavala 1992). According to Bakhtin, there are two opposite tendencies with respect to the dialogical nature of language and self: the centrifugal force that spreads to include a variety of voices, and the centripetal force that confirms and protects against an overwhelming flow and variety (Slaattelid 1993). As we learn various social dialects, some voices are made more authoritarian, at the same time as a multiplicity of voices may also destabilize the unity and authority of language (Zavala 1992:86). It is important in this regard to distinguish between the implicit and the intentional integration of a dominant language, conceptualized by Bakhtin (1981) as organic and intentional forms of hybridization. The organic form of hybridity refers to the unintended and unconscious fusion of language forms, in which the coherent sense of order and continuity is not disrupted (Werbner 1997:5). Such an unconscious form is 'muted', apolitical and does not involve any form of contrast or opposition, but rather maintains the illusion of boundedness (1997:4). In contrast, intentional hybridity is developed to shock, change, challenge, revitalize or disrupt, through deliberate, intended fusions of unlike social languages and images. Such an intentional form of hybridization is more politically and binarily oriented, as it implies a fusion that at the same time separates and is motivated by irony, critique and opposition (Werbner 1997).

While taking place in the course of fusion, intentional hybridization entails the simultaneous reification of experiences and viewpoints. Such a form can be seen to create an ironic double consciousness, a 'collision between differing points of view on the world' (Young 1995:21–5), implying a creative play with metaphors, a transgression of boundaries and fragmentation of categories. This form can be compared to theories of play (Bateson 1973) or cultural bricolage (Levi-Strauss 1964), as entailing the capacity to play simultaneously and interchangeably with two or more ways of classifying reality. Intentional hybridization thus entails a deliberate development of multi-voiced utterances and a rejection of single-styled discourse. By this distinction between organic and intentional hybridity, Bakhtin has recognized the dynamics of cultural and linguistic interchange as involving both accommodation (organic hybridity) and contestation (intentional hybridity) of dominants discourses (Werbner 1997). It can be a way to account for the existence of multiplicity that not only unsettles, but also serves to reproduce and reify the boundaries and categories of language and identity.

This co-existence, I find, is important for understanding some of the dynamics that characterize the ambiguity and interchange between speaking positions among people who migrate. People's quest for progress and *mestizaje* can for instance be seen to correspond with the organic form of hybridization, as it implies an integration of and accommodation to dominant forms. Although the strategic aspect of these redefinitions makes such a dynamic more intentional than unintentional, it still takes place within – and serves to reproduce – the dominant discourse. At the same time, this everyday unsettlement of categories and interchange between speaking positions can also take the form of intentional hybridity, by involving an interchange of cultural forms and the use of dominant idioms to imitate and criticize, to essentialize as well as dissolve. As illustrated among traders at the market, for instance, people's positions in-between languages may entail a creative and playful interchange not only between languages but also the positions from which to speak and with which language is identified. Such an interchange may also involve a means of contesting the linguistic and ideological hegemony, for example as described by the significance of jokes with reference to cultural, linguistic and gender difference. It entails a negotiation and contestation of boundaries through play with differing points of view on the world.

People may thus situate themselves within linguistic and social categories in a way that is characterized by a continual switching of speaking positions, that is, between the views of the world that particularly concern the relationship between the 'rural' and the 'urban', *indio* or *mestizo*. The choice of a speaking position seems to depend upon context, and the relation within which people speak. In this switching between speaking positions, people interchangeably pay respect or disrespect in relation to the other. It entails a dynamic in which a dominant discourse may be challenged through unsettlement of or play with social and linguistic categories in one moment – for example by imitating the voice of the dominant from the position of the marginal – while in the next reproducing dominant categories through an integration of dominant values and points of view. In this manner, the switching of speaking positions can be conceptualized as dialogic encounters that are articulated across multilayered links of power (de la Cadena 2000:10). According to de la Cadena, such relations can be seen as encounters in which the dominant side in one instance may be the subordinate side in another. Subordinate practices may in this manner defy a higher level of domination in one relation, while acting as the dominant side of another, and thus subordinating others as inferior and confirming the hegemonic ground of the dominant (2000:10). People can in this regard be seen to make use of a range of cultural strategies and resources, serving both to accommodate and contest dominant forms through the fragmentation as well as reification of these forms. In processes of mobility and migration, this dynamic may explain the simultaneous destabilization as well as reification of social and cultural forms and boundaries. It can also illuminate how cultural and linguistic practices are reified in different and sometimes contradictory ways depending on context, sometimes through celebration and sometimes through contempt.

Conclusions

This chapter has explored how migration is related to a quest for progress or social mobility and involving a negotiation of social categories. I have illustrated how the search for mobility and progress must be related to the ideology of *mestizaje* in the Peruvian context, in the sense that it involves a search not only for an urban way of living but often also a quest for *mestizo*-ness. This search for mobility and progress is thus often characterized by people's attempts to redefine their position in relation to social categories and as producing a fundamental ambiguity in people's relationship to their Andean background and identity. This is illuminated for instance by the way in which notions about 'race' and 'culture' are made relevant and negotiated also among kin, and how the relationship to family and kin is made an object of rejection as well as extension in the transition from highland to city. Although the search and demand for work represents a decisive factor in these processes of mobility, it is important to stress that migration in this context must be understood as the result of people's attempts to redefine the more general conditions of their lives and identities. Indeed, these processes of mobility may even be seen as an effect of what is often an exclusion from citizenship among people in the highlands on the one hand, and the ideology of *mestizaje* on the other. The ideology of *mestizaje* has in many ways served as a device for assimilation of the indigenous population and contributed in depriving people of more specific cultural and territorial rights (see Hale 1999). In this regard, the previous chapter illustrated how people who have migrated generally do not make claims, for example for land, with reference to an indigenous identity. This is partly a result of the ideology of *mestizaje* as noted above, and people's realization that in the city, such a claim would not be recognized.

The effects of an ideology of *mestizaje* is in many way contradictory, and despite the possibility of unsettling and redefining the boundaries of social categories, there is still a polarization and essentialization in this context of the 'indigenous' and 'Hispanic', and a reproduction of inequality based on class as well as ethnicity. I have therefore argued that the dynamics of this unsettlement may even serve to disguise the existence of inequality and racism, in the sense that the processes of mobility and *mestizaje* involve an unsettlement of social categories and forms that actually serve to reproduce the very same categories, along with a consent to the principles of inequality. The fundamental ambiguities that these processes involve are illustrated by the switching between speaking positions as people often change the viewpoints from which they speak, depending on situation and relationship. People's experiences with respect to language and their management of a position as bilinguals in a Spanish-dominated context have been given particular attention in this regard. I have explored the process from exclusion to inclusion in relation to the Spanish language, and the way in which people's relationship to Quechua is altered and imprinted with ambiguity in the process. Nonetheless, the Quechua language is not necessarily under-communicated in the urban context, but is also made use of in an often playful interchange between languages and viewpoints that works to comment upon and make fun of dominant categories and forms. In this respect, I have drawn on Gramsci and Bakhtin in order to stress the ways in which the interchange between different viewpoints may involve accommodation to dominant forms on one level and a reflective juxtaposition on another.

Chapter 3
Moving through the Powerful Landscape

This chapter explores further the spatial dimensions involved and negotiated in processes of mobility, and deals with the ways in which people often attempt to re-create a reciprocal relationship with their surroundings in an urban context. In the Andean highlands, people negotiate their spatial situatedness through reciprocal means that they see as central for the fertility of the land and animals as well as the well-being of the community (see for instance Allen 1988, Harris 2000). I will discuss how this relational understanding of the animated surroundings is reproduced or changed as people move to an urban context. In so doing, I explore the extent to which the relationship to land and the animated surroundings is important also for the understanding of movement and mobility as such. In contrast to the increasing body of literature discussing how indigenous peoples make demands for cultural rights and access to markets by essentializing and 'branding' their cultural identities and practices (see Comaroff 2009), this chapter explores the ways in which cultural practices concerning the landscape are made relevant in new surroundings, that is, in an urban context, primarily by their centrality in people's everyday lives. Indeed, I will argue that these practices are important for how people accommodate in the city and conceptualize their experiences of movement.

Not only in the Andes but also more generally, people often give meaning to places through the ascription of specific qualities and see landscape as having a certain power over their lives (see for example Feld and Basso 1996). Several studies have stressed the animistic or ancestral dimensions of landscape more specifically, and while some of these explore how the significance of the ancestral landscape can be re-created according to new circumstances (Morphy 1995, Harvey 2001), less has been done on the significance of these dimensions in processes of migration. In the Andean context, the surroundings are seen as powerful and ascribed an agency of their own, in the sense that they are believed to have human-like needs and feelings (see Allen 1988, Lund Skar 1994, Harris 2000, Harvey 2001) that can make them hungry, angry or revengeful. People therefore share with them and make offerings in order to ensure that the spirits of the surroundings are benign and not evil. Landscape in this context is thus not understood as constructed by human agents and as passively acted upon, since people also see themselves as influenced *by* the surroundings. In this regard, Western thinking has been criticized for a categorical polarization of nature and culture, seeing agency as a characteristic only of human beings while seeing 'landscape' as having no active agency (see for instance Ingold 1993, Hirsch and O'Hanlon 1995, Harvey 2001).

While the previous chapter was concerned with the re-definition of ethnic identities in relation to people's ideas about progress, this chapter will reveal how the powerful surroundings are considered sources of potential prosperity and therefore made important in the quest for progress. In light of this, I will discuss how power and prosperity in a cosmological framework are perceived as differently distributed in space and time. Places or surroundings in this context are associated with prosperity at two levels: as central for the re-generation of prosperity through offerings and ritual, and as related to the spatial geography of social and economic differences as described in Chapter 1. Accordingly, different places or surroundings are associated with different sources and kinds of prosperity, and movement in space can itself be seen to create or threaten people's well-being and prosperity. This serves to illuminate the significance of not only sociological but also spiritual or cosmological dimensions in people's understandings of place and surroundings, and therefore of movement.

I begin with a brief discussion about notions of place and space, and how migrants are involved in a process of making places out of spaces in the urban context. I then explore more specifically how people attempt to communicate with the surroundings as sources of danger and prosperity in a process of mobility, and how the notions of soul, kin and community are understood as connected to landscape. Later I describe the rediscovery in the urban context of powers of the past, and discuss the significance of notions about time and prosperity in people's understanding of their surroundings.

Making Places Out of Spaces

In his analysis of pilgrimages in the Andes, Sallnow (1987) argued that space is understood as informed by specific directions, due to a spatial geography that indicates movement in specific directions, such as through pilgrimage to sacred sites. Space can also be seen as intrinsically linked to time (Feld and Basso 1996, Ashworth and Graham 2005), and with respect to Andean views of history, the future is often associated with a place in the west (that is, the coast and its urban centres) just as the past is seen as located in the highlands, thus illuminating how time is seen as located in space (Randall 1982). This indicates how places can be informed by spatial and time-related configurations that give meaning to movement in specific directions or of specific kinds.

When I started my first fieldwork, I was primarily concerned with questions of migration regarding ethnicity, work and gender, but discovered that ritual relationships and offerings represented significant dimensions for my understanding. Many scholars seem reluctant to explore notions about spatial belonging, lest they risk suggesting an essentialist, naturalized and primordial notion of place and identity. At first this complication made me hesitant to explore these practices as well, but I gradually found it important to recognize the significance of these understandings without necessarily essentializing the relationship between people and place. In fact, the relationships to land that I describe in this chapter do not imply that people from these rural areas have not been involved in previous processes of movement and migration. Through forced labour, commerce and ritual journeys, people in the Andes have taken part in processes of mobility for centuries (see Sallnow 1987, Harris and Larson 1995, Saignes 1995).

The exploration of spatial dimensions in social life often involves a distinction between space and place, a distinction that has been understood in a range of different ways. Massey (1994) is among those who have criticized the view of place as bounded, as a site of authenticity, as singular, fixed or unproblematic, and argues that such a conceptualization of place rests on the view of space as stasis. Instead she has proposed to see the spatial in a context of space-time and as formed out of social interrelations on different scales, in relation to which place can be seen as a particular articulation of those relations, a particular moment in those networks of social relations and understandings (1994:5). The most common way to distinguish between place and space is to see space as abstract, as associated with something 'outside', or as not being used and identified with by people, while place is associated with the local and descriptive, with meaningfulness, identification and importance for belonging (Massey 1994:9). In a somewhat different way, I think of space first of all in material and practice-oriented terms, as the use of and movement in space, while I understand place as the conceptualization of space, as it is discursively identified, categorized and personified through naming or categories. In this regard, I see the process in which people in Jerusalén have moved and accommodated to an urban context as involving a negotiation about the transformation of urban space into place – of place-making. For instance through practices of occupation and the collective establishment of housing and infrastructure as described in the first chapter, people can be viewed as being involved in a process of making spaces into places. This does not mean that these urban spaces should be considered as previously empty, but that spaces through settlement increasingly become contested, named and categorized.

The arrangements of festivals in the city also illustrate this process of making urban space into place, and are held on anniversaries relevant to the regions or districts where people come from. Festivals can be seen to entail a re-creation of a rural place within the urban context, through the demarcation in time and space for the performance and visualization of dance and music from the Andes.[1] These arrangements of rural festivals in the city represent an attempt not only to attribute new meaning to urban spaces, but simultaneously to negotiate how a rural place of origin is to be represented (Paerregaard 1997b). It illustrates how distance serves to actualize people's relationship to place, and draws people into new processes of place-making. This process of making places out of spaces is similarly illustrated

[1] In recent years, the ritual fighting (*tinku*) arranged in some part of the highlands have also been arranged in Arequipa.

in the reciprocal consumption of food and drink at social gatherings, festivals and work parties (*faenas*) which also involves offerings of alcohol to the natural spirits. These offerings take the form of reciprocal consumption and are part of the process of making spaces into places by creating a relationship between people and surroundings in the urban context.

One of my informants, Jorge, works as a *curandero* (shaman, healer) in addition to his work in construction, and is simultaneously involved in a range of other projects and plans. One day when I came to visit I found him enthusiastically speaking about a project on which he had been working together with a couple of his *paisanos* (people from the same village or district) from different villages in the department of Puno. He and his colleagues had spent the last couple of years surveying Misti[2] by taking regular trips to the top of the volcano and noting all its changes and possible signs of eruption. In order to continue this project and realize their other plans, they had just sent some applications for economic support to the authorities of Arequipa as well as the Red Cross. The project had been in the planning stages for a couple of years, and at the time of my visit, Jorge was concerned about the risk of new eruptions from the volcano. Jorge explained that their motives for this project are grounded in their belief that within a few years Misti will become more active and perhaps a danger to the inhabitants of Arequipa, and particularly those in Jerusalén as it is located so near. This belief is based on their numerous observations of the crater, as well as their view of its volcanic movement as signalling the day of judgement. The intention of their project is to develop a more formal study of the volcano, in order to predict its movements more precisely. Jorge explained that such a study will create the basis for another part of this project, which is concerned with the construction of a new city, a new Arequipa.

According to their ideas, a new Arequipa ought to be constructed and located further away from the volcano and the actual location of the city. This part of the project involves some specific ideas about how this new city should be constructed, in terms of designing a new and different form of house construction that would be especially developed to tolerate tremors and earthquakes. What they want to accomplish with such a project, Jorge stressed, is to create something new and different and at the same time give poor people jobs in a huge and expansive construction project. They thus want to create a new Arequipa and secure for themselves, as he expressed it, 'a position of power'. As a part of the project, Jorge and his companions have also been arranging trips to the crater, especially for the days around the anniversary of Puno. On these occasions, they take the banner of the department of Puno to place by the crater, and arrange a performance of the dance called *la diablada*[3] – one of the characteristic dances from Bolivia and the district of Puno – including all of its richly decorated and colourful costumes.

[2] Misti is Quechua for *mestizo*, or powerful other.

[3] The *diablada* and its costumes are a spectacular sight, and often performed during carnival. In this dance, the performers wear full masks with long fangs and bulbous eyes,

Jorge and his wife even got married at the top of Misti, an event that was recorded in pictures as well as a documentary they have tried to distribute.

This project of Jorge and his companions illustrates how there is sometimes an explicit urge among people who have migrated to create their own place or position in the city, in this case by seeking to influence and change the area to which they have migrated. Although parts of this project may seem rather unrealistic, it is nonetheless an expression of the various ways in which space and surroundings in the urban context are sometimes re-defined, both symbolically and practically. Projects like that of Jorge and his companions can thus be seen as attempts to make places out of spaces by making them more one's 'own'. In this regard, the somewhat utopian Arequipa of Jorge's vision would be a better and safer place for people who have few resources to live on, and it would be based on the workforce and influence of people from the highlands like themselves. Accordingly, the ceremony at the top of Misti, and particularly its performance on the anniversary of Puno, can be seen to symbolically 'conquer' or 'colonize' places of importance in the city. In this respect, it is also interesting to note the combination in this project between motives and means of a scientific as well as a religious and symbolic kind, that is, the danger of volcanic eruption – followed up by systematic observations – and the belief in a day of judgement.

There are several ways in which the presence of people from the Andes in the city is conceptualized in terms of colonization or invasion, both by the migrants themselves and by *arequipeños*. This is illustrated not only when it comes to the claims to land related to the housing settlements, but also by more general references to the arrival and accommodation of people from the highlands in the city, and particularly with respect to the perceived changes that their presence has produced. People in Jerusalén sometimes talked about their arrival in the city as an 'invasion', that is, in a spatial sense as well as in terms of cultural difference and change. Similarly, I have also heard *arequipeños* speak of the arrival of people from the highlands as a kind of invasion, with comments such as, 'Nowadays the migrants are taking over everywhere, they are the ones who establish businesses, and they are also the ones who dominate at schools and universities'. Similarly, I heard people say that 'Arequipa is not like it used to be, clean and beautiful and surrounded by green agricultural areas, now it has all been changed by the people from the highlands'. As noted in the previous chapter, the presence of migrants is also talked about as a new culture, that is, *la cultura chicha*, a term which is generally given negative connotations and associated with violence, corruption and criminality. In this manner, the notion of invasion is informed by ideas of morality, or what is seen as moral degradation from the perspective of *arequipeños*, and a morally justified change in the view of people who have migrated. It may reflect how the negotiation of place in processes of urbanization also involves a negotiation about power and position in the relationship between 'self' and 'other'.

---

topped by four horns and lizards, and red satin cloaks decorated with snakes (see Harris 1995b).

Communicating with Spiritual Powers and the Landscape

In the rural Andes, people's communication with the powerful surroundings is primarily connected to agricultural activities and cycles, and actualized through ritual offerings, for example to *pachamama* (mother earth)[4] and the *apus* (mountain gods or spirits).[5] These natural spirits are paid through the offering of food, alcohol, coca, herbs, an animal or the like, in order to secure their goodwill and thus the fertility of the fields and flocks.

In the city, many people continue to communicate with and bring offerings to the natural surroundings, such as to the *apus* of Arequipa and particularly to the volcano Misti, as well as to *pachamama*, so that the powerful surroundings will cause no harm but give protection. I have previously noted how the construction of houses in Jerusalén generally takes place through reciprocal labour, through the organization of work parties involving neighbours and kin. For the day of the *techamiento* (roofing), *padrinos* (godparents) for the house are appointed, workers are invited to eat and drink, and offerings (*ch'alla*) are made. The *ch'alla* is not expansive but consists of an offering of alcohol that is thrown along the ground or sprinkled towards the mountains. This is a way to ask for the goodwill of the powerful surroundings and is meant to secure the luck and prosperity of the house and the people living there, and the pattern that the liquid makes on the ground gives an indication of how the offer has been received. Offerings can also be made by coca leaves, and during a workday, offerings of coca often take place during breaks or when people come by for a chat. People invite each other to chew some coca, but first they make an offering by finding three nice and complete leaves that are gathered in the hand. They blow on the coca, saying a few words of appraisal to *pachamama* and the *apus* about whom or what they want them to protect or benefit, roll some earth or ash in the leaves, and then they break the offerings into little pieces and throw them in three different directions. Similarly on festive occasions, when making or greeting *compadres*, when welcoming someone, or saying farewell before a journey, payments are performed through such offerings of coca leaves or drinks. More grand-scale offerings (*despachos*) are performed once or twice a year, generally by hiring a *curandero* (shaman) for the offering of different objects, food and alcohol and often including an animal. In addition to being used in payments, coca is important for spiritual guidance, for instance to *mirar la suerte* (read the luck, or the future). This involves gathering some coca leaves in the hand and, after deciding on the different significance of the different leaves, reading the pattern they make after they are spread out. People often hire *curanderos* to read the coca leaves as well as make payments, for instance in

---

4 *Pachamama* is the feminine principle of fertility, life, growth, *ayllus* and society (Bastién 1992:155), able to give or withhold the rains and the harvests (Lund Skar 1994:173–4).

5 *Apus* are the mountain gods, often seen as the incarnations of ancestors and generally regarded as a masculine principle.

situations of illness, but it is not uncommon that people also read the coca leaves themselves.

While most people in Jerusalén were originally Catholics and the first church constructed in the neighbourhood was Catholic, people have increasingly turned to Evangelical churches during the last decade. Several such churches have now been constructed in the neighbourhood, and among those who have converted are Angelina and Eugenia. Both explained to me that they had converted in relation to a situation of illness, where they had turned to the Evangelical church as a last resort after having tried everything else, including medical experts as well as *curanderos*. They both experienced wellness after this, and therefore decided to convert. In new urban neighbourhoods like Jerusalén there are generally a high number of conversions, and while there are of course many reasons for this, one explanation may be related to the work ethos and restrictiveness that these Evangelical communities tend to promote. It is a strict approach to life that may appeal to people who have few resources, but who are proud to be hard working and aim to save money in their quest for mobility and progress. Amongst those who convert, the expense involved in celebrations or ritual payments – that is, in relation to Catholic saints, or spirits of the landscape such as *apus* or *pachamama* – are also often named as one of their reasons to turn to Evangelism.

I got the impression that conversions are generally initiated by women who, after converting, encourage their husbands to do the same. The reason for this, some people claimed, is that conversion to Evangelism is a way in which women find they can combat some of their problems, of poverty as well as *machismo*. By making their partners convert with them, women see conversion as a way to reduce their partners' excessive drinking and waste of money, and at the same time contribute to a strengthening of work efforts and income. Gill (1990) has similarly underlined the predominance of women in Evangelical churches in La Paz, Bolivia, particularly amongst first- or second-generation Aymara migrants from the countryside. They do thus not resemble the upwardly mobile male entrepreneurs who spearheaded the growth of Protestantism in Europe (Weber 1930). Instead, Gill notes that they comprise the poorest and most marginal residents of the city, many of whom are abandoned wives or single mothers. She nonetheless argues that those who convert generally avoid gender issues related to the church despite the contradiction between the patriarchal orientation of Pentecostalism and the situation of responsibility-taking and hard work in these women's own lives (1990:709). In contrast, converts in Jerusalén often mentioned gender issues as one of the reasons why many women want conversion for themselves as well as for their husbands. From their point of view, family life as Evangelical converts is less troubled by the problems associated with *machismo*, for instance the excessive drinking. What is more, conversion seems to be given meaning through the valuation of hard work and the quest for progress.

While the Evangelical churches often have a critical attitude towards the ritual payments practised among people from the highlands, conversion does not necessarily mean that they leave these practices behind. Angelina and Eugenia, for example, instead search for guidance in spiritual or health-related concerns from *curanderos* as well as in the church. The ritual payments people make in the city are not necessarily defined by an agricultural calendar, nor are they intended to increase the fertility of agricultural land as such, but rather are made to stimulate other forms of prosperity, well-being, and luck, or what could be conceptualized as fertility in more general terms (see Harris 2000). In the city, people make payments in order to appeal for goodwill in relation to for instance work, or business. While payments to the *apus* are performed with appeals mainly for economic success or progress, payments to *pachamama* are made to seek well-being on more general terms, such as to prevent illness[6] and secure the family and household, to avoid theft and other forms of bad luck. Harris has argued that in the rural Andes, the performance of ritual payments are informed by general notions of fertility that are associated not only with production and reproduction, but also fertility as created and maintained through a logic of reciprocity, circulation and exchange. In this view, *pachamama* and the mountains are understood as guardians not only of the fertility of fields and stock – as well as the mines – but also, as in my study, of the fertility of business (see also Harvey 2001). So while the intentions behind the payments may vary, they are based on the same cosmological and ontological understanding of exchange as necessary to maintain fertility, that is, the fertility of agriculture as well as money. Lund Skar (1994) has argued that while wealth in the rural context is characterized by the connectedness to surroundings and land, wealth in the urban context is divorced from agriculture. She thus notes that in the urban context, wealth is no longer synonymous with the total state of interpersonal person-landscape relations that create prosperity in agriculture, since migrants engage in new forms of work that generate wealth on different terms. According to her, the strong association of money with a particular cosmo-vision (Parry and Bloch 1989:20–21) thus necessitates a reinterpretation of wealth in the transition from a rural to an urban setting. Divorced from the land and the context of the ancestors, she argues that wealth increasingly becomes associated with a notion of luck, more in keeping with Western ideas of fate (1994:226). As I will demonstrate, however, rural understandings of wealth and prosperity are not necessarily changed so abruptly as people move to the cities. This is illustrated by the complex and contested understandings of progress among people who migrate, often seen as dependent on social and ritual relationships and not necessarily as individualized or opposed to a sense of community.

[6] *Pachamama* can cause illnesses if displeased by lack of payment, and make people be *agarado de la tierra* (taken or attacked by the earth), the only cure for which is to return to the spot and make an offering (see Lund Skar 1994:174–5).

Notions of Prosperity and Progress

I have previously indicated how, when I asked people why they had moved to Arequipa, they often said that they moved in order to *progresar*, and to '*buscar modernidad*' (look for modernity), or to acquire paid labour, money, goods, or the standard of living and knowledge they associated with the urban *mestizo*. Also in general conversations, I often heard people comment on the extent to which they consider themselves to have achieved progress in the city or not, as well as commenting on the progress of others, such as relatives, neighbours and colleagues.

People sometimes spoke about progress as something quite concrete, as something you either have or do not have, as something you can acquire, lose and then acquire anew. In their perspective, people in Jerusalén were regarded as having acquired different degrees of progress, for instance as reflected by the great variety of employment forms, years of schooling, housing standards and degrees of '*mestizo*-ness' in the neighbourhood. As previously illustrated, inhabitants were especially concerned with the different standards of houses in the area, and a usual comment would be that a person '*tiene buena casa*' (she has a nice house). To have a house with several floors was often referred to as a significant sign of progress – '*esa señora ha avanzado bastante, se ha hecho construir una casa de tres pisos*' (this woman has advanced significantly, having constructed a house with three floors). As I seek to illustrate in this chapter, this quest for a better standard of living is at the same time influenced by the significance of ritual relationships and payments, seen to influence people's success in the urban context and representing an alternative source of power (see Harvey 2001:199).

Angelina sometimes complained about what she sees as her lack of progress, '*no hay progreso*', and that she still has to struggle to make ends meet. Her husband Juan has retired from construction work and now helps her out at the market. She underlined how different her husband is from herself, since she is always struggling to improve things, while he tends to be happy with the way things are. In fact, she said that if only her first boyfriend had stayed with her, life would have been different, since he was a real good worker (*trabajador*) who would have helped her in her quest for progress. Like Eugenia who suspected that some neighbours had directed *brujería* against her to make her continue in misery, Angelina also sometimes said that she has lost her luck due to *daño* or *brujería*. She suspected that someone must have directed *brujería* at her and her husband so that they would not have progress or success. Such interpretations regarding one's lack of progress are widespread, and indicate that notions of progress and prosperity are not only informed by dominant ideas about modernization and modernity, but understood as influenced also by other acts and sources of power, such as *brujería*. Indeed, people's quest for mobility seems to be informed by the significance of ritual relationships and offerings, in the sense that ritual relationships are seen to influence people's success as well as misery in the urban context. People thus perceive well-being and prosperity to be intimately connected to acts of reciprocity, between people as well as in relation to the landscape. As illustrated in the previous chapter, this does not deny however that the quest for progress and the opportunity for some people to achieve social mobility also entail an individualizing dimension.

The power of *pachamama* is not necessarily place-specific, as it encompasses a generalized idea of the earth or ground, implying that its powers may be at work anywhere. Different from *pachamama*, the *apus* are more specific to a certain place and region, in the sense that the powers of an *apu* may be limited to a certain area. This, however, is believed to depend on the size and powers of the particular *apu*, since the really powerful ones can have a wide geographical reach (Lund Skar 1994). People generally prefer to make payments to the most powerful *apu* in their local surroundings, often depending on size and appearance. Lund Skar (1994:209) notes that there are hierarchical relations between the *apus* within the near, and in some cases, quite distant surroundings (see also Sallnow 1987:129). In Arequipa, people sometimes speak about the Misti as more powerful than the mountains of their places of origin, and due to its physical nearness they consider themselves primarily to be influenced by Misti. At the same time, many people continue to appeal to the powers of the mountains that surround their village of origin as well, such as when making visits. For instance, when Angelina and I went to visit her mother in Arapa, one of the first things she did on arrival was to take out the bread that she had brought from Arequipa and present some of it to *pachamama* and the *apus* while saying the names of the different *apus* surrounding us, in addition to Misti. She asked the *apus* for everything to go well on our journey and that her business may prosper. Then she broke the rest of the bread to give to her mother, nieces and nephews. These payments to *pachamama* and the local *apus* when visiting a place of origin come in addition to, and appear to reinforce, the powers that are evoked in the urban context. In the city and when at work in the market, Angelina similarly pays the *apus* or *pachamama* in order to cure illnesses and promote the well-being of her family and, as I will elaborate further in last chapter, to secure success in her business.

It is interesting to see how the *apus* in the city and those of the highlands may require different payments. One day while the *curandero* Arturo came to Angelina's house to prepare a more expansive payment to the mountain spirits, he explained that the *apus* in the highlands are generally paid in a much simpler and less expensive manner than the *apus* in the city. In the highlands, he said, the *apus* are generally paid with some anis spirits. In the city, in contrast, *apus* like Misti, Pichu Pichu, or Chachani prefer expensive drinks like whisky or beer, that is, goods that are generally consumed by people with money. This indicates how the specific objects used in ritual payments can be subject to change in the process of migration. Arturo explained this change as due to the different desires of the *apus* in the city from those in the highlands, and compared it with the way in which the desires of people also may differ or change. As previously illustrated, many people mentioned their wish to *progresar* when describing their motivation to move to the city, it being associated with the access to money and certain goods. This can indicate how the city is associated with a somewhat different kind of prosperity than that associated with the highlands (that is, the fields and flocks and their produce as outlined by Harris 2000), and how different places may also demand different kinds of payments. It can illustrate the way in which different places are associated with different kinds of, or possibilities for, prosperity and therefore how the movement in space can be seen to influence not only people's well-being, but also their prosperity.

In the urban context, the practices concerning the powerful landscape are also made subject to change and negotiation. Some people in Jerusalén said that *pachamama* and the *apus* lose some of their powers in the urban context. According to the *curandero* Jorge, this is because people think there are too many houses and people in the city for these powers to work. Other people simply performed their payments occasionally and without talking much about them, or expressed reluctance to talk about them. Due to the stigmatization of people from the highlands, many under-communicate their Andean background and their performance of rural practices in the urban context for fear of being called *indio* and looked down upon. In relation to such a stigma the use of coca is given particular significance. While many people chew coca especially during breaks since it represents an important form of social exchange and takes away the hunger and fatigue during long working hours, other people avoid the use of coca or take part in exchanges of coca only in familiar settings at home or at parties. A few people also denied the importance of the *apus* and *pachamama* by rationalizing about a lack of proof and effect, or complained about the high expenses involved in ritual payments. On other occasions, I nonetheless met the same people in situations where they did take part. If the situation required it therefore, such as in the case of illness or social obligation, many would seek a traditional healer or make ritual payments while they otherwise did not make payments on an everyday basis. People in Jerusalén are increasingly turning toward the Evangelical churches, where priests actively criticize these ritual practices. One woman who had converted even said she was glad that the Evangelical priests are so critical, since that gives people a legitimate way to escape the high expenses often involved in ritual payments and obligations. These differences illustrate how various logics are made relevant in relation to people's prospects in the city, and therefore how progress may be ascribed with different and contested meanings.

Ritual activity and labour in the Andes are intimately connected (Harvey 2001), and what people say and do in relation to these practices often vary with context as well as with life and work situations. For instance, people involved in factory work or employed as servants seem to be less involved in these practices than people working in occupations such as transport or at the market. As I will discuss in Chapter 7, I found that people involved in trading in particular were concerned with making ritual payments to improve or secure their business. These ritual payments illustrate how land and surroundings also in the urban context are re-created as inherent with specific qualities – and seen as animated by certain powers. It indicates the way in which a reciprocal relationship to surroundings is made important in the process of resettling in new surroundings, by representing an alternative source of power in the quest for belonging and progress.

Spatial Powers and Movements in Space

The powers of the surroundings can also be harmful, and as already noted, offerings are made to ensure that these powers are benign and not evil. In cases when people fall, for instance, it is said that *pachamama* is hungry and '*quiere agarar*' (wants to take or attack)[7] the person for failing to make offerings. Similarly, people who move need to protect themselves by making offerings or bringing stones, earth, or food from the place left behind (see also Allen 1988, Lund Skar 1994, Harvey 2001). Since the powerful surroundings are seen as located and manifested in different local, regional and geographical landscapes, movement from one place to another may disturb the communication between people and surroundings and put the person who moves in danger. Angelina's neighbour Carla once explained that such a danger can arise because the earth of a new place does not yet 'know you' (*conocerte*). This is a situation that can threaten one's health and general well-being, so in order to make the earth or mountains at a new place 'know you', one can bring a piece of earth or a stone in a bag or pocket, or otherwise make some kind of offering. By bringing such objects from the place left behind to a new place, the powers from the place left behind are seen to work protectively against the dangers found upon arriving at new surroundings. When talking about her childhood growing up in a village outside Cuzco, Tarabamba, Eugenia spoke about the first time she was about to leave her village of origin as a little girl. She was to accompany her mother on a trip to the marketplace in a town nearby in order to barter agricultural products. When about to leave the village, her mother found a little stone[8] that she gave Eugenia to put in her *manta* (rug, carpet) to take along on the journey, so the powers of the *apus* from home would protect her against the powers of the new place. These practices illustrate how people see themselves as related to and influenced by the powerful surroundings, and how they seek to mediate between the powers of a place of origin and the powers at a new place of arrival. For a person who moves, it illustrates the significance of re-creating and maintaining a relationship to the surroundings in order to secure well-being.

Food products, as well as coca leaves and alcohol, are significant for dealing with movement and migration in the Andes. The sharing of food is seen as

7 According to Lund Skar, *pacha* sickness illustrates the continuity that exists between the earth and people, and a fall disturbs this continuity by challenging the earth/person boundary. Following a fall, one may pick up and eat a bit of the earth from that spot, and hence avoid being grabbed by *pachamama* (Lund Skar 1994:175), or one may urinate on the spot to achieve the same effect.

8 See Lund Skar (1994: 67–8) about bringing stones (*illas*), seen as containing some of the force of its source, that is, from *apus*.

essential for instance when leaving or visiting a village of origin, and illustrates how people's relationship with their place of origin and their relatives there is often characterized by acts and expectations of reciprocity. The traveller is expected to bring foods from the city when visiting the village, not only to feed relatives and neighbours, but also the *apus* and *pachamama*. The traveller is also given food from the local lands in return, including sacks of food products to bring back to the city in order to reinforce her relationship with relatives as well as the land (Lund Skar 1994, see also Weismantel 1988). This food is seen to be particularly tasteful and nutritious, and is talked about as containing some of the qualities of the land. The qualities of the land are therefore seen to be transferred though the consumption of this food (see Ødegaard 1999).

These ways of dealing with movement through the transference of qualities of the land are closely related to Andean cosmology, that is, as a discourse about people's relationship to place (Sherbondy 1992). In the myths of the Incas, the relationship between people and place similarly represented an essential theme, in the sense that the ancestral origin of the Incas was connected to Lake Titicaca (see Dover, Seibold and McDowell 1992:9). In Peru, children now learn about these myths at school, one of which says that the first Incas, Manco Capac and his brothers and sisters, were created at Lake Titicaca, from where they travelled along subterranean channels to Cuzco. Since this creation of the Incas, their Titicaca origins were symbolically remembered with a ritual for each new Inca king by bringing water from Lake Titicaca to Cuzco to anoint a new king. Such a ritual anointment with Titicaca water also served to legitimize the displacement of the Inca centre from its site of emergence to Cuzco (Sherbondy 1992). Sherbondy notes that this was necessary since, according to the myths of origin, the distribution of peoples was fixed from the beginning of the world. Similarly when ordinary people moved, the re-foundation of an *ayllu* at a new site could be ritually accomplished by carrying water from the *ayllu*'s previous water source into a new territory, where it was poured into the springs of the new land. In this manner, people symbolically re-established their *ayllu* (Sherbondy 1992:57). There are clear similarities between these pre-colonial practices and the current significance of bringing stones, earth, or food, and making ritual payments when moving or arriving at a new place. These practices illustrate how cosmologies create a framework not only for how people are to relate to their surroundings, but also for how they should deal with movement.

In the words of de Certeau, to practice space is 'to be other and move towards the other' (1984:109). He notes that a sense of otherness is particularly made relevant in the course of travelling, as subjectivity is linked to an absence that subsequently structures the place as existence and makes it 'be there'. According to de Certeau, this is the subjective experience of place, created by spatial practices or 'the ways of moving into something different' (1984:109). In addition to the existential or phenomenological dimension as thus underlined by de Certeau, the movement in space in the Andes also actualizes another dimension, that is, the cosmological or spiritual one. This adds another dimension to de Certeau's idea of 'moving into something different', a dimension that is physically as well as psychologically powerful. Due to the powers of places and surroundings, movement can be fraught with danger as well as possibilities.

The understanding of the notion of *ánimo* may further illustrate how the powerful landscape is seen to affect people who move. The *ánimo* is associated with soul and refers to a part of the person, or self, sharing connotations with notions such as spirit or courage, agency, will or intention. As noted by Gose (1994), the *ánimo* can also be associated with energy, and particularly the energy involved in work. The state of the *ánimo* can be acknowledged by the interpretation of dreams (see also Allen 1988, Gose 1994) as well as a person's state of being. Angelina one day told me that she had been dreaming about her village of origin again. She said that she often has such dreams, about life and places in the highlands and herself living and walking in her village of origin. She found it strange that she still dreams like this, especially since she hardly ever dreams of life in urban places such as Arequipa, where she actually lives. Instead she dreams about herself working with the soil and the animals like she used to as a little girl, and about taking salt from the lake while fearing the powers of the enchanted places. Once when chatting to her colleagues at the market, she told them about these dreams. They responded that she ought to listen to the dreams, since they may tell her something important about the state of her *ánimo*. One of them said that the dreams could indicate that her *ánimo* has been left behind in her village of origin and, being unable to come back, it makes her dream about her village. They told her she therefore ought to go back home and prepare herself to *llamar el ánimo* (call the soul to come back). In this manner, the person who has lost the *ánimo* can make it return by calling upon it or attracting it by the display of specific objects, such as some pieces of clothing or sweets. Angelina was for instance advised to use her hat, wave with it, and call her name '*ven, Angelina, ven*' (come Angelina, come). However, her colleagues said that there was no use in doing this while in Arequipa, and she would have to call on her *ánimo* at the place where it was lost, that is, in the village.

Different kinds of changes that people go through can make the *animo* leave the body and consequently alter a person's state of being. As in the case of Angelina, the cause – and recuperation – of this state can be dependent on the movement in space, or the distance or proximity to a specific place. The *ánimo* may also leave the body due to an experience of fear or shock, most often occurring with children (see also Lazar 2002), indicating a general instability of the *ánimo* that for adults similarly can be caused by movement in space. This manner in which the *ánimo* may leave the body and stay behind at another place serves to indicate how people experience themselves as influenced by the powers of specific places, and how the movement in space may affect their well-being. It illustrates how people in the Andes see places as integral parts of their own formation and origin (Lund Skar 1994:71) and demonstrates the significance of maintaining a particular relationship to place and surroundings. If a person does not succeed in communicating with these powers or maintain a positive sense of spatial situatedness, as illustrated in Angelina's case, the essence of a person may split up, and make the person feel ill or have strange dreams. Indeed, the movement in space involves different states of being that in the Andes are made important in processes of curing more generally. Lund Skar (1994) argues that the aim of different forms of curing is to reunite an animated dimension that has been separated from its source and to make it return to the object/subject of its origin. According to her, people may experience a return to a village of origin as an act of curing in itself, by placing their own animated nature within its originating context from which it draws its strength and authority (1994:231–2). This experience of return as a curative act can further be related to the way in which people in the city may also be affected by bad influences that are sometimes activated by people in the village who want to do them harm, such as by *brujería* (harmful acts) or the use of objects containing dangerous powers. In these cases, the affected person may find it necessary to return to the village in order to respond to, or undo, these negative influences. Hence physical presence can be regarded as necessary in order to perform and succeed with ritual acts. If people are unaware that they have been the object of *brujería* in the village, however, return may also be dangerous. After a period during which Angelina's mother had been sick and had no one in the village to take care of her, her mother finally came to stay with her family in Arequipa for a while. Missing her house and neighbours though, she decided to return to the village, only to get worse – and after a few weeks she died. When her son found her, he also found a dead frog in her house, with her hair around it, indicating that someone had wanted to harm her. According to Angelina's daughter María, returning to the village had actually been fatal for her grandmother by activating the harmful powers of the *brujería.*

The above illustrates how the reciprocal relationship to land and the animated surroundings is important for understanding movement and mobility in the Andean context. It highlights the way in which people deal with movement by recreating a relationship to the surroundings through acts of reciprocity. Through these acts, people maintain and re-create relationships with a powerful landscape, engaging in practices of reciprocity that can be seen as a process of place-making. Indeed, this communication with land and surroundings is closely connected to ideas about and communication with kin and community, so that for the person who moves, it is not only her relationship to land that may be jeopardized, but simultaneously her relationship to kin and community. The significance of maintaining these relationships is illustrated through acts of reciprocity, acts that are seen to enable the transference of specific qualities. These acts serve to tie together kin as well as the landscape, and demonstrate how notions of place are intimately connected to kin and community.

New Neighbourhoods and Ancient Powers

As Jerusalén is located just below Misti, there are many stories in the neighbourhood about the volcano's strength and powers, as well as the evil spirits that are at work in its surroundings. Several inhabitants have made a living by removing stones from abandoned mines located on the hillsides rising towards the volcano. As the land here is owned by the state but not officially in use, these mines represent an opportunity for anyone to come and work them. People come to dig out stones that are used in the production of stone-washed jeans and collected in trucks that come by once every week. Those who work like this have to protect themselves from the evil *duendes*, that is, small, bearded and human-like creatures that are said to live in these mines and cause the miners to have accidents or become ill. As a way in which to protect themselves against the *duendes*, people make offerings and pray to God, as well as consume coca or spirits or smoke cigarettes.

Misti's surroundings are seen to be the location for other bad places ('*mal sitios*') as well, some which may cause the sickness *mal viento* (bad wind). These are places associated with evil spirits, and *mal viento* is caused by the presence of souls or *condenados* (condemned spirits) who have not found peace and are angry because people do not pray for them. In cases when people have to pass, or accidentally come across such a place, the payment of coca leaves, liquor and cigarettes – in addition to the words of God – is required as protection against these powers. The influence of spirits in the urban context can in this manner be significant, although more so in the outskirts of inhabited areas such as those close to the mountains. However, while people previously used to know how to handle these evil spirits, many currently fall ill since the knowledge of how to handle them is gradually disappearing. Among the illnesses that these evil spirits or sites may cause is the psychological or emotional disorientation of those who chance upon them. For instance, mental illness in Jerusalén is in some cases explained by contact with such 'bad places' and the supernatural beings residing there (see also McDowell 1992:97). The evil powers of these places can also be used to do *brujería*, for example through the collection of objects found at a bad place in order to harm another person.

Upon returning one day from his job on a construction project, Angelina's husband Juan was feeling very ill. From that day and for several months, he continued to suffer from such bad headaches and dizziness that he was unable to work. When Angelina finally told me what had happened, she explained that while Juan had been digging the ground that day, he had suddenly touched upon a ceramic object hidden underground. It was at that moment he became ill. Thus, not being able to look again at the object, he had to leave it for the other workers to explore. In retrospect, Angelina underlined that Juan became ill since he had come too close to a bad place, a badness that was probably related to the ceramic object. They confirmed this suspicion shortly thereafter when they consulted the coca leaves. Angelina was certain that Juan had actually hit an ancient grave with his stick and the ceramic object contained gold that was meant for him. However, as Juan had not been saying his prayers or chewing coca as she always reminds him that he should, the wealth had suddenly made him ill and was lost to him. For this reason, Angelina was annoyed and said that if Juan had only protected himself when at work in such an unfamiliar place, he would probably have gotten possession of the gold instead of falling ill. Indeed, she said that the gold was obviously meant for Juan. This illustrates how ancient powers are sometimes rediscovered in an urban context through objects or places that are believed to have the power to bring prosperity or do harm. These objects may even be seen to have a direction or intention of their own (for instance that the ancient wealth was meant for Juan to possess), something that Juan in this case failed to respond to. Such an understanding of the intentionality – or agency – of objects is an expression of the animated qualities of the surroundings, and indicates how a source of prosperity is not regarded simply as the object of human manipulation – although it is possible to influence through the payment of gifts or food.

From the house next door to Angelina, we one day heard some loud noises, as if somebody were hitting rocks or digging the ground. The noise continued for the next few days and nights, and we all became increasingly curious about what it might be. After a couple of days, Angelina finally spoke to her neighbour, and came home excited to tell me that they were digging to take out gold found hidden in the ground. The reason they had found this gold, she said, was that the woman next door had suddenly seen a blue light outside her house. She had been quick to find some food in the kitchen to offer, and had then discovered that the blue light came from gold hidden under the ground on the same spot where they were about to construct a new house. We were told we should not tell anyone, however, since this gold was obviously meant for the woman next door. It was she who had seen the blue light and knew what it meant, and in addition knew how to respond by immediately offering food.

Some of these powerful places and objects found when making use of new land in Jerusalén are seen to originate from the time of the Incas, and among these are the sites of the powerful *gentiles*. The *gentiles* are a group of ancestors who used to rule the universe, but were forced underground because their age was over, hiding there with all their ancient objects and wealth (see Lund Skar 1994). Through this relationship between the *gentiles* and the autochthonous powers of the landscape, Lund Skar argues that people in the Andes find the present world to be infused with the past (1994:241). As illustrated in the case of Juan coming upon an ancient grave, the ancestors' powers[9] are also expected to possibly come to the surface in cases when grave sites and objects are found under the ground, as when digging new land for housing, construction work or mining.

Both cases above illustrate how the result of such encounters with spatial or ancient powers depends on the ways in which people respond. In other words, there are specific ways of responding in order to make sure that such powers are benign and not evil. Not everyone knows about these approaches though, and only those who know can enjoy the enormous prosperity that these powers may

---

9 While the places of ancestors in the highlands are generally seen as potentially dangerous and therefore approached with care, some land occupations in the city are made on top of ancestral graves. According to Lund Skar, this is because the ruins of the earlier settlement bear a resemblance to that of their own ancestors and as such, may be used to give certain validity to their claims to land (1994:192).

represent and bring. In this regard, prosperity seems to be associated with a kind of power that can originate and be materialized in new as well as old forms. It can be seen to reflect Harris's (2000) point that agricultural fertility and money are not necessarily opposed in Andean thought, since money comes from the same sources that ensure the harvest and reproduction of flocks. According to her, money is associated with natural fertility as well as the state, and prosperity can be seen as having different sources, one ancient, underground, and the other less ancient, that is, today's money (2000:73).

People's occasional encounters with the *gentiles* or ancient objects and prosperity can be related to an idea of the possible return of the ancestors and earlier times, and thus the current significance of ancestral powers also in the urban context. This possible return of ancient times and powers reflects what has been considered a circular understanding of time in Andean thought (see Harris 2000, Mannheim 1991, Lund Skar 1994, Harvey 1997), and how richness and prosperity are seen to circulate. Lund Skar (1994) notes that central to the notion of circulating times in the Andes is the capacity of ancestors to intervene in the human world, and the expectation that they – when the time comes – will retain their powers and overthrow the current rulers.

What characterize some accounts of ancestral places and powers are thus the sequential reversals seen to represent a focal dynamic in Andean historicity through different *pachakutis* (world orders, or epochs) (Mannheim 1991:92). The notion of *pachakuti* indicates how power and prosperity can be seen to circulate in time and space, and illustrates how notions about time and place, power and prosperity are interconnected. Similar ideas are also evident in how some migrants view their own lives. Many people were concerned that they were not able to progress in the city. They spoke about the stubbornness of poverty, that there are no jobs, that they cannot afford the food or things that they need, and that in the city, nothing comes for free but has to be bought with money. Once when Angelina and Pedro, a friend of hers, discussed these issues, they agreed with Angelina's claim that, '*La vida es y siempre va a ser pobre. Aunque uno tiene plata por un tiempo, la plata se va después y siempre se queda pobre*' (Life is and continues to be poor, although one perhaps may become rich for a little period. The money will finally be spent and one always ends up being poor again). So while I most often heard Angelina underline her own progress, especially in relation to her business, she also commented that she would probably soon become poor once again, and live like the sick old women who come begging at the market. The reason for this, she said, was that previous times always tend to return. In this manner, a person's power and prosperity can be expected to take abrupt turns, in the sense that someone who is prosperous and powerful at one point will eventually turn poor. As illustrated in Angelina's claim, for instance, she sees prosperity as something that may come one moment just to leave in the next for someone else. In general, people seem to understand prosperity as basically characterized by instability. This instability is further illustrated in the understanding of *brujería* as harmful acts with the potential to ruin someone's ability to make money.

Due to the way in which the past in Andean perspectives on history is seen to co-exist in the present, Harvey (1997) has noted how the past can be brought out and actualized in particular ritual circumstances. Similarly, Harris (2000) has contrasted these notions of time and history with the Hispanic versions of history, and described them as two kinds of history related to different sources of power. In the Hispanic version of history, that is, the history of the modern nation state, there is change and displacement of the traditional by the modern. In the other kind of history, the distinction between the Hispanic and the non-Hispanic is understood in terms of religious periodization, or a kind of history characterized by continuity and the enduring understanding of alternative sources of power. Different parts of history may thus be seen to co-exist and interact, through an interchange that is reflected in the possible return of ancestral powers (Harris 2000). In the migrant context, this interchange between different parts of history – as well as sources of power – may be related further to the meanings people attribute not only to prosperity but also progress. On the one hand, people associate 'progress' with a 'modernity' found in cities, and on the other hand they see it as dependent on and influenced by the powers of the past and the surroundings. Different sources of power and prosperity are therefore seen to co-exist in the urban landscape, and in their quest for mobility and progress, people appeal also to the powers of the landscape.

Conclusions

This chapter has explored how notions of powerful surroundings are made important in processes of migration and mobility, and how a reciprocal relationship to the landscape is in different ways re-created in an urban context. People's accommodation to the city therefore does not entail a one-sided process of, for example, a bureaucratization or commercialization of spatial categories, since space is simultaneously understood on spiritual terms, as animated and powerful. Indeed, the powerful surroundings are made important for people's quest for belonging and progress in the urban context, such as through ritual payments to maintain relationships and to seek protection and success in work or business. At the same time, these practices also become objects of change and negotiation, and some people regard them as a tradition belonging to their rural past, insignificant for their lives and prospects in the city. Others see them as a necessary means of protecting themselves and ensuring the possibility of progress through the engagement with the surroundings as sources of prosperity as well as danger.

Indeed, movement and mobility can be seen to actualize the significance of spatial powers, in the sense that the surroundings are perceived to affect people positively or negatively in the process of moving. This ontological continuity with rural life can serve to make places out of spaces, in the sense that the powerful surroundings are appealed to as mediators in the attempt to make hostile space into meaningful places, or places of identification and possible prosperity. As illustrated in the notion of *ánimo*, people's ideas about soul and well-being are understood as connected to their relationship with the surroundings, and illustrate how places are seen as an integral part of people's formation. The understanding of place is furthermore connected to ideas about kin and community, and the dangers connected to movement thus throw an interesting light on personal experiences of movement in relation to collective structures. My contribution has been to explore how the reciprocal relationship to kin, land and the animated surroundings in the Andes is important for understandings of movement and mobility as such. Movement in space can be seen as potentially dangerous, at the same time as it involves the potential for communication with new sources of prosperity, and movement can itself thus be seen to create or threaten people's well-being or prosperity. In this regard, I have explored how the powers of the surroundings are associated with prosperity, and how movement may actualize different sources of prosperity and power. Indeed, prosperity and power are perceived as differently distributed in space as well as time, thus informing the movement in space as related to different spatial (and time-based) configurations and directions. People understand their relationship to the surroundings according to ideas about circulating times and powers, in the sense that places are imagined as locations for different visions of and aspirations for the future as well as the past, in the form of hopeful visions for the city or expectations to the powerful ancestors. In this manner, different sources of powers and prosperity are seen to co-exist in the city, that is, in urban, as well as ancient forms.

Places are often associated with qualities that people seek to re-make and reconstruct in processes of mobility, and as noted by Hirschon (1998), 'home' cannot necessarily be reduced to a place of origin, but may be made and remade on an everyday basis. Not only in the Andes, but also more generally, people who move often attempt to keep memories of, or create continuity with, a place of belonging, for instance by bringing along certain objects (Frykman 2007). Among people who fled to Sweden during the war in the former Yugoslavia, for instance, Frykman illustrates how specific objects were made important in the efforts to maintain a relationship to particular places of belonging, so the refugees could stay connected and be remembered. Frykman underlines that these objects represent in many ways an attempt to bring places with them. This is common in processes of mobility and can be seen as efforts to make places out of spaces as people seek to reconstruct a place of belonging. The practices that I have described here illustrate people's attempts, not merely to bring places with them, but to actively relate to their new surroundings and thus engage in processes of place-making. By seeing themselves as influenced by their surroundings, they seek to recreate these influences in processes of mobility, and re-conceptualize the surroundings as mediators in their quest for belonging. In processes of mobility, people can thus be seen to involve themselves in processes of re-creating places and creating new ones, and making mobility into a process of place-making.

Chapter 4
Relations of Trust and Prestige

The focus of this chapter is the understanding of sociality in processes of mobility, and the significance of practices of reciprocity and ritual kinship, or *compadrazgo*.[1] I will explore the significance of practices of reciprocity for people's accommodation in the city and the creation of social networks, and how questions related to trust, respect and prestige are often negotiated through these relationships. So while the previous chapter was concerned with a relational understanding of the landscape and notions of mobility, this chapter is more specifically concerned with sociality and practices of reciprocity. The significance of reciprocity in the rural Andes is reflected in often elaborate festivals and fiestas, practices of gift giving and ritual payments, communal work and rituals of transition. I will explore how – in the process of establishing themselves in the city – people accommodate these practices to an urban context and sometimes re-create their forms and meanings. While practices of reciprocity and collectivism represent central values in the Andean highlands, it is nonetheless important not to forget, as noted in the introduction, that Andean socialities are not characterized by an absence of individual interest and agency (see Albó 1975, Bradby 1982, Allen 1988, Weismantel 1988, Urton 1992, Lund Skar 1994, Gose 1994, Abercrombie 1998, Harris 2000, Lazar 2002, 2008, McNeish 2002). This is reflected also in what may appear as the somewhat contradictory dynamics of people's responses to new situations, such as when settling in the city. An important concern here is therefore how practices of reciprocity work to confirm notions of 'community' and communal obligation on the one hand, and serve as a means of personal progress or prestige on the other. In this manner, I explore how practices and values of reciprocity articulate with notions of progress and prosperity.

While practices of reciprocity may be important for how inhabitants sometimes confirm their identities as people from the highlands, these practices may be important also for how they seek to involve people from the city in their social networks. This chapter therefore explores how inhabitants seek to extend their networks of trust and care by involving people from the neighbourhood as well as people in relations of reciprocity. In this manner, I aim to highlight the ways in which people seek to (re-)define themselves and their position through specific ritual and relational practices, and how they negotiate the question of belonging in the urban context. Although my focus in this chapter is primarily on relations of *compadrazgo*, the significance of reciprocity must not be understood as limited

---

[1] Ritual or spiritual kin; co-parenthood.

only to this practice, since indeed, the significance of reciprocity in this context goes far beyond *compadrazgo*.

Compadrazgo in the Urban Context

The will and ability to give is celebrated as an important value among people in Jerusalén. This value is important for how people relate to each other and, as it represents a significant idiom for sociality, is important also to how people see themselves and others as social persons. Relations of *compadrazgo* are established on a wide range of different occasions, for example on behalf of a child in relation to baptism or *corte-del-pelo* (hair-cutting ritual),[2] the first communion, confirmation or the fifteenth birthday; in relation to marriage; work parties (for instance in relation to roofing, or *techamientos*); inaugurations of buildings or places; or the acquisition of new goods. In this respect, *compadrazgo* in the urban context represents a practice that ensures the initiation and confirmation of social relationships on different occasions and of different kinds. In the appointment of *padrinos*,[3] people ask non-relatives as well as relatives. What is common in both cases however is that there is a preference for appointing a person who is particularly respected, valued or seen to possess prestige in some way. As I will come back to, there is a tendency for parents to appoint people from the city as *padrinos* for their children, while they appoint other migrants like themselves for occasions which do not involve children, occasions such as house roofing parties or the like, which involve the expectation of mutual work help. As a relationship of *compadrazgo* is initiated, the individuals involved start addressing each other by the self-reciprocal term *comadre* (female) or *compadre* (male).[4] People say that this is to underline their respect and care (their *cariño*). The child involved is referred to by the non-reciprocal term *ahijado/-a*, and a child's spiritual parents are referred to as *padrino* (male) and *madrina* (female).[5]

---

[2] For the first cutting of a baby's hair, an occasion for which *padrinos* are appointed and gifts are exchanged.

[3] *Madrina* (female) and *padrino* (male) are the terms used for sponsoring or giving roles in a *compadrazgo* relationship.

[4] *Compadre* (male) and *comadre* (female) are the reciprocal terms for people who have entered relations of *compadrazgo*.

[5] In the literature, the link between the sponsors and the children is conceptualized as *padrinazgo*, and is generally not made important to the same degree as the *compadrazgo*, that is, the link between the parents. What first of all characterizes relations of *padrinazgo*, is that the *padrinos* are expected to give the child presents for birthdays and perhaps contribute in the guidance and education of the child, while the child is expected to show particular attention and respect towards the *padrinos*. In this manner, *padrinazgo* represents a vertical or asymmetric relationship in the sense that the *ahijado* is always subordinated to the *padrinos*, while this is not necessarily the case between the adult *comadres*.

While she was young and not yet married, Juana worked as a servant in the centre of Arequipa, in a house where she was given a small room in which to sleep. After several years in the city, she met her future husband Javier, whom she partly knew from her childhood in Chumbivilcas. Before getting married, they agreed it was no longer convenient for her to work and live in the house of other people. Instead, they wanted to find a place of their own, and they finally found a place in Jerusalén, a small terrain that had been occupied by others but was now to be sold. The terrain had not been prepared for housing at all, so they had a lot of work ahead of them. Without knowing their new neighbours when moving in, Juana was happy to learn that her next-door neighbour was a woman about the same age as herself, more specifically Eugenia who has been presented in a previous chapter. Juana and Eugenia are both from the department of Cuzco, although from different districts. In the same way as Juana, Eugenia was struggling to make the place habitable and ends meet, and during these first years in Jerusalén they both took work as servants in some periods or tried to make some soles[6] from selling things in the streets. While Juana's husband Javier temporarily made good money by working in a well-established hotel in the centre, Eugenia's husband brought in little from his work as a mechanic as previously noted. For that reason, they were often short of money, and unlike Juana, Eugenia had no relatives living in Arequipa during these first years whom she could ask for help and support. Some days she did not have enough to buy food, and on such a day she went to Juana to ask if she could borrow some money so that she could cook for her family. After that they started to lend each other things and invite each other for meals and small parties, and when Eugenia was about to baptize her son, she convinced her husband that they should ask Juana and her husband to act as *madrina* and *padrino*. He agreed, and they presented their request together with a case of beer. The request was accepted, and they held a big party in Eugenia and her husband's house. They thus became each other's first *comadres*. As the years have passed and their children have grown, there is still a continual movement and exchange between the two houses, such as when Juana and Eugenia invite each other to share small plates of food because, they sometimes said, 'we are *comadres*'. After having more children and thus several occasions to create relations with *compadres*, both Juana and Eugenia have also established other relations of *compadrazgo*, mainly with kin or neighbours. However, they still tend to refer to each other as their closest *comadre*, so if anything happens they continue to turn to each other. As Eugenia used to say, '*en ella tengo confianza*' (I trust her).

This illustrates how the initiation of *compadrazgo* may work as a way to create or confirm relations of trust, care and support in the absence of relatives in the area or neighbourhood. In this regard, the practice of *compadrazgo* can represent a way to initiate relations with someone you do not have any previous relation to, or otherwise someone with whom you want to confirm and strengthen

---

6 During my fieldwork in 1997 and 2001, the Peruvian currency sol was equivalent to around $0.50 (US).

an already existing relationship. As time goes by, as in the case of Juana and Eugenia, people will generally become *compadres* with a range of different people and thus gradually expand their social networks in the city. Others may be more concerned with strengthening already existing relationships with a few selected persons, in some cases by making *comadres* mainly with kin or by appointing the same *compadres* for different occasions. *Compadrazgo* may thus serve as a way of re-creating a social network in the process of accommodating to the city, or to reinforce the relationship to kin in the urban context.

One day Angelina received the news that the president in the women's organization, Leonarda and her husband were about to arrange a roofing party for the new house of their oldest son in Cerrito de Belén. Both Angelina and I were later appointed as *madrinas*, in addition to eight others, including Carla (who is among the leaders in the women's organization), a representative from one of the state agencies involved in the area[7] as well as some of the neighbours, most together with their partners. Angelina said she was glad not to have been appointed as the first *madrina*, however, because of the greater expense it would have entailed.[8] Nevertheless, she spent several days worrying about the money she would have to spend, money that she needed for other purposes. She could not decide if she should present one or two cases of beer, for instance, and kept worrying about the impression that people would get of her being poor or pitiful if she presented only one. After discussing it back and forth for a while, she decided to bring two. When we were walking towards the house, greeting the other neighbours and about to go in, she said she felt ashamed though, and regretted that she had not brought three cases at least. Everyone must think I am really poor and even feel sorry for me, she said worriedly. Later she commented that on arriving at the party and placing her cases of beer in front of Leonarda and her husband at the open place in front of the house, she had felt quite awkward by having to present her beer in the presence of the other guests who were already seated.

As the other *padrinos* arrived, they all presented their cases of beer to Leonarda and her husband. The first *padrinos* presented five cases in all, to the joyful appreciation of the guests, while the subsequent *padrinos* presented between one and four cases. As it was getting dark and the roof was finished and left to dry, all the *padrinos* and *madrinas*, responding to a sign from Leonarda, went up on the roof to stand in line facing the other guests who were gathered on the ground. The atmosphere was characterized by silent formality, and the *padrinos* and *madrinas* were all nicely dressed and discretely preparing their speeches as well as a few more gifts. Each of the *padrinos* or *madrinas* in turn then had to make a speech in which we all congratulated the work party and the owners and wished luck on the house. After each speech the *padrinos* broke open a bottle of sparkling wine and

7 From the state programme Programa Nacional de Asistencia Alimentaria (PRONAA).

8 In cases when several *madrinas* are appointed, the first *madrina* is supposed to give the most plentiful gifts, while second *madrinas* are expected to give somewhat less.

lit some fireworks. When all the speeches from all the *padrinos* were completed, we remained there to throw sweets down to the other guests, both to children and adults, while they were shouting at us: *madrina* and *padrino*.

Among some of the other guests, the appointment of so many *padrinos* for this occasion was subject to criticism during the evening. In their perspective, the appointment of fewer *padrinos* would have represented more of an honour for those who were appointed. At the point of this *techamiento*, the women's organization ASOMA had for a long time been headed by Leonarda as its president. Her name is well known by most people in Jerusalén due to her different positions of leadership both in women's groups as well as in the neighbourhood committee. During her period as the president of ASOMA, she has established relations of *compadrazgo* with several women in the group, not only among the other leaders, but also among members more generally by appointing them as *madrinas* for other similar occasions. I several times heard her criticized for this, not only among members of the organization, but also among those who were her own *comadres*. Nevertheless, it seemed she continued to enjoy a position of certain respect, and I often heard it said that there was nobody else in the organization who could take her position. As a result, she also ended up continuing as president in ASOMA for at least three consecutive terms. Indeed, Leonarda's wide network of *compadrazgo* relationships seems in many ways to have strengthened her position as a leader, and perhaps particularly so through her *compadrazgo* relationships with other members in leadership positions. *Compadrazgo* can in this regard be important for how some people work to gain confidence and support also within social organizations.

Ritual relationships seem to be of general importance for people's attempts to create relations of trust and support, as well as to increase prestige and accumulate influence. Similarly among traders at the market, relations of *compadrazgo* are important for the creation of networks of co-operation, confidence and support. For instance, after several years working as a trader at the market, Angelina has become *comadre* with several other traders. One of them is Juliana, who sits on the ground just beside her stand selling shoelaces, and with whom Angelina spends much time speaking and having meals during the day. They look after each other's goods when they have to leave their places, they invite each other for meals and lend each other money. Another of her *comadres* at the market is Paulina, who works as a smuggler (*contrabandista*) and who comes each week to supply goods at the market. This relationship was initiated when Paulina one day asked Angelina to be the *madrina* for the baptism of her little boy. After they became *comadres*, Angelina started to buy all the goods of *contrabando* that she needs exclusively from Paulina, although there is a range of other *contrabandistas* who regularly come to offer their goods. Angelina also has other *comadres* at the market, and each time she meets them, she is careful to call them *comadre* with a special *cariño* (care or love), as she calls it, and invites them to enjoy some coca or something to eat or drink. In addition to these relations of *compadrazgo*, Angelina also has other traders and customers with whom she has a special relationship, her *caseras*,[9] as she calls them. At the marketplace, women thus base their business networks on relations of reciprocity with colleagues as well as customers. These relationships seem to gain particular importance because of the often insecure nature of this kind of trade, characterized by intense competition and the risk of being caught, fooled or of losing investments. As I will come back to, it is a context in which personal and ritual relationships gain increased significance in the attempt to create confidence and support in the realization of business.

In many of these relations of *compadrazgo*, same-sex relationships tend to be of particular importance, in the sense that *compadres* of the same sex often come to create a particularly close and trusting relationship. Similarly in the highlands, *compadrazgo* is made important for a same-sex dimension in the form of mutual work help, such as between *comadres* who cook together while the *compadres* plough the fields (see Gose 1994, Paerregaard 1997a). In the city, these same-sex relations created through *compadrazgo* are also made important for work-help, such as when constructing houses or arranging grill parties (*parilladas)* in the neighbourhood. So when people need work help, they generally ask their *compadres* in addition to kin, affines and sometimes close neighbours. In return for work, people receive food and alcohol at the festivities that generally follow the arrangement of work help (or *faenas*). Next time it may be the *compadre* who was previously called for work help who needs the same favour in return. In this manner, there is an interchange of labour and food between *comadres* in a way that may take the form of generalized reciprocity, in the sense that the return of a favour or gift may be delayed and the interchange is not necessarily balanced (see Mauss 1954, Sahlins 1972). This generalized reciprocity seems to be central for people's experiences of communality and equality in the relationship between *comadres*, and is made important also in relation to the expectation that people contribute to the arrangement of fiestas and festivals.

The Appointment of *Padrinos* for Children

The appointment of *padrinos* for children is seen as particularly important and as potentially of great significance for their future. This is because the *padrinos* of a child are expected to serve as an extra set of parents and thus an important part of their social network providing advice and support. For this reason, people tend to appoint *padrinos* for their children who are somehow considered as having social prestige, for instance with a good income or job. The first occasions for the appointment of *padrinos* for a child are the Catholic baptism and the hair-cutting ritual (*corte-del-pelo*, or *rutuchi/-kui*). *Corte-del-pelo* is a ritual of transition for

[9] *Casera* can be translated as homemaker or customer, but in the market context it is used to refer to customers as well as traders, and to indicate a special relationship or attentiveness.

the first cutting of a baby's hair.[10] In the cities, however, this kind of ritual is regarded as a typical 'Andean' practice and is often frowned upon or looked down upon. Despite this and the expenses required for arranging a party and preparing food in honour of the *padrinos*, most people in Jerusalén nonetheless choose to arrange this ritual for their children.

When Iván, the second-born child of Carla and Teófilo, was about one and a half years old, they decided to baptize him as soon as possible because he had been ill for several months and they were afraid of losing him. They also decided to arrange the *corte-del-pelo* on the same day as the baptism so that it would only be necessary to arrange one big party for both occasions. Although arranged for the same day, they needed *padrinos* for both occasions, hence I was appointed the godmother[11] for the hair-cutting ritual (together with a friend of mine as the godfather), while a representative from the state institution PRONAA, Arturo, was appointed as the godfather for the baptism. Just after the baptism at the local church of Jerusalén, all of us went to the house of Teofilo's brother where the party was to be given and the hair-cutting was to take place. Those of us who were the *padrinos* were given the most central and comfortable seats at the main table, and when food was served it always came first and most plentifully to us. In general we were treated with particular attention and respect, and after a while we also had cases of beer placed at our feet. This was in order for us first to serve ourselves, and then serve the beer around to the others. In so doing, we were to administer the toasting in a certain order depending on status or closeness of relationship to Iván's parents. As the godmother for the *corte-del-pelo*, I was encouraged to start cutting Iván's hair. So I did, and as I had been told, I placed some money, together with the hair I had cut, on a decorated plate. I turned the scissors over to the godfather for the baptism, who similarly cut the baby's hair and in return placed some money on the plate. This act was subsequently repeated by all the other guests with gradually decreasing amounts of money placed on the plate as it was circulated. Each time, the amount of money was read out loud, in response to which people applauded in recognition, especially if the amount was high. We made two rounds of hair-cutting, and the completion of the interchange between hair and money was marked as the newly established *compadres* went out to dance while the others watched and clapped to the *huayno*.[12] After this, the *padrino* for the baptism retired, although he was told that the party was just

---

[10] This ritual for the first hair-cutting of babies is probably of ancient origin, and related to similar practices such as the Incas' of keeping toenail-clippings.

[11] I accepted this appointment despite my hesitation and after stressing the difficulties I might have in meeting their expectations concerning my future support for the child, that is, due to the geographical distance between Peru and Norway among other things. Indeed, there are many ethical dilemmas involved in being appointed as godparent for a child during fieldwork, since the expectations to this relationship may be difficult to live up to.

[12] A kind of music and dance that is popular among people from the highlands, characterized by the typical Andean vocal and accompanied by guitars and organ.

about to begin. Most of the other guests stayed behind, dancing and drinking until early morning. After the fiesta I learned that my appointment as the godmother for the hair-cutting was subject to criticism among Carla's friends and neighbours. They thought it would have been more appropriate to appoint me – '*la extranjera blanca*' (the white foreigner) – as the godmother for the baptism instead of the *corte-del-pelo*. According to them, the baptism would have been a much more respectable occasion for me to be made a godmother rather than the more typical Andean *corte-del-pelo*.

The appointment of godparents for this kind of occasion can be a way of integrating the baby into a network of social relationships and reciprocity. It can be a way of extending kinship relationships in the urban context by drawing people into relations of obligation and care for their children, and therefore significant to the process of establishing the child as a social person. In the hair-cutting ritual, the baby's hair that the godparents and other participants remove can in this respect be seen to metonymically represent the person, and the exchange as an act of trust and relatedness between the parents and *comadres* (co-parents) involved. The hair that is cut on these occasions is considered special and is said to bring prosperity and good luck, or could alternatively be used to perform *brujería* (harmful acts). This indicates how *brujería* is associated with a failure of social relationships, a point I will return to. The choice of a specific set of godparents is given significant thought on these occasions, for instance whether to appoint middle-class people from the city or people from the neighbourhood. When appointing godparents from outside the neighbourhood such as in Iván's case, that is, an official representative and a person such as myself from another country, parents sometimes seek to include people from the urban middle-class in the network of their child and symbolically add this dimension to the identity of the child by relating it to a specific set of godparents.

After Angelina's youngest son Pablo was born about 20 years ago and when it was time to arrange the *corte-del-pelo* for him, she and her husband decided to ask some of their new neighbours in Jerusalén become his *padrinos*. They were people who had just moved in at that time, and Angelina had a good impression of them. After the fiesta that was arranged and as Pablo grew bigger, she and her husband gradually lost contact with their neighbouring *compadres*. When I asked Angelina why, she explained that she had discovered that this family actually lived from stealing: 'They had nice clothes and said they were *contrabandistas*. I believed what they said. But later I discovered that all the members of this family – also the women – are thieves. They wear knives and when they have parties there are always fights.' As Pablo was growing up, I several times heard Angelina refer to these *padrinos* on occasions when her son had been behaving badly, saying that her son had become badly behaved (*malcriado*) because of his *padrinos* who are thieves. In this manner, *compadrazgo* relationships (or, more specifically, *padrinazgo* in this case) can be seen as important for the definition and creation of social personhood. Indeed, it illustrates the importance of who are chosen as the *padrinos* of one's children, as the qualities of the *padrinos* can be transferred to the *ahijados* and thus influence his or her character and development. I have also heard people say that it is first at the initiation of a relationship to *padrinos* that a baby becomes gendered, that is, becomes a girl or a boy (see also Canessa 1998). For instance, one of the godchildren of Angelina and her husband is a little boy who always used to wear a ponytail before his baptism and *corte-del-pelo.* After the ceremonies his hair not only became short for obvious reasons, but his mother also stressed that '*ahora es hombre*' (now he is a man). In this manner, the relationship to *padrinos* may entail a transference of qualities not only with respect to personal prestige or qualities, but also with respect to gender. For adult personhood too, the relationship with *compadres* is important for how people establish, confirm or negotiate their personhood and position, for example through the qualities that people are ascribed through their relationship with *compadres* or *padrinos*. *Compadrazgo* may be, in other words, a way to position and define one another as social persons, and a relation in which the identity of one's *compadre* may act as a source of identity to one's self (see Strathern 1988:92).

The Morality of Giving and Rituals of Respect

The relationship between *comadres* is established through the ritual exchange of food and alcohol. It is common that the person(s) who appoints *padrinos* (that is, the receiving *compadres*) is expected to show those who are appointed (that is, the giving *compadres*) particular attention and respect.[13] When a person or a couple want to ask someone to act as *madrina* and/or *padrino* and thus become *compadres*, it is usual to first come with small gifts of alcohol or plates of food and then present the request. After initiation, the relationship is later expected to be maintained through continual acts of confirmation, such as through gift giving and acts of reciprocity. There is an expectation that both the giving and the receiving *comadres* shall give the best of what they can afford, and serve them the best and most plentiful selections of food. Each time Angelina's *comadre* Verónica comes to visit her at the market, Angelina always buys her the best food she can find and some bottles of beer. Through these gifts, Angelina sometimes said that she wants to show her *cariño* (care or love) because Verónica is her *comadre* and has always treated her well and helped her in times of difficulty. The gifts offered in these relations are thus often treated as a sign of trust, gratitude or respect, and serve as expressions for the qualities and intentions of the giver. The serving of guinea-pig (*cuy*), a prized delicacy in the Andes, is seen as a particularly appropriate way of showing respect to your *compadres*, and is often served when entering

[13] Amongst some Aymara-speaking people in Peru and Bolivia, Ossio (1984) notes that even the parents of a child – that is, the parents of the *ahijado* – may be treated and referred to as *ahijados*. Accordingly, the term *padrino* may be extended to the children of the actual *padrinos*. This is not the case in an urban context such as Jerusalén, however, where the parents of an *ahijado* instead are addressed by the *padrinos* as *comadres*.

or confirming a relationship of *compadrazgo* (see Weismantel 1988, Allen 1988, Archetti 1997). In the urban context, it is not that common to keep guinea-pigs, but it continues to be seen as appropriate food for a feast and for making *compadres*, although it is not necessarily created in the household but bought.

Although the different ways in which *compadrazgo* relationships are initiated and practised make it difficult to describe, there are some more or less standardized patterns of etiquette for interaction and the exchange of food, alcohol, money or other gifts. These are based on quite clear ideas and expectations about who is serving or inviting, giving or receiving and in this manner reflect the position people have in relation to each other. In this respect, Lund Skar underlines the difference between symmetrical and asymmetrical dimensions in the act of drinking together (1994:111). The symmetrical kind of drinking is when one person pours a drink and gives it to the next person to the right. This person finishes the drink and then pours a new drink for the next person on the right. In contrast, there is an asymmetrical aspect of drinking when it is the same person who pours the drinks for all the others present (see also Allen 1988), such as on the occasion of Iván's hair-cutting when I as the *madrina* poured all the drinks. In this manner, the asymmetrical aspect of drinking is made particularly relevant at the initiation of *compadrazgo*, when the giving *comadres* pour drinks for the receiving *comadres* as well as the other guests. Despite these often strict codes for drinking, the act of drinking may in itself serve to bring about more confidence and intimacy in relationships of *compadrazgo*, by making people relax and by reducing distance or barriers. The act of drinking together may in this regard also serve to underline a dimension of equality and intimacy in *compadrazgo* relationships. At the initiation of a relationship with a *comadre*, a certain amount of alcohol is exchanged and consumed, and there is often an expectation that they should stay all night and consume significant amounts of alcohol. It is not uncommon that a *comadre* insists that the other shall drink, for instance, and to decline would be seen as an offence. At the initiation as well as the confirmation of a relationship between *comadres* then, the interaction is often characterized by drunkenness. *Huayno* music is essential at such gatherings, and the newly established *comadres* are supposed to dance first while the other guests watch, and later with the other guests joining in. I often heard people say that unless they have been drinking for a while, they are unable to dance a *huayno* in the way they are expected to.

As between kin, the *compadrazgo* relationship is expected to be binding and reciprocal over time, and supposedly so for life, although this is not necessarily realized in practice. People often mentioned respect (*respeto*) as well as trust (or *confianza*) as important dimensions of their *compadrazgo* relationships. The significance of these dimensions will vary depending on the relationship and change over time, and *compadrazgo* relationships may also be characterized by a certain tension regarding the degree of *respeto* and *confianza*. Between *comadres*, one can be asked for advice and help to solve a problem on the one hand, and be invited to parties and drunkenness on the other. This, however, can also depend on who you make your *compadres* (that is, people's status or class position), in the sense that the degree of respectfulness and trustfulness may vary according to the different positions of the people involved. For instance, the making of *compadres* with people from a higher social standing may make respect a more central issue than confidence.

The significance of the ability to give is illustrated by the way in which acts of giving, sharing and throwing parties are often contrasted with negative qualities like greed and selfishness. In relation to the hair-cutting ritual, it is for instance interpreted as a sign of greed if someone cuts the baby's hair without arranging the baptism the same day, or at least a short time afterwards. It is said that cutting the baby's hair in this manner, without also arranging for its christening, is equivalent to selling the baby's soul to the devil. It implies that you cut the baby's hair just to obtain the money, without a willingness to make an effort to arrange the baptism and a party. This interpretation of the failure to throw a party indicates that the understanding of the devil in the Andean context is not necessarily due to the association of the devil with money as argued by Taussig (1980), but rather with the failure to give and share (see Harris 1995b). In most of the cases that I know of, the babies' hair has nonetheless been cut long before they have been baptized. This is generally accepted on the condition that a lot of people are invited and a party is given. What is not accepted are the cases in which the hair-cutting is arranged and *padrinos* appointed without throwing a party or serving the *padrinos* the adequate kind and amount of food and drink. This is seen as particularly disrespectful towards the *padrinos*, because it entails a failure of an essential act of giving and thus the performance of respectfulness otherwise meant to honour the *padrinos*. Nevertheless, it is not that uncommon to appoint *padrinos* and have a baby's hair cut without giving a party, particularly in times of unemployment or poor finances. I have been appointed the *madrina* myself a couple of times on such occasions, but have been advised to decline the appointment as long as a party is not to be given.

As long as a party is given the invitation to become *comadres* is in most cases accepted. It is considered an honour to be asked, particularly for occasions such as a baptism or confirmation, although it may represent a significant expense in terms of gifts, food and alcohol. A refusal may also be taken as offensive, similar to not accepting a gift or an invitation to eat and drink. People who decline an invitation or gift in this manner are regarded as conceited or believing themselves to be better than the person who makes the offer, and attempting to appear more as a *criolla*. When I first got to know people in Jerusalén, I was continually invited to eat. I experienced this as a way of bringing me into relations of reciprocity and of testing me as to whether I would eat the food eaten by people from the highlands, and the fact that I did was always received with approval. On receiving an invitation or a gift, people may reciprocate there and then, often by going to buy some alcohol, but reciprocation may also be delayed. These exchanges can be regarded as the basis on which *compadres* are expected to support each other. It implies a range of obligations related to the exchange of gifts, food and drinks, a supporting hand and work help at work parties, as well the sharing of good advice and influence. Through the exchange of gifts and services, the significance and quality of the relation is confirmed, implying a reciprocal recognition of each other as social persons – complete and adult social beings.

Inequality and Mobility, Self and Other

Originally a Catholic institution, *compadrazgo* was introduced in Latin America by the Spaniards and informed by Catholic ideas with respect to baptism and spiritual guidance. According to Gudeman (1972), the Catholic *compadrazgo* originally served to re-order the 'spiritual' and 'natural' domains of life into two different sets of persons – the 'spiritual' and the 'natural' parents. In the Andes, *compadrazgo* has been given new meanings and forms since the time of colonization, however, in the sense that the Catholic practices have been subject to change (see Ossio 1984). In general, practices of *compadrazgo* in the Andean context differ from the Catholic by the way in which such relationships are a lot more common and widespread in the Andes. Relations of *compadrazgo* are initiated on a number of different occasions, and may in addition extend across a possibly greater number of persons. While the Catholic institution is related primarily to the baptism of children and first communion, *compadrazgo* in the Andes is made use of on a great variety of occasions as previously noted, and illustrates the importance of these relationships for people's everyday lives. Arguing that the Catholic *compadrazgo* has been incorporated into similar institutions that existed long before the arrival of the Spaniards, Ossio refers to pre-Hispanic practices of name giving in which there was a ritual sponsor serving a role equivalent to the contemporary *padrinos*, such as in Andamarca, Ayacucho (1984:130). What is more, the significance of *compadrazgo* for work help is similar to the significance of the *ayni* relationship in the rural Andes, as *ayni* represents a relationship for the mutual exchange of work help, goods and the communal maintenance of sacred sites (see Gose 1994:13). So although the institution of *compadrazgo* is Catholic in many of its functions and expressions, there are nevertheless certain aspects of *compadrazgo* in the Andes that differs a lot from the Catholic. Ossio underlines for instance that *compadrazgo* is not necessarily constrained by the Catholic dogma, and that the Catholic ideas of baptism have not been completely integrated by people in the Andes (1984:119). He also notes how one of the contrasts between Andean baptism and that derived from the Christian tradition is that the former not only incorporates the individual into a religious society,[14] but into a particular stage of social development. So while the Christian idea is that the individual is incorporated from the realm of humans to the realm of God, the Andean idea is that the ritual serves to transfer the

[14] Due to the cyclical understanding of history in the Andes, the idea of original sin from which the Christian baptism is supposed to save the soul has not been completely incorporated. Instead, these rituals are thought to bring a person to the next stage in the life cycle and therefore important first of all for the constitution of the social person (Ossio 1984).

baby from an amorphous condition to the realm of humans, and therefore essential for the making of personhood, that is, complete social beings.[15] Similarly as the Catholic *compadrazgo* through history has thus been reinterpreted, integrated and given new meanings, *compadrazgo* relationships continue to be reinterpreted in processes of mobility as people accommodate these practices to an urban context and give *compadrazgo* new meanings and forms.

Already during the first period of colonization, *compadrazgo* was widely practised by the Spaniards in their initiation of social relationships with indigenous people, indicating the high degree of contact and exchange that characterized this encounter from the beginning (Harris and Larson 1995). For instance, *compadrazgo* was made important for oiling commercial relationships since the time of colonization, such as between *mestizo* intermediaries and Indian wool producers, and may thus have facilitated the integration of Andean people to markets (Harris 1995:362). *Compadrazgo* relationships increasingly became one of the tactics indigenous people also used to integrate themselves in social networks in processes of migration (Saignes 1995). By documenting the migratory processes during the early periods of colonization, Saignes argues that one should thus not overlook the early mobility of the Andean peasantry, nor the flexibility in their status, nor the opportunities migrants had to enter into contacts with Spaniards (ibid:189). The economic interests of the Spaniards, as well as the significant extent of mobility and migration among Andean people – for example in relation to tributary work and mining, exchange and trade activities – all contributed to a significant involvement of the Andean population with the Spaniards. During the 1700s, one of the tactics Andean migrants used to integrate themselves during the processes of breaking up, migrating and resettling, was to develop real or ritual kinship ties as a way of compensating for the loss of kinship networks of mutual aid (ibid:188). By stressing the significance of *compadrazgo* in this period, Saignes illustrates how such relationships seem to have reflected – and to a certain degree served to reproduce – the influence from two systems of social articulation. On the one hand, there was the Andean system of a divine rule and governance through ties of vertical subordination, and on the other the hybrid system of modern Europe, which combined hierarchical principles derived from feudalism with mercantile humanistic values founded on initiative and personal qualities (ibid:191). Saignes notes that the encounter between these systems of authority was actualized through migration and resulted in a gradual transition from a society founded on filiation, ascription, kinship and estate, to one based on residence, achievement, territoriality and class. It was a change that allowed the formation of new identities linked to co-residence in both the rural and urban

---

[15] As noted by Ossio (1984:126), this is illustrated in marriage rites in Andamarca, where the *padrinos* from the baptism later escort the young people at their marriage, by leading the new couple through the socialized space of the village all the way to the groom's house. This reflects, Ossio argues, the role of *compadres* in the Andes of introducing those who are getting married to society.

setting and the forging of a more universalistic basis for social ties through an equal and rotating access to civic and religious offices (ibid:192). A previous hierarchical basis for social relationships was in this manner partially replaced by a horizontal relationship – through ties of *compadrazgo* – which legitimated peoples' incorporation in their new place of residence (ibid:189). In this process, *compadrazgo* was made significant in a reordering of social relationships. As the new markets forced Andean people into more impersonal, anonymous exchanges, they may also have had certain interests in, and gained some advantages through relationships of *compadrazgo*, due to the contacts, security or protection that *compadrazgo* relationships may have represented. Indeed, people living in poor and marginalized circumstances seem to have sought to overcome aspects of their marginality through relations of *compadrazgo*, that is, through the possibilities it offered for the creation of new relationships of reciprocity and interchange. This is a dynamic that resembles the significance of *compadrazgo* also in contemporary processes of mobility.

The *compadrazgo* system was at the same time central to the ways in which the Spaniards exploited indigenous people during colonization. For instance, Harris (1995:363a) argues that much of the land that passed out of Indian control in this period often changed hands in dubious ways, and in many cases through bonds of debt or relations of *compadrazgo*. She also underlines how some *mestizo* salesmen established a variety of *compadrazgo* relationships in one specific or several communities – in one instance as many as 600 – and gained great economic advantages as a result of these relationships (ibid:362). It is therefore important not to exaggerate the equalizing or egalitarian dimension of *compadrazgo*, but, as I will discuss later, rather to explore the co-existence of equalizing and differentiating mechanisms. *Compadrazgo* has generally been seen to represent one of the many forms of clientelism and paternalism[16] in Latin America, for example as connected to notions of *caudillismo*, or *gamonalismo*.[17] These social institutions have affected the general formation of politics in Latin America, that is, through the importance in official contexts of personal relations and motivations (Molyneux and Dore 2000). Indeed, *compadrazgo* and similar institutions represent and reflect relations of power and inequality in a way that, through acts of reciprocity, entail a personal and intimate character.

In Jerusalén, and especially among people who have worked as servants or the like, it is common to appoint their employers as *padrinos* for their children. Most women here have worked for a period as servants in the houses of more well-situated families, that is, before they had their own children. Many of them have

---

16 It is worth noting that a *padrino* and a patron are not the same thing, as relations to *padrinos* are associated with kinship and conceptualized as a second set of parents, while relations to a patron are often more distant and formal.

17 *Caudillismo* refers to relations of patronage in Latin America, in Peru referred to as *gamonalismo*, that is, the relations between land-owners and 'commoners' in Peru (see Gose 1994, de la Cadena 2000).

also lived in the houses of their employers and spent most of their time working for the family, in a situation in which everyday life and relations between employer and employee are in many cases of a quite intimate character. Although some women mainly complained about their experiences as servants, others seemed to appreciate and seek to reinforce the relationship to their employers through bonds of *compadrazgo*. When Juana talked about her previous employers, she often underlined that it was through them that she had learnt to work in the urban context, to speak Spanish and a range of other things about the ways of *mestizos*. She said she also learned how to act in order for people in the city to trust her. While the first family where she worked had treated her badly, the second family had been nice to her, and later, she had therefore appointed these employers as the godparents of her children. Some people thus value these relationships despite their unequal and sometimes exploitative character. What might otherwise appear as a contradiction in this relationship may indeed illustrate the complex dynamics of power in people's relationships with the upper social classes. It illustrates the importance for many of making the employer and/or *padrino* care about them and their family, for example through relations of *compadrazgo*, probably because of the sense of security that such a relationship is expected to represent. What seems to motivate people in these relations of *compadrazgo* with employers is thus an attempt to create a certain degree of trust and care in a relationship otherwise characterized by distance and inequality.

In contemporary processes of mobility, the above illustrates how *compadrazgo* is made important for the creation of networks of trust and support not only between kin or other migrants, but for how to relate in a more familiar manner with people from the city. In the urban context then, relations of *compadrazgo* appear to become increasingly more flexible as they are no longer determined by marriage or kinship as has been the case in some rural areas (Ossio 1978, 1984). As a result, the question of how relations of *compadrazgo* are actually practised becomes more open for negotiation, with respect to who is to be appointed and what is to be expected from the relationship. This must be seen in relation to the ways in which the authority of older kin also tends to become more fragmented in processes of migration, with the result that non-relative patrons, *compadres* and *padrinos* sometimes come to take more central positions in people's networks. In light of Saignes' (1995) historical argument about *compadrazgo* as noted above therefore, the contemporary practices of *compadrazgo* still seem to work as a vehicle for social change. They represent a means to initiate or consolidate social relationships in processes of mobility and thus a manner in which to (re-)define one's social position and belonging. Through practices of *compadrazgo*, people are enabled to enter social relationships with different people within the framework of specific codes for reciprocity and performances of mutual respect. Indeed, *compadrazgo* may serve as one of the ways in which people seek to re-position themselves by placing 'the other' into a specific relation and position to 'the self'. In processes of mobility therefore, *compadrazgo* is made particularly important in people's attempts to negotiate, reproduce or reformulate forms of belonging. These practices can serve as a vehicle of reproduction as well as change through and of social relationships, by becoming subject to a process of de- and reconstructing 'the self' in relation to 'the other'. While 'the self' is always constituted in relation to others, as social and relational, *compadrazgo* is interesting because of the way in which these relational dimensions of self seem to be explicitly acted upon through acts of reciprocity, for example in the sense that they may serve as a way of expressing, reproducing or negotiating relations of authority, inequality and difference. It thus makes a useful entry point to an understanding of how social categories and forms of belonging are handled and negotiated. At the same time as enabling people to establish relations of trust and support, however, *compadrazgo* relationships may at the same time enable people to perform authoritative and demanding roles in relation to each other, such as in cases with greater social distance between *compadres*. So while *compadrazgo* may indeed serve to legitimate people's incorporation into new places of residence, it may also serve to underline and reinforce social differences.

Vehicle of Change? The Negotiation of Identity

Many people underlined their preference to become *compadres* with other people from the highlands, or as they said, '*gente de la sierra*'. The sentiment that '*Es gente humilde, como nosotros*' (they are poor people, who are more like us) was often talked about as important for understanding and trust in relations between people. It was also said that poor people from the highlands are more likely to fulfil their obligations as *compadres*. In this manner, relations of *compadrazgo* can also work to create or strengthen ties between people with more or less similar social standing, such as between people in the neighbourhood. What is more, the preference among some people to make *comadres* with people more specifically from the same or neighbouring rural areas also indicates a desire to confirm social relationship connected to their Andean background. In general, people choose as their *compadres* someone who is regarded as higher or better positioned than themselves, or people who are looked up to in some way, like older relatives, respected neighbours or well-situated people from the centre, such as employers, teachers, politicians, the representatives of NGOs or state institutions as in the case described above, or anthropologists like myself. It is particularly for occasions such as the baptism of a child or first communion that people from the centre are appointed as *padrinos*, or as sponsors for large fiestas or anniversaries.[18] In addition to the prestige connected to making *compadres* with people seen as significantly more educated or well-situated than yourself, this kind of relationship is also seen to open certain opportunities. In order to get a proper job, for instance, many people

[18] The sponsor is often called *madrina* or *padrino* also in relation to more impersonal occasions such as a fiesta or anniversary, although the relationship established is not of the same continuity as the regular bonds of *compadrazgo* between two individuals or couples.

said that the key is to have a *comadre* or *madrina* in a good position from which to gain help and assistance. However, there is a widespread opinion that *gente grande* (well-situated people) are not to be trusted to fulfil their responsibilities as *compadres*, a view that is often explained by what is seen as the self-sufficiency and egoism of people from the city. By appointing such people as sponsors or *padrinos* you therefore run the risk that they fail to show up or soon forget all about you, with the result that a long-lasting relationship and obligation is never established. I several times heard people warn each other about this kind of risk, especially when someone was thinking about asking a well-situated person to become the *padrino* of their child. People are also sometimes sceptical towards the idea of bringing someone well-situated to their house and neighbourhood on these occasions, because they fear they will criticize the poor housing and standard of living. In such cases, the degree and manner of participation by more well-situated *padrinos* is often characterized by a maintenance of distance, for instance as indicated in relation to the baptism and *corte-del-pelo* of Carla's little boy Iván. The *arequipeño* bureaucrat who acted as *padrino* for the baptism came to the church and spent a few hours in the house for dinner, but left soon afterwards before the party and drinking began. On other similar occasions, I have also seen that people from the city often refuse to accept the drinks they are offered, or frown upon the food they are served, or otherwise ridicule the dancing of *huaynos*. This indicates how the *padrinos* on such occasions sometimes try to maintain the ideas about *mestizoness* by participating in a different way.

It is furthermore important to underline that the giving *compadre* is never located in a status group below the receiving *comadre* (see also Gudeman and Schwartz 1988), and I have never, for instance, heard about a case in which an employer asks a servant or other employees to act as *madrina* or *padrino*. People who work as servants are thus not given the opportunity to return the favour of the giving *compadres* in this relationship, and as such they cannot place themselves in the position of the reciprocally and spiritually equal. This illustrates the dimensions of authority and inequality in relations of *compadrazgo* that are made relevant especially when crossing the boundaries of class and/or ethnicity. It illustrates how acts of giving are essential for demonstrating or confirming autonomy and agency, and particularly so through the gift that is given without the expectation of reciprocation. As people in Jerusalén may be able to receive but not give in relations of *compadrazgo* with middle- or upper-class people or employers, it illustrates their lower status and lack of autonomy *vis-à-vis* their *compadres*. These relationships may therefore serve to reinforce an asymmetrical dimension in the distinction between receiving and giving *compadres*, and thus reproduce authority and inequality in the relationship between different social classes. In *compadrazgo* relationships between people in Jerusalén, in contrast, the same people may act as both giving and receiving *comadres* for each other. This is a way to articulate a dimension of equality or equivalence in the relationship, although the character of these occasions (for example baptism or roofing-party) is generally not of the same kind but hierarchically ordered and valued.

When arranging large communal events or festivals, inhabitants in Jerusalén often ask politicians or representatives of state and NGO agencies to act as sponsors (or *padrinos*). This was the case in 1997 when the neighbourhood committee asked the Mayor of Mariano Melgar and his wife to contribute as sponsors for the anniversary of Jerusalén. As sponsors they were expected to present flowers, beer and prizes for the winning dance group and football team, in addition to the honour of their mere presence. In this, as in many other cases, however, the sponsors did not arrive as planned, and I was asked to give a speech in their place. The mayor and his wife did not show up this day at all, and while some people were disappointed, others just shrugged and said that the untrustworthiness of elites was to be expected. From the perspective of inhabitants, this kind of sponsorship may on other occasions be a way of acquiring some extra resources for some big arrangement, and to attract the attention or goodwill of a politician or district official and perhaps get donations for construction works *(obras)* in the neighbourhood as a result. From the perspective of the sponsor, this kind of contribution can serve as a way of creating political support, although, as I will illustrate in a later chapter, inhabitants do not necessarily feel obliged to respond as expected in these relationships.

On some occasions, people in Jerusalén are also appointed as sponsors themselves for events, for instance, in their village of origin, that is, as sponsors for fiestas or festivals either personally or as the representative of an urban organization that works to support the village (see also Lund Skar 1994, Paerregaard 1997a). On these and similar occasions, those who have migrated may bring gifts and resources not only for their kin but the entire community, sometimes by donating to local institutions such as the local school. These gifts may represent a mutual recognition and connection between those who have left and those who have stayed behind, while also serving to demonstrate a distance in terms of material or educational resources. Among those who have migrated, such donations illustrate the concern for the progress of a village of origin.

Notions of Collectivity and Prestigious Goods

Relations of *compadrazgo* are generally entered into, not as an individual, but as a couple, family or group of kin. Indeed, *compadrazgo* in the Andean context seems to be characterized by a collective organization and understanding, as illustrated for instance by the inclusion also of the kin and affinals of those who have been directly involved in creating the *compadrazgo* relationship. For instance, the kin or affines of a person's *ahijado* or *compadres* may also treat and refer to this person as *madrina* or *comadre*, and vice-versa.[19] After I became Carla and Teófilo's

[19] According to Ossio, the term *compadre* has even been incorporated into kinship terminology to designate the co-parents-in-law of a married couple, and the siblings of an intermarrying couple (1984:122).

comadre through the hair-cutting of their son, Teófilo's mother also started to call me *comadre*. What was more, although I was the *madrina* for Iván and not for his older sister, Mary, she also started to call me *madrina* and was encouraged to do so by her parents. Also in other cases, I have heard that the use of the term *comadre/compadre* can similarly be extended, to be used by other family members to address a person who has become *compadres* with someone in the family. This may serve to illustrate Ossio's (1984) argument that there is a collective aspect to the Andean *compadrazgo* that differs significantly from the Catholic. According to him, this also reflects how the Andean *compadrazgo* requires bilateral kinship as its foundation, rather than being a substitute for a disrupted kinship system as has often been argued (ibid:119). He refers to historical material indicating that children also used to inherit ties of *compadrazgo* from their parents, and that currently, the *compadres* may similarly be linked with the real or classificatory siblings of the couple to whose child she or he is the *madrina* or *padrino*. In turn, the child may be linked with the real or classificatory siblings of the *madrina* or *padrino*. In continuation of this, Ossio argues that contemporary practices of *compadrazgo* in the Andes are associated with affinity both at the symbolic level and within the system of kinship relations, by representing an alliance mechanism complementary to marriage. Affines and *compadres* often take up the same roles on different social occasions, and in certain parts of the highlands, Ossio notes that all the children born of a marriage will also be sponsored at baptism by the *compadres* selected at the parents' marriage. In the city, people generally appoint different *padrinos* for different occasions, although I have seen that some parents similarly have appointed their *padrinos* from marriage to be the *padrinos* also for their children. When appointing *padrinos* for their daughter María, for instance, Angelina and Juan asked the *padrinos* from their marriage. The extended use of these relationships and terms may, as illustrated in my experience after the hair-cutting of Iván, involve all from individuals to whole groups, and entail the expectations of equivalent relations of confidence and/or respect. Similarly when Leonarda's son was to construct the roof for his house, it was his parents and not the young man himself who appointed the *padrinos*. By arranging the roofing party on their son's behalf, Leonarda and her husband were included in the (re-)creation of these relationships, at the same time as their son was brought into the social network of his parents.

I have previously indicated how practices of *compadrazgo* are made subject to innovation and change in the urban context, and so also are the objects involved in gift giving. This is illustrated for instance in the arrangement of roofing parties, or *techamientos*. At roofing parties in the city, *padrinos* are not only expected to present a wooden cross as in many parts of the highlands, but to also bring beer and sweets for the *compadres* and the other guests, as well as fireworks, flowers and a bottle of sparkling wine. For the *padrinos* (or giving *compadres*), *techamientos* in the city thus involve more monetary expense. Roofing parties similarly represent a significant expense for the receiving *compadres*, that is, those who arrange the event and want to see their house constructed. In the urban context, this couple has to cover all the expenses of food and music, while in many parts of the highlands it is common that the guests, including the *padrinos*, all bring some food. In the city it is also more common to appoint not just one couple of *padrinos*, but several. Since all the *padrinos* are expected to bring at least one case of beer each, the beer for this kind of party is often plentiful.

People's quest for social mobility and progress is in many ways related to a fascination with all that is considered urban or 'modern' and some people carefully make sure, for instance, to be photographed with their newly purchased commodities and clothes. The acquisition of certain commodities can also represent an opportunity to appoint *padrinos*, and when someone has bought something new, like a television, a refrigerator, a computer or some other expensive, big or technical artefact, they sometimes appoint *padrinos* for the occasion. Similarly in the highlands, *padrinos* are appointed on occasions when an animal has given birth. The principle for these occasions seems to remain the same, in the sense that *padrinos* are appointed when there has been renewal and reproduction of some kind – or, in other words, when something has been invested in and 'given birth'. This notion of 'giving birth' has been related by Taussig (1980) to the fetishism of money and the quality it is ascribed in a capitalist system of reproducing itself. In an Andean context, however, the notion of 'giving birth' is related to a more general notion of fertility (Harris 1995b), created by various forms of reciprocity and exchange, with people and the surroundings. In the city, the inauguration of new objects is most often practised in cases when someone has acquired technical commodities of some kind, thus illustrating how the acquisition of such goods simultaneously work not only as a sign of modernity, but also as an opportunity for reciprocity. It is interesting to see this ritual demarcation connected to the purchase of goods in light of Friedman and Ekholm's (2008) distinction between exo-sociality and endo-sociality described in the introduction. By ascribing particular importance to and including objects that are considered somehow different from the 'traditional', this ritual demarcation can be seen as an example of exo-social practices. On the other hand, the re-creation of reciprocal practices related to the purchase of goods can also reveal an endo-social aspect, since the cultural logic on which some of the subsequent exchange is based partly remains the same and is thus being reproduced. Indeed, while there is a significant innovation and change of reciprocal practices in relation to such things as the exchange and consumption of goods that are somehow considered urban or 'modern' (for example technical artefacts, sparkling wine), the performance of these practices is realized within the same understanding of sociality.

People often worry about how they will raise money for these occasions of reciprocity, however, and some even borrow money from kin or neighbours to meet their social obligations. It is considered shameful not to respond to such expectations of reciprocity, and as illustrated in the case of Angelina in the beginning of this chapter, it is important also to give generously. In the city, social and ritual obligations involve expenses that are first of all monetary due to the absence of agricultural lands that provide produce and animals that could be used to feed guests or as gifts. In the city, people's participation in these occasions of reciprocity is dependent on the capital they gather through wage labour or small enterprises. In this regard, people sometimes complained that in the city, everything must be bought, and they spend considerable time worrying about expenses if they are appointed or involved in ritual and social occasions. When people nonetheless respond to these obligations, it indicates how social relationships and acts of reciprocity continue to be associated with the (re-)generation of prosperity. This is a discussion I will come back to.

Competitive Giving

Practices of reciprocity and ritual obligation entail festive occasions and forms of consumption that serve as a way not only to create or confirm social relationships, but also to express or gain certain prestige. Indeed, these occasions seem to represent an opportunity for people to create or demonstrate prestige and success through gift-giving and festive consumption. Gifts are generally presented in the view of other guests, and such prestations tend to be commented upon by the people present, or responded to by applause. This was the case during the hair-cutting of Iván, when the money collected during the hair-cutting was counted in front of the guests, who responded with applause. In general, there is a significant prestige related to the ability to give. If such social and ritual obligations are not fulfilled, one may be seen to fail not only as a social and responsible person, but also to fail as a person who is seen as economically able or potent. In order to be considered a truly successful person therefore, successfulness needs to be socially or ritually displayed. The lack of such an ability to give and share is not only given negative associations, but is seen as anti-social.

It is not unusual for people to appoint several *padrinos* for the same occasion, for instance as illustrated in the *techamiento* for Leonarda's son. Different sets of *padrinos* will then be ordered hierarchically in terms of first and second *padrinos*, an ordering that has implications for who is to first give their gifts and speech, who is to receive the first and biggest plates of food and so on. In this manner, there is a hierarchical ordering between the *padrinos* also in terms of who is supposed to give the best and most expensive gifts. Although the first *padrinos* are thus the ones supposed to give the most expensive or plentiful gifts, I have heard of cases in which the first *padrinos* have been out-competed by some of the other *padrinos*. Angelina said she had witnessed one such instance, and underlined that it was regarded as disrespectful towards the first *padrinos*, and was meant to challenge or shame them. Competing with the first *padrinos* in this manner is thus another way of saying that what they have given is not good, expensive or plentiful enough. In this respect, the things that are given on these occasions may be used to judge the value or prestige, prosperity or intentions of the giver and her relationship to the receiving *compadres*. To fail in such prestation may, therefore, also imply a loss of prestige. This significance of competition and prestige at festive or reciprocal occasions also comes to expression in relation to dancing. For instance, dancing is often conceptualized in terms of competition with respect to who gains over whom in terms of style and energy[20] in the fast movement of feet (*zapateo*, or tramping) that characterizes the *huayno*. In particular, people tend to encourage and clap for the competitive dancing between *comadres* by comments like '*te esta ganando*' (he/she is winning over you). Before such occasions, therefore, Angelina always brought me to practise some *huayno* in the yard, probably so that I should not make a fool of myself and lose in competitions.

These practices of festive reciprocity and consumption are sometimes regarded as a provocation by middle- and upper-class *arequipeños* however. I have several times heard people from the city criticize the fact that poor people spend more than they actually have or earn on just one party, only to have to live on 'charity' the next day. While such practices have appeared as a paradox also to scholars, Harris (1995b, 2000) notes that these scholars fail to realize the fundamental understanding of social relationships and exchange that these practices involve, namely that acts of giving are believed to be significant for the creation of prosperity as such. In this perspective, the act of giving does not simply involve a 'spending', but involves at the same time an act of 'investment'. This corresponds with the way in which money in these relations may also be given other meanings than the mere economic, and is used in ritual exchange such as during the hair-cutting and certain marriage practices.[21] In the hair-cutting ritual, money is exchanged with hair, in a way that initiates social relationships as well as contributes to the advancement of a social being from one stage in the life cycle to another. In this respect, money is ascribed not only a monetary value, but may also work as a medium to express the qualities of a person or a relationship, and contribute to the sociality and fertility of a social being. As Harris noted (1995b), money in the Andean context is given multiple symbolic values by being related to fertility, sociality and stages of a person's life cycle. The meanings attributed to money can therefore be seen to transgress the mere capitalist notion of money by forming part of different moralities of exchange. In contrast to the view of both money and commodities as 'signs of modernity' (Giddens 1990), Harris therefore argues that money may also become integrated in systems of symbols other than that of capitalism. It may take up meanings related for instance to the fertility of social relationships as well as the productivity of the soil, etc. (Harris 1995b:308–10). This dynamic illustrates the inaccuracy of presenting money and capitalism as global forces that 'penetrate' local society, as there may simultaneously be a

[20] This kind of competitive dancing can be related to the often oppositional and competitive character of social relationships actualized during festivals and ritual fighting (*tinku*) in rural areas (see Lund Skar 1994, Gose 1994, Harris 2000).

[21] At marriages in many parts of the highlands, for instance, the marrying couple receives money from the guests. This money is attached to the clothes and hats of the marrying couple, who may end up being completely covered with money. In the city, the guests generally give presents instead of money.

creative reinterpretation and recreation of symbols, in the sense that money and commodities may be transformed into local idioms and take up new meanings. In this manner, money may even lend a new drive to reciprocal relations in a local context. Indeed, as I have tried to demonstrate, the quest for mobility and progress may also lend a new drive to practices of reciprocity, instead of causing social disintegration as is often argued.

This does not mean that social relationships in this context represent a harmonious whole free from accusations and distrust. Indeed, while acts of reciprocity may serve to create relations of trust such as between *comadres*, there is also a continual negotiation of these acts as well as degrees of trust. People talked a lot about envy also in relations between kin, neighbours and *compadres*. In periods when her business went well and she was able to buy good meals during her days at the market, for instance, Angelina said that she feared the envy of people around her, including her closest colleagues, for seeing how well she ate. She always shared her food with people who stopped by for a chat, with neighbouring colleagues, *comadres* and some of the *contrabandistas* who deliver goods, as well as the poor people who come to beg. Sometimes when arriving at her pitch in the morning she found pieces of flowers or corn in a circle around her pitch, however, which she interpreted as a sign that someone has directed *brujería* against her so that she would fail in her business. The fear of envy is in this regard often related to a fear and suspicion of *brujería*, and as I will come back to, distrust seems to be negotiated through accusations of corruption as well as *brujería*. What is important to note here is that when people experience themselves to be affected by *brujería*, they generally suspect relatively close neighbours, colleagues or also kin. On the one hand, this can be because people are more likely to compare themselves (and their degree of success or progress) with people in their immediate surroundings, and that envy is therefore most likely to be expected in close relationships. On the other hand, the existence of *brujería* in these relationships may also indicate that envy is associated with the failure to give, or to reciprocate, and that the fear of *brujería* thus can be seen to draw its significance from the significance of reciprocity and trust in social relationships.

Conclusions

Practices of reciprocity seem to gain particular significance in relation to the marginalization and discrimination that many people experience due to their Andean background, and serve as a way to establish and negotiate relations of trust and support in the urban context. At the same time, practices of reciprocity seem to gain importance – and be made objects of change – through people's quest for mobility, and thus work as a way to create or demonstrate prestige, status and social positioning. This chapter has therefore illustrated how people's quest for mobility and progress can be seen to articulate with and even reinforce certain practices of reciprocity. An important point in this regard is that the quest for progress does not simply entail a dynamic of increasing individualization, but may also include an intensification of the cultivation of social relationships. Practices of reciprocity can work as a vehicle of change and mobility for instance through the relationships of *compadrazgo*, by representing a flexible institution that in an urban context is made important in the accommodation to the city and the initiation of new social relationships. A central argument in this chapter is therefore that *compadrazgo* represents a practice through which people seek to re-position themselves in their accommodation to the city, through the initiation of social relationships that work as a way in which to negotiate the manners and means of belonging in an urban context.

The practices of reciprocity are characterized by festive occasions and forms of consumption that serve to initiate or confirm social relationships and a sense of community on the one hand, and create prestige or an image of personal successfulness on the other. By including people and objects that are considered different from the 'traditional', or particularly prestigious in some way or another, these reciprocal practices may represent an example of exo-sociality in the framework of Friedman and Ekholm (2008). The cultural logic on which these exchanges are based seems to remain the same, however, and therefore to involve also an endo-social aspect in the sense that giving is not simply seen as an expense, but connected to the understanding of exchange as significant for the re-creation of the sources of prosperity, a dimension I will return to. Alongside the innovation and change of these reciprocal practices in processes of migration therefore, the performance of such practices continues to take place within the same understanding of sociality.

The relationships and positions that are (re-)created through these practices must also be seen as constructed within and on the basis of relations of power and inequality, and I have therefore intended to explore the subtle forms of power that I see as being negotiated as well as reproduced through relations of reciprocity. Such subtle forms of power are made relevant through the ability to give and to receive, and the negotiation of trust and respect, autonomy and dependence in a way that makes *compadrazgo* serve as a vehicle of mobility as well as a reproduction of certain inequalities.

Chapter 5
Mobility, Work and Gender

The processes of mobility that I describe in this book highlight the extent to which ideas about a separation between private and public spheres are actualized and negotiated as people from the Andes move to the city. Indeed, cities are often associated with a dualist opposition between private and public, production and reproduction in a way that has strong gendered associations and implications. Previously I have illustrated how urbanization involves an unsettlement of dominant social and spatial categories and boundaries, and this chapter will demonstrate how there is also a fundamental gendered aspect to this unsettlement. Building on my previous discussion about the significance of work to processes of mobility and people's self-understandings, this chapter will focus on work with specific reference to gender, and especially how the work practices of women serve to actualize different imageries of gender.

Through this focus on work, the chapter explores the ways in which gender articulates with other differences such as ethnicity and class. I discuss the complementarity of gender relations in the rural Andean highlands in relation to *mestizo* notions about *machismo*, and the way in which they represent different discourses on gender that are (re-)created and negotiated in processes of mobility. I explore how people's quest for mobility and progress actualizes different and competing discourses on gender, and the significance of gender for notions about progress as well as ethnicity. The intersection of gender with ethnicity and class becomes particularly evident in a migrant situation that often will actualize a pluralization of different ideals and practices (see Moore 1994a). I am concerned with the relationship between gender as represented and gender as practised, and how people may practise gender in a way that implies a negotiation of ideals, expectations or stereotypes. As demonstrated in Chapter 2, processes of mobility are interesting for possibly involving a tension between discourses and the subject positions in which people attempt to position themselves. Moore uses the notion of subject position to address the relationship between gender identity and gender discourse, that is, gender as lived and constructed, and how people attempt to position themselves in relation to these discourses. She argues that discourses on gender and sexuality work to construct women and men differently as social persons and to embody different principles of agency (1994a:50). I seek to highlight how a negotiation of, or interchange between, subject positions may serve to contest or reproduce dominant gender discourses, and how the practices of indigenous women, for instance as workers and traders, seem to negotiate dominant discourses and categories connected to ideas about *indio* and *mestizo*, female and male, private and public.[1] This demands a dynamic treatment that looks at how such different 'spheres' and categories are constructed, contested and possibly reproduced. In this regard, the chapter discusses why the trading activities of women – in the Peruvian context as elsewhere – are often associated with and considered as an extension of the household, and explores what kind of ideological construction this is, in light of its gendered connotations and considering that most traders are women.

In the first part of this chapter I describe in detail the situation of one particular family in Jerusalén in order to highlight people's involvement in same- and opposite-sex relationships such as in marriage and between the generations, in neighbourhood and work relationships. The situation of this family is in many respects similar to many other families in the neighbourhood, and in other respects less similar, and I use this as a way to illuminate the negotiation of gender relationships and imageries. In the second part of the chapter, I explore how gender is made relevant for general imageries of difference and 'otherness'.

Gender and Work

In Jerusalén, it is common that women and men share the responsibility of bringing in an income. On the one hand, this is because their economic conditions demand that everyone contribute to the economy of households, and on the other hand it is related to cultural notions of work and gender. People engage in a variety of work forms, both through self-employment such as trading or by opening shops from their houses in Jerusalén, as well as in wage labour such as construction, industrial production, the service industry or the mines. Those with formal employment in Jerusalén are most often men, while women in Jerusalén are more often informally employed by working as servants or in trade, that is, in the streets or at the many outdoor markets in the city. A few men, often young men or men of age, are also self-employed or involved in work at the margins of the formal economy, such as in taxi- and bus-driving,[2] or building houses for kin and friends. There are also a few women who have formal employment, and work in such jobs as

[1] Indeed, the distinction between public and private spheres as an analytical tool and as explanation for the subordination of women has been criticized as problematic. For instance, with the differentiation between gender as ideology and gender as practice within feminism and post-structuralism, contrastive oppositions related to male-female relations such as culture-nature, active-passive, public-private have come to be seen as a disguise for power mechanisms and specific gender ideologies. The focus has thus come to be the ways in which we should understand gender both as a *practiced* and as *conceptualized* difference, as well as the power mechanisms that mediate between the two.

[2] Lazar (2002) similarly notes that parts of men's employment also operate on the edge of the formal economy, such as in taxi- and bus-driving, where the fares they charge are regulated but the drivers are self-employed and generally not paying taxes.

cleaning public buildings or working in factories for the production of textiles or industrial products. In addition to other kinds of work, many women are involved in production forms that take place outside the factories, that is, by performing tasks that are out-sourced to be produced in homes. The *waipi* that many women do is an example of this. *Waipi*[3] is the name for some textile materials that the women receive in small pieces in order to untangle and return – generally to car-mechanics who use them for washing cars. During my fieldwork in 2001, this kind of work was not particularly well paid – three soles for one kilo of *waipi* – but it is nonetheless a popular way for women to earn some extra soles since it can be done anywhere and at any time, both at home and in the streets.

In the literature from the Andes, gender relations are generally described as complementary (or as balanced and equal),[4] and as such are often contrasted with what is conceptualized as the *machismo* or male dominance in Peruvian society more generally. In the Andes, various ethnographies have illustrated how women and men perform different, but complementary roles and tasks (see Isbell 1978, Lobo 1080, Allen 1988, Gose 1994, Lund Skar 1994, 1997, Paerregaard 1997a, Harris 2000, Lazar 2002). For example, Harris (2000) has documented the gendered division of labour in rural parts of the Northern Potosí, where women herd and – on the principle that labour defines ownership – own sheep and goats, while men mind the llamas. In the fields, men plough and women sow, and similarly weaving responsibilities are divided by gender (2000:170–71). On the basis of this, Harris has demonstrated the close association in the Andes between labour and property rights, and argued that it creates a frame for an ideology of equity. In the rural Andes, Gose (1994), Skar (1994) and Paerregaard (1997) have similarly noted that while women and men perform different tasks and sometimes work within separate gender groups, they take a complementary part in the sowing as well as the harvest, in the herding of animals as well as communal work.[5] Women are often responsible for the main meals and men for the preparation of textiles, and at communal work parties, women collectively prepare the corn beer and food, while men lead the communal work. Women also play a major part in local or inter-regional exchange and trade (Silverblatt 1987, Allen 1988, Zulawski 1990, de la Cadena 1996, Lund Skar 1997, Harris 2000, Weismantel 2001, Seligman 2004, Femenías 2005). In this regard, Lund Skar (1997) has illustrated how the activities of women within trade is in some cases related to their responsibilities in herding – the products of which are more often made object for sale than are agricultural products.

3 *Waipi* appears to be a mixture of an English word (wipe) with a Quechua ending (-i).

4 In this respect, there has been a tendency in the ethnography of the Andes to focus on complementarity in gender relationships as representing the same thing as egalitarianism. As noted by Harvey (1994), however, complementarity in the Andes does not necessarily entail egalitarianism.

5 In rural areas, a conceptual distinction between the 'house' and 'outside' is not made significant as it is in urban areas.

In Jerusalén, great value is ascribed to the ability of women as well as men to perform different work forms ranging from income earning to household chores. Similarly in relation to the up-bringing of their children, I often heard people stress the importance of teaching young people how to become good workers. To some extent, the complementarity between genders therefore seems to persist when people move to the city. This does not mean, however, that relations and understandings of gender complementarity are not made subject of negotiation and change. It has been argued in the literature that in the city everyone, regardless of age or sex, shares in the struggle to make a living (Lobo 1982, Paerregaard 1997a). It has also been argued that migration results in the greater influence of *machismo* on gender relations (Stolcke 1990, Yeager 1994). With respect to people's increasing orientation and migration toward Cuzco from the rural community Chitapampa, de la Cadena (1995) notes that the work of women was increasingly seen as of less value than the work of men. While women take up what is seen as marginalized roles in their work as servants or traders, men find easier access and better opportunities to enter the process of *mestizaje*, and the city is thus increasingly regarded primarily as a male domain, while women are seen as more 'Indian' (1995:341). In Jerusalén, I similarly got the impression that women's work was regarded as somehow less important than that of men, although their opportunities to earn an income were sometimes better and more predictable than men's.

As neither Angelina nor Juan got the opportunity to study when they were young, they long had the ambition to give their children a chance to study and become professionals. Education is, however, expensive, and while María started to work after secondary school, their youngest son Pablo enrolled in military service after he turned seventeen years old and later went to Chile to work in construction and mining. Their second youngest son, Esteban, who lives with his aunt, is the only one who has studied and continues to do so with the support of his aunt, while the oldest, Jayme – who also lives with his aunt and with whom they hardly have any contact – works in transport. While lamenting that only one of their children has thus had opportunity for the education that they wanted for them, Angelina and Juan also stressed the value of children learning how to work and get a job.

When Angelina started to work in trade, their children usually came to assist her when not at school. Her daughter María was especially helpful in selling as well as in watching out for the goods. During the period when Angelina was still participating in the women's organization ASOMA, she also used to bring her daughter with her. After María finished school and tried different kinds of work – as a servant, in a textile factory and in a kindergarten[6] – she finally established a market pitch on her own, although at another market. Through this business, she earns enough to take care of her family in periods when her husband Eduardo is unemployed. When he is out of work, María often leaves her pitch to Eduardo

[6] Financed by Ministerio de Promocion de la Mujer y el Desarollo Humano (PROMUDEH).

while she goes to help her mother at the market. In the period after Angelina had become a *tesorera* (treasurer) in the market association, María became increasingly involved in her mother's work. Since Angelina does not know how to read and write, as well as being troubled by an eye disease, she found it difficult to manage all the papers, budgets and accounts, and was dependent on María to arrange the paperwork for her. Before this, María had been to Lima a couple of times to work as a servant. She has gone in order to work intensively for short periods and save money since the pay in Lima is better than in Arequipa for this kind of work. While she was away, Angelina and Eduardo looked after their boy Alejandro. From each of these travels María has returned home after just a couple of months since she missed her family too much. Angelina similarly underlined how much she has missed María during her travels to Lima, but nonetheless she continued urging her to leave Arequipa, find work and earn money. They both stressed that the chances of earning good money are particularly good abroad, and María has several times been planning to leave the country in order to work and send home money. She has a friend from school who went to the United States, and according to the letters, she soon found work. Now she is apparently earning good money and has stayed on to live there through marriage to a U.S. citizen. María and her mother often spoke of the possibility of María visiting this friend and of asking her to find María a job. If María ever gets the chance, the plan is that Angelina and Eduardo will look after Alejandro just as they did when María went to Lima. In addition to the United States and Norway, she has also discussed the idea of going to Chile and Argentina to work as a servant. In the meantime, she started to travel to Bolivia in order to bring *contrabando* (smuggled goods) to sell from her pitch at the market. I never heard anyone criticize María's choice of leaving Arequipa and her child in order to work, and my impression was that her dedication to work and trade was rather seen as an expression of her dedication as a mother.

To work at the market – and still live with her parents in Jerusalén – was not what Angelina had wanted for her daughter, and she often lamented the fact that she had not been able to help her to study and become a professional. Although blaming herself for not having helped her children to achieve the progress she had wanted them to have, Angelina sometimes also blamed the children for not working hard enough in order to achieve progress for themselves. For instance, she sometimes criticized María for not working hard enough and for being disorganized, and not knowing how to run a business or talk nicely to people. At the same time, there were also occasions on which she underlined how much of a hard-working *trabajadora* María is, and how *viva* (smart and outgoing) she is, especially compared with her husband Eduardo who is often unemployed. Angelina also increasingly urged her youngest son Pablo that he ought to start contributing, grow up and become responsible, and while she previously used to make a fuss of the boy for being particularly tall, bright-skinned and clever at school, she started to criticize him for being lazy. She said that at the end of the day, daughters are the ones who really are good and loyal to their mothers, and that it is typical for sons to be less thankful, caring and helpful, as they forget about their mothers more easily. Although both her sons Esteban and Pablo may sometimes still contribute with their assistance, it is first and foremost her daughter María who is really involved in Angelina's business. In the period when I lived in their house, it was also primarily María who assisted Angelina and Juan in the household, although her younger brothers were also given duties to wash, clean and do the shopping. Whilst thus involving her daughter in all matters of daily life, Angelina did not seem to expect the same degree of involvement and closeness in her relationship to her sons. This illustrates how girls and boys are often introduced to different arenas of work and interaction by their parents, and there is thus a gender dimension in the way in which parents include their children in their activities. What is more, the gender dimension of a daughter's inclusion in a mother's work at the market for instance serves to illustrate the definition of certain forms of work as female.

The strong desire among parents for their children to succeed in life represents a common concern amongst people in Jerusalén, and I was often impressed by the effort and sacrifice many parents made in order to help their children. These efforts also seem to involve a certain tension or ambiguity in family and kin relationships, however, as illustrated for instance in Angelina's concern that her children ought to learn how to work in a way that simultaneously involves a concern about laziness among the younger generation. Such a tension in generational relationships is partly related to the possibility – or impossibility – of achieving progress for the family or younger generations, materially or by increasing cultural capital through education, marriage partner, place of residence, etc. Indeed, this kind of tension is informed by the possibility of failure, and the degree to which people blame each other or themselves for the lack of progress and negotiate with one another as to how improvements can or are supposed to be made. While parents may on the one hand urge their children to leave the family to work and earn money as illustrated in the case of María, parents are also often dependent on their children for assistance in work and household, for reading and writing. In this manner, there is often an ambiguity in generational relationships related to the way in which people work to achieve progress and improve the socio-economic status of the new generations by urging them to leave and work, study, travel and learn things, at the same time as households are often dependent on the mutual help and support between generations.

The Position and Imageries of Women Traders

Previously I have illustrated how young people often start working in the city by finding a position as a servant, work that they later leave when they find a partner and have children of their own. Due to difficulties finding other kinds of work, many start working in trade, especially women. The reasons why there is a majority of women in trade and at outdoor markets are many, and part of the explanation is the often low levels of literacy and education among women from the highlands. It can furthermore be seen as a continuation of the importance of women's role historically in the Andes, through their involvement in rural areas in market activities and bartering, often by travelling long distances (Allen 1988, Zulawski 1990, de la Cadena 1996, Lund Skar 1997, Harris 2000, Weismantel 2001, Seligman 2004). Trading is thus not necessarily something women first learn in the city, but is also important in rural areas.

When I first asked women in Jerusalén whether they worked and what kind of work they did, many of them said that they were unemployed, since there were no jobs to get. Later I found out that many of these women actually work as traders and *contrabandistas* (smugglers). Lazar (2002) has similarly noted that women often call themselves housewives, although it is extremely unusual to find a family that relies solely upon the man's income (ibid:199). In addition to involving a majority of women, it seems as if the association of trade with the household is related to the way in which trading often involves a reliance on family, kin and neighbourhood networks. In contrast to other kinds of work, trading can also be combined with child rearing, since children can be taken along and if necessary looked after by colleagues. Also *contrabandistas* bring their children along on their journeys, even when newly born and despite their often hazardous ways of travelling.

Scholars have sometimes argued that women's economic activities in trade can be considered an extension of domestic duties due to its association with primary needs and food products (for example see Goddard 1996). In this manner, it has been suggested that this work confirms rather than challenges their reproductive roles. This argument is in different ways problematic however. It seems to assume, for instance, that the trading activities of women are related first of all to food and primary needs, which is not necessarily the case. It also overlooks the fact that women traders are sometimes the main breadwinners of their households. While the trading activities of women are sometimes related to food and primary needs and especially so as an entry point for making business, their activities also involve other products, as well as activities and social relationships that go far beyond the household. Traders generally stay out in the streets all day, from dawn to a few hours after sunset, and they generally have all their meals in the streets, either bought or brought. The social networks that women create through their trading also involve relationships through which they create new spaces of action as well as new languages and modes of expression. In fact, women traders are neither housewives nor wage-labourers, and they engage in the economy in a way that does not depend on a rigid separation of the home from the workplace. They can rather be seen to transgress or unsettle such symbolic boundaries and, as suggested by Weismantel (2001), blend what is conventionally regarded as productive and reproductive spheres. What is more, the argument about women's involvement in trade as an extension of household activities does not account for the way in which women traders are also, as I will come back to, associated with immorality and indecency. About traders in the Andes, Babb (1989) has made the important argument that they do not operate within what can simply be considered a 'reproductive' sphere or by selling small-scale food products, since trading at these markets for a long time has also involved mass-production. Criticizing the widespread view of market women's labour as strictly distributive in nature, she stresses for instance how many kinds of food processing take place in the market that would readily be interpreted as productive if done in a factory (for example, by breaking down bulk quantities of food products into portions, and making small ready-to-cook packages).

In local discourses, the perspectives on market women are highly ambiguous, since these women are considered to be very hard-working on the one hand, and associated with immorality, indecency and as a threat to the husband's role as the main breadwinner on the other. The image many people have of these women traders – and the *contrabandistas* in particular – is that they are extremely rough and often rude in their forms of speech and behaviour. Even at the Feria, there are many stories circulating about the toughness of such women, such as how they cross the borders by paying the customs officials to let them pass when caught, or how they sometimes even fight them physically or destroy their goods in front of their eyes, so that neither of them can benefit. It is said that many of these women carry big quantities of dollars under their *polleras* (several layers of skirts), and are often known for being clever at *manejar dólares* (dealing with money/dollars). In this manner, the trading activities of these women create an imagery of powerful women, in a way that stands in stark contrast to the dominant image of the disempowered female migrant, or the woman who is primarily reproducing her position in the home by dealing with nutrition and basic needs. Some of these women also enjoy considerable success and manage to expand their businesses and start investing on a grander scale.

Verónica, one of Angelina's *comadres*, came from Cuzco as a little girl. She soon began to sell in the streets, first starting with sweets and cigarettes as many people do. To begin with, she did not speak Spanish, and she has never finished her education or learnt how to read or write. Little by little however, she advanced in her business and, having gathered some capital after years of selling sweets from early morning to late at night, she started to sell small benches instead, but still by just trading in the streets. This turned out to be a good idea, and she went on to invest in her own small factory located in a central part of Mariscal Castilla, producing benches and furniture. The factory is quite successful and has now been expanded with several employees. Verónica's husband runs a mechanic store, and in both businesses – which they run independently from each other – their children work as assistants. After a few years of first doing small-scale business then, some women go on to run businesses on a grander scale. Like Verónica, a few even manage to start their own factories, or begin investing in land, houses, trucks and buses. The argument that women's activities in trade only serve to extend their position as housewives and reinforce their marginalization may therefore be illustrative in some cases but cannot be generalized.[7] In many cases, the income

[7] See Zulawski (1990) for an historical account of the importance of women's trading activities in processes of migration.

of female traders may even be higher or at least more predictable than the income of the men in their households who often go in and out of formal employment. At the same time, it is of course also important not to romanticize the possibilities involved in trading, since there are also traders who never really succeed but continue to work small-scale all their working careers.

While some of the women in Jerusalén who work in trade are single mothers and sole providers, most of them share the task of making an income with their partners. In periods of employment, the income of men tends to be higher than that of women who work in trade,[8] although the income of women traders often appeared to be more predictable than the income of formally employed men. In construction, people are often hired only for three months at a time, and construction workers are particularly exposed for dismissals. María's husband Eduardo has been in a difficult situation for several years now because of this. He used to work in construction, but has only had short-term contracts resulting in frequent unemployment for long periods of time, and in these periods he started helping María at the market. Employment within construction is also very vulnerable to economic and political instability, since employees tend to lose their jobs as soon as the enterprise no longer needs them. This was particularly so with the economic instability created by the long-lasting election period of 2000 and 2001. It caused an economic downturn that lasted more than a year due to a decline in investments, a weakening of enterprises and economic activity in general. Due to problems of unemployment, the income of traders in this period also decreased, but was nonetheless not so dramatically affected and at least it continued to bring in some kind of income. In such periods of economic instability and unemployment therefore, the income from trading turns out for many to be essential for the economy of households. As noted above, these are periods in which some husbands choose to assist in trading at the market, helping their wives to sell and look after things. In cases when husbands start working with their wives at the market, it is often by taking the role as assistant, while the woman continues to make the important decisions with respect to the business. Some of the men who start assisting their wives in this manner gradually establish their own separate business, however, often by trading with the same kind of merchandise as their wives, such as in the case of María and her husband. There are also cases in which husbands take part in their wives' trading on a permanent basis.

[8] Minimum wage for the formal sector was about 350 soles a month in 2001, which is higher than the average income of many traders, at least if compared with those who work small-scale and not as *contrabandistas*. Traders who work small-scale often reported that they did not earn more than between 5 and 15 soles a day, while grand-scale traders, *mayoristas* and *contrabandistas* can earn a lot more.

Interdependency and Relational Selves

I have previously described how Angelina sometimes ascribed her family's lack of progress to her suspicion that someone had performed *brujería* on her and her husband Juan. After he became ill and stopped bringing in an income from his previous work in construction, they had to depend on the money Angelina brought home from her work as a trader. As a result, she also had less money to invest in her business. When discussing this situation, she underlined that in order for a market woman to progress and have success, it is necessary to have a partner who earns money. She compared her own situation with traders who own their own shops down in the area around the Feria, and pointed out that all of them have partners who make their own money. She added that in order to achieve progress, both man and woman, husband and wife need to be working and be good *trabajadores*.

Previous ethnographies from the Andes have emphasized the significance of being a couple to the ideologies of gender complementarity in Andean cosmology (see Silverblatt 1987, Harvey 1994, Abercrombie 1998, Harris 2000, Lazar 2002). The couple is significant not only as an economic unit, but also as a cosmological model of personhood, in the sense that the relationship to a partner is a relation through which one comes to be considered an adult and complete social being (Lazar 2002:197). In Jerusalén, to get a partner is similarly seen as a central dimension of adulthood and personhood. Whether or not a relationship is formalized through marriage is not considered to be of particular importance (see also Lobo 1982, Lazar 2002), since more importance is given to the fact that a couple lives together and has children. Independently of whether a couple has been formally married or not, people often call their own partner as well as the partners of others by the terms for married (*esposo*-/a, or *marido*), the main characteristic for which is that they live together and have children. While people increasingly stress that young people ought to wait longer before they get a partner and children, the relationship to a partner is still regarded as important not only for the recognition of adulthood, but also for the quest for social mobility. The significance of being a couple for the ascription of personhood is particularly connected to parenthood which, as previously illustrated, in turn involves the establishment of other reciprocal relationships through ties of *compadrazgo*.

When young people are about to establish themselves as a couple, the question about where they are to live is significant. This is because young couples often lack resources to establish a house of their own, and therefore have to move into the house of the girl's or the boy's parents. When discovering that Angelina's daughter María and her boyfriend Eduardo were expecting their first child, both their families made an effort to gather money in order to arrange their marriage. A couple of years before, Angelina and Juan had acquired a plot of land for María in the more recently established neighbourhood El Mirador, and after the marriage she soon moved there with Eduardo. However, since their new house was robbed a number of times and due to the location of the house much further up the hillside and the fact that it still lacked water and electricity, they soon moved back into María's parents' house as previously mentioned. By that time Angelina and Juan's house had been extended with more rooms, so the young couple could have a room and an outdoor kitchen of their own. Although they thus started living in the house of her parents, María and her husband were nonetheless addressed as an adult couple, as *señor* and *señora*. Their economy was also separated from that of her parents, although they shared some responsibilities with Angelina and Juan, for example with respect to meals.

As mentioned in a previous chapter, it is not unusual that young couples live in the house of the girl's parents, although some may stress that to live with the boy's parents is the 'right' or 'ideal' thing to do. In the case of María and Eduardo, the fact that they ended up staying in the house of her parents can be related to several factors. One of these may be that Eduardo's father lives with a woman who is not Eduardo's mother, and as they now have other younger children to take care of, there seems to be less space for Eduardo. While Eduardo agreed to live with María in her parents' house, he nonetheless continued to spend a few days and nights every now and then in the house of his father and stepmother. In this regard, María made me aware that there were certain conflicts between Eduardo and her, and some of them were related to their housing situation. In periods when he was absent, she also worried that he might be unfaithful, a suspicion that she saw as confirmed on occasions when he came home in a somewhat aggressive mood and apparently with '*la cabeza caliente*' (hot head). When speaking with Eduardo I got the impression that he went over to his parents primarily in order to be closer to his brother and work in the disco he runs next to their house. When considering the different accounts of the people involved, however, the periodic absence of Eduardo from his wife may also be related to what seemed to be his somewhat negative attitude toward living in the house of his parents-in-law. This attitude appeared to be reinforced by the way he and his mother-in-law did not get along very well.

Despite the importance of marriage in the formation of social personhood, people in Jerusalén told me that in the city, couples leave each other to a greater extent than in the highlands. In cases when couples split up, they are often made object of rumours and sometimes criticism, especially if it is the woman who leaves and even more so if she at the same time leaves her children behind. One of Juana's neighbours is a woman who apparently had left her husband for another man. While Juana is in a friendly relationship to this woman, she sometimes spoke negatively of her as a strong-willed and somewhat self-centred *machista*, thus indicating that she regarded her behaviour (for example to leave one's partner) as more typical for men. In other cases, it is not uncommon that one of the parents has to temporarily leave the family for purposes of seasonal work. Although it is generally men who leave the family in this manner to work, for instance in the mines, there are also cases in which women do so – leaving the responsibility of children to her parents and/or the father.

Violence in Social Relationships

There were several occasions on which María's husband had hit her, and I got the impression also from other women that violence in the relationship between husband and wife is not unusual – and even considered somewhat inevitable. What is important to note in this respect is how authority, responsibility and/or the position of bringing an income often seem to legitimize the use of violence. For instance, Lazar (2002) highlights how violence is legitimated with reference to work and responsibility in a case in which the mother of a newly 'married' daughter argues that it would be alright for her husband to hit her if he had actually worked (ibid:199, see also Harvey 1994). In María's case, Eduardo's violence does not seem to be accepted. The reason for this may be that Eduardo's family does not hold any particular authority over the young couple that might legitimate the violence of a husband. In María's case it was her parents and not his who acquired a house for the young couple to live in, and on discovering that they did not feel safe there, they moved to the house of María's parents and not Eduardo's. This was also María's own objection after an incident in which Eduardo had hit her. She questioned his reason or right to act in such a manner given that he not only lives in her parents' house but also uses her pitch at the market in order to gain some money since he is generally out of work. According to María, it was Eduardo's work at her pitch that on this occasion had made him hit her in the first place, since he was frustrated by the actions of a nearby female trader who had imitated their attempts to specialize in certain products. In this case and for the first time as long as I have known her, María wanted to report Eduardo to the police, and she told him to leave the house permanently. On previous occasions when he had hit her, she had always decided to put up with the situation, thinking that reporting or divorcing him would be unfortunate for their son. This illustrates Lazar's point that couples involve juridical measures only as a last resort, since involving the state represents the failure[9] of emplacement in kin networks (2002:208). As similarly noted by Harvey (1994), women often try to endure violence so that they are able to provide a full set of parent-child kin relationships for their children, and instead of involving juridical measures, couples sometimes consult with kin or *compadres* for good advice on how to work things out. In María's case, it was primarily Angelina who had tried to speak to Eduardo in order to help her daughter. This apparently failed, and according to Angelina, he did not even have the decency to respond correctly and respectfully in front of her. As a result, María finally decided to leave her mother out of it and go directly to the police to report her husband.

Violence in kin and family relationships is not uncommon in the Andean context, and is made an issue particularly in the relations between older and

[9] As noted by Lazar, involving the authorities in marital conflicts implies a different conception of the self, that is, as a bounded individual with rights and responsibilities as recognized in law, that is, a 'citizen' in a legalistic sense (2002:208).

younger generations. With respect to kinship relationships, Harvey (1994) argues that also marital violence should be understood as created in the negotiation of hierarchy and respect in relations between kin, more specifically in the relations between kin and affines. In the Andean town Ocongate, she notes how relations with affines may be notoriously tense, and often represent a particular challenge for women, since young couples in this context often reside in the house of the husband's family and are expected to respect the authority of his kin group more than her own (1994:76). Harvey's argument in this respect is that marital violence should not be understood primarily in terms of gender as it often is, but as a negotiation of hierarchy and the claim for authority by the husband's kin group. In the city, groups of kin do not necessarily hold authority in the same way as in rural areas, however, since kin become more geographically dispersed and their authority is often questioned. Marriage, household and inheritance practices are also subject to change as I have previously illustrated, but the problems of marital violence do not seem to decrease.

While I most often heard women speak about the violence of men, there were also stories about women who beat, primarily in the form of defence but also with the indication that in some cases the woman can be the aggressor. It is interesting in this regard to note Angelina's reactions when I was in Peru with my fiancé just before getting married. Although jokingly, she kept saying to my fiancé that he better treat me nicely, or she would beat him ('*te voy a pegar*', and '*te pego*'). This indicates that it is not only men who may use violence or threaten with violence, and reflects how violence is not necessarily viewed as an inherent part of masculinity (see also Lazar 2002:205).

In some of my talks with Eugenia, she underlined how she used to suffer from the beatings of her husband, until one day, he stopped. In response to my question as to why he had beaten her, she said that he probably had a lover and therefore came home to relieve some tension on her. A common response among women to the question why men beat was similarly that they have a 'hot head' (*una cabeza caliente*) because of a lover or an experience that makes them angry. The consumption of alcohol was another common explanation, or it was said that men hit in cases when their wives have not cooked for them, or not looked after the children well enough so that they have fallen or had accidents. Yet another explanation for the violence of a husband was jealousy (*celos*), or the situation that the woman had children from a previous marriage. I even heard people say that single women with children ought not to marry again because a new partner is expected to increase the problems of violence, because of jealousy or competition. After Eugenia's husband stopped beating her, she explained that it was because he had finally stopped drinking. She also related it to the fact that she had started to work in Arequipa and make friends on her own, with the result that she was no longer as dependent on him as she used to be. In addition, she underlined that as the children were getting bigger they had already made a few attempts to pay back their father in kind for beating their mother. Also Angelina sometimes spoke about how she suffered when Juan previously used to beat her. According to Juan, however, it is normal for wife and husband to fight, especially while they are young and full of passion and jealousy. He admitted that he sometimes lost his temper with Angelina and beat her, but underlined that she gets back at him now that he is older and weaker. This illustrates how it is often when young that women experience being beaten, and less so when growing older and increasing their authority (see also Harvey 1994, Harris 2000). This is important also to see in light of Harvey's (1994) argument as noted above, namely that marital violence is not just a question about the relationships between partners, but also about kin relations and age, interdependence and autonomy. The decrease of violence as relationships age and change thus seems to confirm the suggestion that violence is informed by the negotiation of interdependence and autonomy. In Eugenia's case, for instance, she used to be beaten in a period when she most depended on her husband, a situation that changed as she gradually found more autonomy and independence from him through friends, work and her grown-up children. It indicates how violence may to some extent be related to the situation in which the husband considers himself more responsible by earning an income, and in a way that is also seen to legitimize his violence (see also Lazar 2002:199).

María's case and the violence of her husband show, however, that the above explanation is not sufficient, and that the dynamics of responsibility, dependency and autonomy can also have contrary effects than those suggested by Harvey. The violence in this relationship cannot be understood in terms of María's dependence on her husband, but rather his dependency on her and her family, since he works on her pitch when unemployed and lives in the house of her parents. The difference between these cases may thus illustrate that the negotiation of interdependence and autonomy through violence may work rather arbitrarily, in the sense that it is not necessarily the one who feels responsible or depended upon that turns to violence, but as in the case of Eduardo, also the one who experiences dependence. This dimension is not included in Harvey's analysis and is perhaps also more relevant in a migrant situation. It can nonetheless serve to question Harvey's argument that violence in marital relations is more about kin and affinity than gender, since the agent of violence in this case is the same (the male), although the relationship of dependency is turned upside-down compared to the situation outlined by Harvey. In continuation, this is a debate that can serve to illustrate a somewhat different point made by Moore (1994b) among others, namely that men's violence is often caused by feelings of frustration for not living up to ideals of masculinity, that is, as the one who earns an income. This is likely to become particularly acute in the migrant situation, due to people's preoccupation with survival and progress combined with male unemployment and women earning an independent income. In other words, while women gain more independence in relation to kin and household through earning an income, this does not mean that there is less violence. Later in the chapter I will come back to the way in which violence is sometimes talked about and problematized as a 'backward' and 'barbaric' practice that is associated with people from the highlands – in contrast to an idea of the more 'civilized' city. In a later chapter I will also discuss how marital violence is a central theme in the courses and campaigns of state and NGO agencies in new urban neighbourhoods.[10]

The Interference of *Brujería* in Social Relationships

The significance of a relational understanding of personhood is illustrated by the possibilty to influence people and their social relationships through powerful acts. As previously described, ritual payments and the use of powerful objects are seen to have the potential to enhance or prevent people's chances for progress, for instance through *brujería* or *daño* (harmful acts).[11] In my talks with Eugenia, for instance, she often blamed her lack of progress on her neighbours' use of *brujería* so that she and her husband would be miserable and not achieve any progress. As previously noted, she attributed this to the fact that unlike her and her husband, who are both from Cuzco, most of her neighbours are from Puno and that people from the Puno region are not to be trusted. It is interesting to note here that Eugenia's suspicion expresses the idea that harmful acts may affect the progress of a couple and not only of the individual person, thus indicating how these acts can also affect and interfere in the relationships between people or between partners.

Indeed, acts of *brujería* and *daño* also have the potential to affect the relationship between husband and wife in a negative way. A friend of María had for a long time suspected that her husband was unfaithful. She went to a *curandero* who told her that another woman had performed harmful acts so that she and her husband would be unhappy in their relationship. In order to counter this negative influence, the *curandero* told her to put some of her menstruation blood in her husband's drink. By drinking this he would be affected by her substances and become so attracted to his wife that he would stop seeking other women. This kind of attempt to influence a relationship in a specific way is widespread and indicates how the relationships between partners may be subject to positive as well as negative influences through the use of powerful acts and objects. Such acts can be seen as the cause of problems, for instance with infidelity in a relationship, and is also used as a response in order to reverse the problem. Through the use of powerful substances, this woman sought to change her relationship to her husband by directing his physical attraction towards herself, so that he would stay at home

10 In Latin America, the women's movement's campaign of Violence Against Women has been very influential during the last couple of decades (Lazar 2002). As a result of the lobbying efforts of women's NGOs, many countries have established legislation on domestic violence, and NGOs assist female victims of violence to bring legal cases against their aggressors.

11 *Brujería* or *daño* in this context cannot necessarily be categorized in terms of sorcery or witchcraft in correspondence with the way in which these notions was used since Evans-Pritchard (1937). In fact, many of these practices seem to have characteristics of sorcery as well as witchcraft as they conventionally have been conceptualized.

more. Similar acts are also used to make a person fall in love in the beginning of a relationship.

As previously noted, notions of self and personhood are understood as defined primarily through social relationships, and through these relational senses of self, different kinds of collectivity are underwritten (Lazar 2002:183). Lazar explores marriage as one of the primary relations that constitute the self, and sees it in relation to how relational senses of self are simultaneously created through other networks, for example as part of a neighbourhood. She underlines that the processes involved in creating these kinds of relational persons also leave open the possibility of 'failure', and therefore show that individuals are embedded in their communities in a dynamic and not automatic way (ibid:183). What I would like to stress in relation to this is how the significance and potential harmfulness of powerful acts must be understood in terms of the relational notions of self and personhood. As I will come back to, powerful acts can be seen to gain meaning through the ways in which people try to influence each other negatively or positively through relational means. People's use and fear of harmful acts can therefore be seen as essential to the possible fragility of social relationships, and as illustrating how 'failure' in social relationships can be caused as well as amended through powerful acts and objects.

While both women and men can be affected by harmful acts and blame their economic as well as marital misfortunes on other people's envy or powerful interference, they can use it in different ways, and it may influence women and men differently. Among men in the Andes who experience impotence or cannot have children, or otherwise fail to behave in a way expected of a man, Glass-Coffin (1998) has described how it is not uncommon that they blame it on magic or witchcraft. Similarly in cases when the husband is controlled by his wife, Glass-Coffin notes that it is sometimes ascribed to magic or witchcraft. For a woman, like in the case of María's friend illustrated above, her suspicion that her husband was unfaithful was ascribed to another woman's harmful acts that made him cheat on her, drink too much and escape his responsibilities to wife and children. This kind of harmful act may thus be used and interpreted differently by women and men, and the experience of María's friend illustrates Glass-Coffin's point with respect to the significance of magic for the negotiation of gender roles and ideals. For instance, the suspicion of Maria's friend that the other woman had directed *brujería* at her and her husband may have served as a way for her to demonstrate the indecency of the other woman on the one hand, whilst maintaining her own decency on the other. In this respect, it is also worth stressing that although men can be blamed for the use of magic or witchcraft, accusations of this kind are more often directed at women (Glass-Coffin 1998, Machaca 2005).

As I will come back to, the fear and suspicion of harmful acts and *brujería* is an enduring concern among traders at the market. The possibility of powerful and potentially harmful acts are therefore given significance for how traders get involved in co-operation as well as conflict with other traders, and it was not uncommon to hear their suspicions about envy or use of *brujería* among other traders, as well as claims about how mean other traders can be and that some cannot really be trusted. Among the traders, this was often connected to their continual evaluations and negotiations over their own and other's success, a subject that was made the object of conflict and distrust as well as fears and accusations of harmful acts. The relational significance of personhood and the possible 'failure' of social relationships are thus illustrated also in the relationships between colleagues. What is interesting in this respect is how this fear of *brujería* seemed to be associated primarily with the envy of other women and not the envy of men, something that on the one hand can be related to the imageries of womanhood, and on the other hand to the ways in which women primarily cooperate with other women and at the same time seem to compare themselves and their degree of progress with other women and not with men.

Competing Gender Representations and Ideals

While ethnographies from the Andes primarily have stressed the complementary and egalitarian relationship between the genders (Lobo 1982, Harris 2000, Lazar 2002), the literature on Latin America more generally has underlined the significance of male dominance and patriarchy, for example through the notion of *machismo*[12] (see Yeager 1994, Archetti 1999, Melhuus 1996, 1997, Gutmann 1996). My contribution in this regard is to explore to what extent notions of *machismo* interact with indigenous notions of complementarity in a migrant context and discuss their significance in relation to people's ideas about progress.

The notion of *machismo* has often been seen as accompanied by the ideals of *marianismo*, which refer to the submissive and sacrificial position of women (Stevens 1979). These notions reflect a gender complex closely related to Catholicism, wherein God as the authoritative father and the Virgin Mary as the self-sacrificing mother have created a basis for patriarchy (Stevens 1979, Melhuus 1997). Central to this differentiation of gender categories is a division of labour that relates ideas about work to ideas about sexuality, and the expectation that men work to sustain the family, while women should limit their activities to reproductive functions and the boundaries of the home (Yeager 1994). Gender categories are in this manner seen as informed by a distinction between *la casa* and *la calle*, and articulated through moral discourses based on notions of honour and shame (Melhuus 1997:232). In the literature (see Melhuus 1996, Gutman 1996), it has been noted that the use of the term *machista* – as a personifying noun or adverbial/adjective for the generalized term *machismo* – often refers to a male who is financially responsible for his family, and who makes decisions on their behalf by representing his family in the public sphere. It refers to a male who makes sure that the activities of his woman are limited to the household in order to

[12] Machismo, derived from the generic term *macho*, meaning male, is often used synonymously with masculinity (Melhuus 1996:240).

secure her respectability as a woman and his own honour as a man (Stevens 1979, Gutman 1996, Melhuus 1996). The significance of *machismo* in the Peruvian context seems to be more complex and ambiguous than for instance in Mexico. In Peru, the participation of women in work, colonial wars and guerrilla fighting has laid the grounds for other perspectives on the position of women than those outlined above, at the same time as ideas of *machismo* may nevertheless be seen to represent a dominant imagery on gender (Castro 1994). It is important to underline in this regard that the ideas associated with *machismo* are primarily a characterization of middle- and upper-class discourses,[13] and not the general practice – nor necessarily the ideal – among working classes or more marginalized groups such as people from the highlands. Gender relationships in the Peruvian context seem to be influenced by ideas of *machismo* as well as those of Andean complementarity, and can be viewed as offering two competing ideals that both contradict and mutually inform each other (see also Widmark 2003). They represent different imageries of gender in a way that reveals how gendered values and expectations are informed by discourses on class and ethnicity (see for example Moore 1994a). Among people who have migrated, the income-earning of women as well as men is related to economic necessities as well as cultural values. Although there is a gendered division of labour in Jerusalén in the sense that women often work as servants and traders and men within construction or transport, these work practices are not necessarily based on a gendering of the conceptual boundaries between street and household as noted in relation to the middle-class ideals of *machismo*. Nonetheless, middle-class ideas about gender do seem to gain potency among migrants in their accommodation to an urban context and quest for progress. In the following, I will highlight the different ways in which people in Jerusalén understand and make use of the term *machismo* and relate this to their understanding of progress. Although I in this manner do not intend to suggest that the concept and values of *machismo* are something that people 'encounter' for the first time in the migrant context, I nonetheless underline that their use of this notion must be seen in relation to their Andean background and accommodation to urban life.

When the term *machismo* was mentioned and discussed in the conversations I had with women and men in Jerusalén, it was generally as an interpretation of behaviours as well as qualities related to responsibility and independence, work and income, but also to drinking habits, jealousy and particularly outgoing, dominating or aggressive modes of behaviour. This indicates how people understand and use the concept *machismo* or *machista* in a variety of different ways. Similarly, Lazar (2002) notes that in contrast to the income-bringing and responsible *machista*, some people also say that men who do not sacrifice themselves for the sake of the family are *machistas* (ibid:211). In this manner, the idea of *machista* can refer to positive as well as negative qualities, and to those who live up to their

[13] It is at the same time important to note that the situation of the Peruvian middle class has changed dramatically during the last two or three decades, with increasing numbers of women acquiring higher education and professional careers.

responsibilities of bringing in an income, *as well as* to those who do not – and both are part of the ambiguous gender imagery of *machismo*. In Jerusalén, the term was also used when referring to young boys who act childishly, violently or irresponsibly, and to mature women who drink, fight and work in the streets. Indeed, people sometimes referred to cases in which it was the woman who made her male partner suffer, by working and staying in the streets all day, or by drinking, quarrelling and talking dirty. These women were also referred to as *machistas* or (*mari-*)*machas*. The *machista* notion was thus applied in a variety of ways according to different situations and expectations, and there did not seem to be a singular or necessarily gender-specific meaning in people's use of the term. In the midst of this polysemous nature of the concept, the idea of *machismo* generally appears to be associated with some kind of energy, an energy that is spent in work or in the opposite, such as fights and alcohol. In this respect, anger is somehow characteristic of the *machista* or *vivo* (that is, energetic and outgoing person), and represents a kind of 'energy' that can either be positive or negative.

In the literature, the notion of *machista* is reported as referring primarily to men. I was therefore somewhat surprised when I heard it used to describe the behaviours also of women in Jerusalén,[14] and in a way that I had never heard it used about women considered middle-class *mestizas*. This can be an illustration of how, in the process of accommodating in the urban context and learning the Spanish language, Spanish words and expressions can be given new or expanded meanings and associations. As I will come back to below, it also reflects how women from the highlands are ambiguously positioned in relation to dominant discourses and ideals, for example concerning ideas about ethnicity and 'race', work and spatial categories. In particular, I understand the use of *machista* as it refers also to women to be related to the way in which the work practices of these women involve a transgression of boundaries between what is considered private and public spheres in the urban context. The significance of work for the conceptualization of personhood was reflected also by the way in which women spoke about themselves as well as other women more generally. I often heard that women who were positively valued were described as good *trabajadoras*, because they worked hard and gained an income. Such a positive valuation of hard-working women could involve most kinds of work, from household and the upbringing of children to that of trade, servant-, factory- and construction work. Also when talking about themselves, women frequently emphasized that they are *trabajadoras* and that they have the knowledge and experience of hard work. In this manner, they also made a contrast between themselves and other women who do not know how to work (*las que no saben trabajar*), frequently meaning middle-class *mestiza* women who do not know how to work because they do not have to.

---

14 A similar use of the *machista* term when addressing women is also briefly mentioned by Stølen (1996) in rural Argentina.

The Idiom of Suffering

Women often underlined the suffering they had experienced or were going through. Among them was Angelina, who frequently talked about all the suffering she had endured in her life. In particular, she often mentioned a recurring eye disease she was bothered by and that she explained as being caused by her crying and suffering so much. She related the disease particularly to the time when she and her husband in desperation had started to work in the mines just above Jerusalén. It was the hard work and dust she had to endure there that had caused the eye disease.

In the literature from Latin America, the image of suffering is related especially to womanhood and the role of women as mothers and wives in a society where men dominate (Stevens 1979, Melhuus 1997). Womanhood is seen as characterized by suffering, and by suffering one becomes a good woman. The self-sacrifice and suffering of women is in this manner contrasted with men's domination and selfishness (Yeager 1994, Melhuus 1996, 1997). In Jerusalén, women spoke of their suffering also with reference to their experiences of giving birth and raising children, and to the things they had to sacrifice and endure with husbands who drink and sometimes beat them. In addition, they stressed how they had suffered through a life of hard work, poverty and a continual struggle for economic survival. Some women also related their suffering especially to their situation as people from the highlands, such as the ways in which they lacked the necessary competence in Spanish and other kinds of knowledge needed in the urban context, and how this reinforced their experiences of being exploited and discriminated against. In this manner, women related their suffering not only to womanhood – and what was conceptualized as the problems of *machismo* – but also to the struggles of hard work, poverty and discrimination. In this manner, suffering appears to be made into an idiom that not only refers to the suffering of motherhood, but to difficulties in life more generally due to poverty and discrimination. Such an idiom of suffering thus seems to reflect not only the Catholic significance of the suffering Virgin, but also being informed by the value of hard work as an essential moral quality. This furthermore reflects how there is not necessarily a contradiction between the imageries of women as strong and hard-working on the one hand, and as self-sacrificing and suffering on the other – unless one thinks about the latter position as 'weak'.

The experience of suffering among people in Jerusalén was also underlined by men, and particularly in situations when alcohol was consumed. Like women, I several times heard men on such occasions stressing their suffering due to hard work and experiences of poverty and discrimination. When alcohol was consumed it was not unusual to see men weep for their sorrows and talk about their suffering. The idiom of suffering is thus made relevant among men as well as women and represents a recurrent theme also in the *huayno* and the *chicha* music. This general significance of the notion of suffering helps to illustrate some of the ambiguity of gender imageries when influenced by conditions of poverty and experiences of discrimination. It is important to note furthermore that men's emphasis on suffering can also be related to the particular social expectations that they encounter, for instance to behave as responsible income-earners in a situation characterized by marginality and discrimination in their relationship to the wider society. Hence, while men stress their identity as hard-working highlanders, they simultaneously experience problems in finding work and bearing financial burdens. In this situation, the wish to handle and fulfil the role of a responsible income-earner is sometimes impossible to achieve, so that two incompatible imageries of the self as gendered seem to co-exist (see Moore 1994b). What is more, the fact that men are generally dependent on formal employment in conditions that are often unstable – while their wives continue to work in trade – may also increase men's experiences of being marginalized and not living up to ideals of manhood.

The notion of suffering as outlined above can be related to the value among people in the Andes of being able to endure (*aguantar*) (see Harvey 1994, Lazar 2002). Lazar argues that being able to or having to endure is seen as an extremely important value, related for instance to the ability to work hard or show stoicism under violence. To endure is thus a source of pride and may be an effective response to centuries of colonial exploitation. In this manner, Lazar notes that 'the political implications of not demanding, or being able to demand, and the historical exploitation of altiplano people as hard workers, are both linked by the concept of *aguantar* with women's attitude to violence within the home' (2002:211). This confirms my point underlined above, namely that the suffering of people from the highlands is made an important idiom among men as well as women, whether it is caused by poverty, hard work or violence. By gaining meaning at the intersection between gender, class and ethnicity, the notion of suffering is an example of idioms through which people conceptualize and give meaning to their everyday lives and experiences.

The Gendering of Ethnic Stereotypes, or the Ethnicization of Gender

Ambiguous imageries are evoked not only in relation to women who work in trade, but also to indigenous or migrant women in general. This is illustrated particularly vividly in the representation of the Peruvian *chola* in the television series 'Paisana Jacinta'. In this series, the *chola* character is given a very manly and rough expression, and is even acted by a man. This illustrates an imagery of migrant women as somehow inappropriate and less or non-female. As the character is acted by a man, and with an extremely rough and rude expression, it reveals a view on the urban indigenous woman as somewhat anomalous, as someone who unsettles social boundaries and categories related to gender as well as ethnicity.[15] In this manner, gender imageries are also made significant in representations of 'the other', and thus given importance in general conceptualizations of difference, such as between highland and city, or migrants and middle-class *arequipeños*.

[15] At one of the shows of 'Paisana Jacinta' in Puno, several women came to protest against the racist attitude of this television series.

In Jerusalén, many people said that the problems of *machismo* – with reference particularly to violence and excessive use of alcohol – are primarily a characteristic of new urban neighbourhoods. When I asked why this is so, the answer was often that *machismo* is a tradition of the rural highlands and represents an uncivilized behaviour that people bring with them to the city. Despite what is otherwise regarded as the gender complementarity in the Andean highlands, this was a common characterization made by *arequipeños* as well as by people in Jerusalén. When commenting that her sister back home in Arapa was beaten by her new partner, for instance, Angelina made a similar reference to *machismo*: 'People from the highlands are not so intelligent, they have little education and are therefore like animals… They do not know the difference between right and wrong, they only know the difference between what hurts and what feels good. Therefore they beat.' According to Angelina, this explains the problems of *machismo* among people from the highlands. In this manner, the ascription of *machismo* to a rural background seems to be informed by more general descriptions of life in the highlands as *salvaje*, or underdeveloped, ignorant and backward. The idea of *machismo* is thus used to underline the backwardness that people often see to characterize the highlands in contrast to the urban Arequipa. *Machismo* therefore becomes part of an essentialized image of the Andean highlands, reflecting a stereotypical idea about people from this part of the country also among the migrants themselves. In Mexico, Gutmann (1996) has noted a similar mechanism in the sense that *machismo* is associated with the past or with poverty, violence and an excessive use of alcohol among frustrated working-class men. In the Peruvian case, the image of *machismo* seems to bring together a characterization of poor Andean men as drinking too much and having a tendency to violence for which women have to suffer. It demonstrates the significance of gender for ethnic stereotypes, and how gender is 'culturalized' and 'racialized'. In this manner, notions of *machismo* can be seen to inform, and be informed by ethnic- and class-related stereotypes, whereby gender imageries take on specific meanings.

Interestingly, the few women in Jerusalén who primarily stay at home without working were referred to as really having acquired *progreso* or success, that is, by affording not to work. If a woman can live according to a non-working ideal of the middle-class it may thus be regarded as a sign of success. This reflects an understanding of mobility and progress that is associated with the acquisition of certain modes of living related to the middle class.[16] Similar considerations are also reflected in relation to the upbringing of children, in the sense that the wish among parents for their children to move forward and progress may have different implications for girls than for boys. While parents generally hope that their young daughters as well as sons will acquire a professional career by attending school and continuing into higher education, daughters are more often expected to stay at home

[16] This is in spite of the fact that many middle-class women do not necessarily prefer to be housewives, at least not those that I learned to know.

after school and not hang about in the streets. In this manner, young unmarried women are often protected from things that take place in the streets. Although there are girls who are encouraged by their parents to leave the neighbourhood, travel and work, as in the case of Angelina and María, it seems more common to expect boys to seek experiences or progress outside the neighbourhood. So while parents seem to make the same effort with respect to the education and progress of daughters as they make for their sons – for instance in the sense that it is generally the oldest who is prioritized both with respect to education and the inheritance of land independently of gender – there nonetheless seem to be certain differences with respect to how girls and boys are treated. While daughters are often included in the work activities of their mothers such as at markets or in organizational work, the ambition of many parents is that their daughters in the long run will not have to work as servants or in *la calle* as their mothers have done. In this regard, many people seek to raise their daughters more in correspondence with middle-class ideals.

In family and kin relationships, therefore, the orientation towards progress can be seen to entail certain gender differentiating mechanisms. The limitation of young girls' movements is increasingly given significance in the urban context, and reflects an increasing concern that they do not become teenage mothers but finish their education. It is interesting to relate this to Ortner's (1996) argument that young girls' possibilities for upward marriage in male dominant societies depend on their respectability, an important sign for which is virginity. She makes an historical point in this respect, by stressing the change from a concern with women's dangerousness in egalitarian societies to a concern with their purity in hierarchical societies, and relating this change to the emergence of the state and the increasing significance of social mobility (ibid:57). In this manner, Ortner sees the ambiguities of femaleness *vis-à-vis* social categories as connected to the ways in which imageries of womanhood remain bound to idioms of purity and pollution. She notes that the symbolization of this ambiguity shifts from danger to purity in cases when there is an upward direction in the crossing of social boundaries, thus increasing the concern with women's purity and creating a need for protection. Among people from the highlands, it seems to be a general concern with mobility and progress that makes daughters a subject of protection in attempts to transform a kind of 'dangerousness' (like the 'dangerousness' of indigenous market women) into 'purity', in order to make daughters different from their hard-working, market-trading mothers.

Conclusions

This chapter has highlighted how gender relationships and values are often negotiated in people's quest for mobility and progress. I have explored the significance of gender in kin and inter-generational relationships, and how gender relations and ideas are negotiated in connection to work, marriage, violence and practices of *brujería*. Migration encompasses two partly contrasting discourses on gender, that is, Andean notions of gender complementarity and the working couple on the one hand, and the gender ideals of the middle class on the other. In people's search for mobility and progress, gender ideals associated with the middle-class are increasingly made significant, at the same time as these ideals are also challenged and unsettled, for instance through the work practices of migrant women and their transgression of dominant social categories such as *casa* and *calle*. I have discussed this in light of how the imageries of migrant women are imprinted with ambiguity in the process, and related it to the importance of gender for ethnicity and processes of 'othering'.

While I have illustrated how the understanding of women's trade as an extension of household work is partly reproduced also by the women themselves, this work simultaneously involves a blending of activities and functions conventionally understood in terms of private/public, reproduction/production. The increasing significance of these trading activities at the margins of the formal economy can be seen as a response to the conditions of urban marginalization in a globalized economy, and is based upon the use of social and cultural resources and networks of kin. Indeed, the risk and insecurity involved in this work is minimized through the reliance on social networks and kin in which women play a central role. As I will return to, the majority of women in this kind of trade may even serve to reproduce the informal conditions under which these economic activities are realized.

Chapter 6
Neighbourhood and State

This chapter follows up the discussion of the relationship between community and state in the development of new urban neighbourhoods from Chapter 1, here by focusing more specifically on local organizations. I discuss further the ways in which the authorities have often responded to the development of new urban neighbourhoods by appropriating inhabitants' practices and initiatives into policy, and how these local organizations have gained political significance also in wider political discourses and strategies. I continue my discussion of notions and practices of communal work from Chapter 1, and relate this to gender by reflecting on the ways in which the workforce of women in particular are made important in the initiatives to develop and improve these new urban neighbourhoods. Indeed, women have not only played an active role in the work organized by the neighbourhood committees, but have also been involved in women's organizations working to improve the conditions in the neighbourhood. This chapter is therefore especially concerned with the women's organization in Jerusalén, Asociación de Organizaciónes de Mujeres de Arequipa (ASOMA), and the relationship of this organization to the authorities through its involvement in different projects of state and municipal institutions. In this manner, I seek to demonstrate the significance of gender for the re-creation of a somewhat ambiguous or hybrid space for citizenship among people from the highlands as outlined in Chapter 1, and thus the significance of gender not only for governance in development projects but also for the maintenance of a certain level of illegibility. This state-community interaction represents a useful angle from which to explore the relations of power and agency in which people in this neighbourhood are involved. I am especially concerned with the negotiation of gender imageries at the conjuncture between local organization and official institutions, in the sense that it may reveal important notions of development and modernization in relation to gender.

People's participation in social organizations can illuminate questions of power both as institutional structures and as decentralized social relationships diffused through different spaces of interaction (Gledhill 1994). I therefore focus on the accommodation to, and contestation of, dominant discourses within the multiple social spaces that popular organizations can be seen to create. Gledhill has underlined how a focus on social movements and organizations may reveal the complex processes by which groups construct or reconstruct identities for themselves in their negotiation with dominant groups and the state (1994:200). Focusing on how the strategies and language use of institutions and local organizations or actors often influence each other, this chapter explores how notions of the indigenous, communal work and gender appear to be made and un-made through social mobilization and policy making. I will also discuss how notions about mobility and progress are negotiated in terms of collective obligations and personal achievements among the participants, and relate this to the negotiation of leadership.

Social Organization in Jerusalén

Women's Organization, State and NGO Institutions

In the beginning of the 1980s, women in Jerusalén were encouraged by the local municipalities to meet in *clubes de madre* (mothers' groups) as was common in many newly established neighbourhoods in this period. In Jerusalén, these groups came together to form ASOMA in 1993, consisting of four different women's groups that previously worked separately: Corazón de Jesus, Nueva Esperanza, Santa Rosa de Lima and Carmen del Rosario.

From its initiation, the women's organization has been involved in different projects for development and modernization organized by the municipality, state and NGO agencies. The ASOMA organization has in this manner become a channel for the distribution of food and technical assistance in the neighbourhood. Among the projects that women in ASOMA are involved in is the *vaso-de-leche*, that is, the distribution of milk powder for all children under six years of age. Another programme in which ASOMA takes part is the *comedores populares* (communal, or soup kitchen), through which the organization receives food products for preparing meals to sell cheaply in the neighbourhood: rice, beans, corn meal, soya, wheat and the like. The communal kitchen project, like the milk programme, is intended to secure nutrition in poor areas. The milk programme is coordinated by the municipality, while the communal kitchen is coordinated by the Programa Nacional de Asistencia Alimentaria (PRONAA), a state institution which also coordinates other programmes such as the school breakfasts, some of the resources for which are donated by the EU.

During my first period of fieldwork in 1997, the participants in ASOMA totalled about 200 women of different ages ranging from around 20 to over 70 years old. A few of the older women had lived in Jerusalén since the occupation, and many of the participants had known each other for a long time, while a few had newly arrived to Arequipa from the highlands. The working groups were divided according to sections of the neighbourhood, so that neighbourhood relationships were reflected in the division of groups. The selection for leadership positions in ASOMA takes place through election, and is supposed to be organized on a rotational basis. In addition to the positions of president, treasurer and secretary, each of the four mother's groups are represented by a leader in ASOMA's central committee. The holders of these leadership positions act as representatives for the organization and are the ones who primarily have contact or meetings with the authorities and NGO institutions. They are also the ones who are expected to obtain external support for the organization.

In addition to their participation in the programmes of the municipality and PRONAA, the women in ASOMA were also involved with a Belgian NGO called Taller. This NGO has provided support in the form of materials and food products (*víveres*) for the construction and management of a bakery on the ASOMA estate. Before this, the NGO also helped them to buy the terrain that the organization now owns, and provided courses of different kinds. Through the support of the NGO – mainly in the form of donations, but a few things also in the form of loans – the bakery was established as a joint or micro-enterprise with the aim of creating an income for participating women through the sale of bread and cookies. Since the initiation of the mother's groups in the 1980s, the women have also been supported by other NGO agencies, among them a local Christian organization that donates materials and food as well as gives courses. The women have also previously been involved in small enterprises, such as the production and sale of shoes, sweaters and shirts, in addition to a shop that they ran for a time but that has now been closed. The courses that the women take part in are referred to in terms of *capacitación* (training), and are arranged both by official institutions such as PRONAA and the NGO Taller. Some of the courses are focused on practical training with respect to organization and leadership, the running of business, production forms and the like, while others are organized around information about human and women's rights as well as health issues, such as marital violence and issues related to sexuality and family planning. In order to become a member in ASOMA and take part in the projects, women have to pay a few soles (five in 1997). Otherwise, membership requires that the women contribute by participating in the workforce, the absence from which must be compensated for with a fine.

In return for their work performances the women receive materials for construction, production or consumption. From the NGO, for instance, the group received materials for their construction of the bakery, and each participant received food products in return for their compulsory performance of work one day a week. In addition, the women in ASOMA also made occasional agreements both with PRONAA and the local municipal authorities for their performance of works not only at the estate but also for the improvement of the neighbourhood or the surrounding area, like the clearing of roads, maintenance of community buildings, the park and so forth. For the performance of this kind of work the women generally receive food rations or money in return, the food rations consisting of products like milk, *quinoa* (a grain produced in the Andes), beans, rice or wheat. Common to all these official and NGO projects is their reliance on the work efforts of the women. There are also private actors who contract the organized women to perform different tasks (see also Blondet 1990), for instance to prepare different kinds of wool or cloth, or to untangle rags (*waipi*) for car-washeries.

In ASOMA's communal kitchen, the preparation of meals is supposed to be organized on a rotational basis among a group of ten women. From this group, pairs of women are supposed to cook together once a week under the administration of their leader Carla. Often the women did not meet as planned, however, and it was generally Carla who took care of much of the cooking herself. Some of the other women said they did not have time to work in the kitchen because of other responsibilities. Others said they could not even afford to buy this food, or they found it not to be nutritious or plentiful enough. Those who did make use of the communal kitchen however said that they found it very helpful. In a period when Carla had been ill for several days and not able to follow through with her work in the communal kitchen, she was worried that the PRONAA officials would remove the support should they discover that no meals were being prepared. There is a fine to be paid to PRONAA for this kind of failure, and eventually the sanctions may entail the removal of support for the kitchen. Carla was also worried about what the others might think if she was not at work for several days and that she could be accused of just being lazy. Carla could not find anyone to take her place, and she later heard that some people from PRONAA had actually come to check if the kitchen was functioning as planned. According to some other women who had been working on the estate that day, they had all assured the people from PRONAA that it was only on this day that there was no food being prepared. In this case – and to Carla's relief – the support was not withdrawn. In this manner, PRONAA sometimes come to control the work performance of the women's groups in order to make sure that the resources are used as they are intended.

The heavy rainfalls related to the El Niño phenomena in 1997 caused severe destruction in Arequipa. In certain parts of the city, roads and houses were destroyed to such a degree that it took a great deal of work and resources to rebuild them. The municipality in Mariano Melgar asked the women in ASOMA to perform the reconstruction work, not only in their own neighbourhood, but also in the surrounding neighbourhoods. In return, they would receive payment in cash. After the job was completed, the women complained about bad payment and humiliating treatment, and one woman even claimed that they had been treated as if they were servants or some kind of animals. A couple of years before, the women in ASOMA had similarly been recruited to work on a municipal water project outside Arequipa, in Majes, a job for which they never received the payment they had been promised. The construction and maintenance of school and health care buildings in areas like Jerusalén are also accomplished by the work effort of inhabitants, that is, through the participation in communal work of both pupils and their parents. The expense for materials is raised in different ways: through the collection among parents of *cuotas* (fees of contribution), the arrangement of social events like dances and *parilladas* (grill parties),[1] or the small chores performed by pupils such as gathering garbage among households to sell at the Parque Industrial. The state institution PRONAA also assists with the provision of some materials and technical assistance, under the condition that parents perform the work. PRONAA also provides schools with food products for the school breakfasts, for which

---

1 When people need to gather extra money, it is common to arrange Sunday grill parties to sell meals to the other inhabitants.

parents can volunteer to do the cooking, a responsibility which is most often taken on by the mothers. In this manner, state institutions such as PRONAA have come to occupy a central position in the institutionalization of arrangements for voluntary and/or communal work. It is an example of the integration by the state apparatus of local organizational initiatives and necessities, but in a way that often serves to reproduce the informal and unpaid character of people's work conditions in these areas. As previously discussed, these arrangements have become a way to solve economic dilemmas for the state as well as inhabitants in relation to the country's fast-growing urban areas. From the perspective of inhabitants, these arrangements are a way of getting support from local and state authorities. What is interesting in the continuation of this is that in most cases it is women who take responsibility for these communal work obligations, probably because they presumably do not have any responsibility to earn an income.

The representatives of PRONAA, the municipality and NGOs who come to have meetings or arrange work and courses are generally middle-class *mestizos* born in Arequipa, mostly women but also a few men. It is important to underline in this regard that interaction between participants in ASOMA and official representatives was generally characterized by inequality and distance. So, although most of the official representatives were women, the common identification as 'women' did not seem to outweigh the significance of ethnicity or class in these relationships. In general, the women's interaction with these officials was characterized by their concern that the representatives should at least show them the proper respect. At the same time as the involvement of official agencies was organized in a top-down manner, there were also situations in which the women appeared to seek or claim their autonomy in relation to the external officials. For instance, while meetings and courses with state or NGO officials were generally held in Spanish, the women often spoke Quechua during these encounters, not only when speaking between each other, but also when making comments in the middle of a course or formal meeting. These comments were often made in a joking manner, although they were also sometimes negative with respect to the projects or presence of the officials. Either way, the use of Quechua worked to exclude the monolingual Spanish speakers and express a sense of autonomy and difference in their relation to the officials. With respect to the food rations that the women received, the women did not always use these rations for the proper purpose in the perspective of the donors. For instance, some women sold their rations of food at the market in order to gain some profit, or used the milk distributed through the *vaso-de-leche* programme to produce cheese and sell it at the market.

Political parties sometimes send representatives to ASOMA in order to make appeals to the women and make them attend party meetings, use their party logos and give them their votes, sometimes in return for food, clothes or materials. Ever since the foundation of these women's groups, political parties have thus worked to gain their support, especially before elections. During the presidential campaign of Fujimori in 2000, for instance, women in ASOMA were told by some of the officials from PRONAA that support to the organization would be withdrawn if they did not attend the meetings of Fujimori's party and give him their votes. In general during his campaign, Fujimori's party apparatus directed a lot of attention towards organizations like ASOMA, by making visits and giving away food, clothes and materials. After Toledo gained the presidency in 2001, however, PRONAA's staff was almost completely replaced due to accusations of corruption, especially for the way its funds had been misused during Fujimori's presidential campaign. This indicates how inhabitants in these neighbourhoods are seen to represent great potential in terms of votes, and how local organizations in particular are used as an important entry point for political appeals. At one point, a local office of Alianza Popular Revolucionario de América (APRA) also tried to formalize the relationship with ASOMA. However, in this as in other cases, the ASOMA participants declined and later told me that they chose to attend political meetings solely in order to make use of the advantages the party had advertised. In this manner, the women generally refused a more long-term involvement with political parties. They said that such loyalty may result in the loss of opportunities in relation to other parties and shifting authorities. In the following section I will describe everyday life in ASOMA as I experienced it, based on my fieldwork in 1997.

Everyday Life in the Organization

On a regular weekday at the ASOMA estate, the women with responsibility for the communal kitchen generally met up early to start cooking while the other members with work duty that day arrived a little later to continue working on whatever project they were occupied with at the time. At noon they usually sat down together to have a meal from the kitchen. During my first fieldwork, the kitchen was built with stone and covered with plastic so as not to let the sand blow in, and the food was prepared on kerosene-fuelled equipment. In contrast, the newly constructed buildings on the estate – like the bakery that was gradually constructed while I was there in 1997 – are made of concrete and painted, as would be the room for storage of food rations, which in addition was given a lock. On Fridays, the different work groups got together for an encounter in order to discuss how things were going and make plans about future projects. These Friday encounters were also sometimes used for meetings and courses.

On one of the early mornings when I arrived at the ASOMA estate a group of women were already busy digging a ditch. The ditch was supposed to be about one metre deep, to be filled with the foundation wall for the new storage room. All the women were equipped with small hammers with which to break up the big rocks hidden beneath the dry earth. The work was hard and the sun burning hot as it reached the estate, but people continued to talk and laugh while using their hammers. Sometimes the conversation made people forget their work, in response to which they were reminded by the work leader or others to keep on working. Those who came late for the work session were similarly met with a joking tone, like '*buenas noches*' (good night) or '*has comido toda la noche?*' (have you been eating all night?), suggesting that the person might have had sex all night.[2] Those who had been missing from work sessions for some time were met with comments such as 'we thought you were dead'. At the end of the day many complained that their muscles were sore, and one woman had hit her hand with the hammer and been ordered to stop working. I was hardly allowed to take part in the work, and when I did the women were always reminding me not to hurt my hands. While working on the ditch, everyone had their regular places to work, often next to a good friend or *comadre*.

The women in ASOMA spent two months finishing this ditch. After that they started to dig a new ditch in order to get water to the estate, since at the time they had to fetch water from outside. Then they began to lay bricks and paint the inside of the bakery. In the afternoon on one such day and not long before the work was finished, people were getting hungry as they had not eaten since the lunch at the communal kitchen. At home supper had to be prepared, there were clothes to be washed and children to be looked after and some were on their way to work at the market. Before leaving, they agreed to make everything ready for the next day, for the construction of a second floor for the bakery. A pile of stone bricks had to be taken up to the roof to have everything ready for laying the bricks the following day. The discussion went back and forth for some minutes with respect to how this work should best be done. Some claimed that it was better if everyone carried the bricks individually in their *mantas* (wool rugs or blankets), while others preferred *pasa-mano* (hand to hand), so that everyone could stand in line and hand each other the *mantas* with the bricks inside. A couple of women underlined that this method was more fun, and they agreed to finish the task by *pasa-mano*. The work was advancing rapidly, with the blankets moving from hand to hand, and then sent back to be filled with bricks again by some of the women on the ground. The woman who lifted the bricks up to the roof had the heaviest job, but was continuously encouraged to keep working. Others went on with the conversation while working, and every once in a while someone shouted to the opposite end of the line: 'What are you up to over there; you're not working properly?!' Someone answered that it was the baby that interrupted all the time; he did not let her work and wanted milk all the time; and 'I have to take care of the baby, don't I?' The woman who answered had her baby tucked inside a blanket (*manta*) on her back, in order to have the baby safe and close to her at the same time as her hands were free to work.

The women generally showed joy and pleasure over working and meeting with other women in ASOMA, and in periods without work (that is, without donations) I heard several of them say that they missed the company of the other women. Together they always had conversations and made jokes, told each other about joys and sorrows, and during breaks they knitted or helped each other to do *waipi*[3] while eating something from home or from the communal kitchen. The women

2 See Harvey (1994) about the association between sex and eating.

3 That is, the manual untangling of rags to sell for car-washing.

generally addressed each other as *vecina* (neighbour) or *compañera* (companion, colleague), or otherwise referred to the other women as *las señoras* or *las mamas*. Some were also given nicknames.

The women often underlined the more informal or interpersonal dimensions of interaction as part of their motivation for taking part in ASOMA (see also Lazar 2002). During work and meetings, social spaces were created in which the women came together in small groups, discussing problems and exchanging advice with respect to family life, health and business, experiences of migration and life in the city. In this manner, ASOMA represented an arena to establish new friendships as well as relations of *compadrazgo*, thus creating a possibility for mutual exchange of help and support between women. As one woman formulated it, this is because in ASOMA they work and eat together. The expression of another woman that, '*somos familia del trabajo*' (we are family through work) further illustrates the relationships that are sometimes created through this kind of organizational work. Indeed, if we understand this work as a process of objectification (Starthern 1988), the different conditions and motivations for work in such an organization can be seen to entail both reifying and personifying dimensions. On the one hand, the women work for food rations and material improvement, and on the other hand they also work for the production of social relationships as such.

Background and Motivations for Participation

I several times heard women in ASOMA underline that what brings them together is that they are all poor women from the highlands, although they come from a range of different areas and some are Quechua and others (a few) are Aymara-speakers. Many said that they see ASOMA as their way of trying to build up a society for themselves and their children, in a well-constructed and modern neighbourhood. In this respect, participation in ASOMA was often spoken about in terms of *progreso*. Some of the women stressed that the work they were doing in ASOMA would one day benefit their children, by improving the neighbourhood and building an estate for coming generations to use. The new building that the women constructed above the bakery was for instance supposed to become a communal activity house to use for parties and for the members to arrange marriages, baptism parties and funeral gatherings.

One day we had the sad news that Ana, the leader for the distribution of the milk programme, had been hit by a car. After just a few hours the news had spread and many of the women gathered in the ASOMA estate. They started to gather money for medicine and soon agreed who should go to visit her in hospital. A couple of days later Ana died, and some of the other leaders were quick to start arranging for the funeral. They made contact with her family and the following days Ana's sons kept coming to the ASOMA estate so they could prepare the funeral together, a ceremony that was planned to be held in ASOMA's bakery. The women gathered money to cover expenses for the ceremony, garlands, food and a banner to put over her coffin that said: 'ASOMA, Mariano Melgar'. The women also made and served all the food for the occasion, and made a general effort to share the responsibility for the funeral with Ana's family. There were also other cases similar to this in which a crisis in the life of one of ASOMA's members would prompt the women to take responsibility for gathering money or arranging street parties (*parilladas*) to raise money to help. In this manner, participation in ASOMA can represent a network of support to supplement the external involvement and donations.

Many women claimed that their motivation to participate in ASOMA in the first place was to meet *paisanas* (people from the same village or area, or people from the highlands in general) and to speak Quechua. While the women's perception of a common Andean background thus seemed to form an important basis for their motivation, this was not officially or explicitly made into an important aspect of the organization. The situation and rights of indigenous peoples were hardly referred to, in contrast to the greater and more explicit emphasis on the situation of women and their rights, particularly through the courses arranged by official and NGO institutions.[4] The absence in ASOMA of specific and explicit cultural claims can perhaps be understood in terms of people's general aspirations for social mobility and urge to escape the Andean stigma, but may also be a result of the way in which the authorities have come to handle these organizations during the last couple of decades, for example by focusing specifically on women. The women nonetheless expressed the importance of an Andean background more informally in social interaction, and in their marking of rural festivals and the use of dresses, music and dance from the highlands at parties. In this regard it has been claimed (see Solomon 1997) that the inclusion of cultural elements and events in organizational arrangements is often an effect of the expectations of NGOs or authorities to create performances of 'cultural authenticity'. This was not the case in ASOMA, however, as festivals and dances were included and arranged on the initiative of the participants themselves, while the state and NGO officials gave little attention to questions of 'indigenous culture' in this respect, except for the emphasis on notions of collective work.

Participation in this kind of organization is generally seen as an indication of a person being poor. Some women stopped participating in ASOMA once they acquired a stable job or income, and others said they would have done the same if they had found stable employment. For instance, Juana told me that she for a while had been well established as a trader at the market by selling fruits and vegetables. She was making good money and had started thinking about expanding or buying another house closer to the centre. One day, however, she was robbed and lost all she had invested, something that made her lose the motivation to work in trade. On later occasions she said she regretted having withdrawn from her business and that if she had managed to continue, she would probably have been living in the centre

[4] Being concerned with women's issues of a more immediate and practical kind, ASOMA was not conceptualized as a feminist organization. Many women were also sceptical about referring to themselves by the term feminist, apparently because they see the term as indicating some sort of hostility toward men.

by now and would certainly not have been working in ASOMA. She told me about how a friend of hers had withdrawn from participation in ASOMA as soon as she got a steady job as a cleaner at the hospital. This illustrates how people participate in ASOMA because of a lack of other opportunities, and how participation in this kind of organization is associated with low incomes. Participants in ASOMA also seemed to evaluate each other's economic position and whether other members actually had the *need* to take part, for example, whether they had too nice a house, a steady job or education. For instance, a woman called Bea started in ASOMA shortly after it had been initiated. In the beginning, she experienced that the other women disliked her coming to join in the work, since they seemed to be wondering what she was actually doing in ASOMA, she who lived in one of the biggest and nicest houses in Jerusalén. Bea was later accepted however when they learned that she is a single mother who was working more or less as a servant in the house owned by two cousins working in trade. Later, when I was back in Arequipa in 2001, Bea had become even more dependent on the kind of network and security that ASOMA represented. At that point she had moved out of her cousins' house because of a disagreement. Without anywhere else to go, she had asked the other women for permission to stay and live on the ASOMA estate, and thus started to live in the storage room with her children.

Some people find themselves more in need than others of the food rations provided through work in ASOMA, and a few chose to work more than the compulsory once a week in order to receive more food rations. It was first of all single-mothers who used this kind of arrangement, and among them was Margarita who lost her husband in 1992. She said that for her, ASOMA represents a certain material stability that adds to her income from selling food (*chuño*[5]), at the same time as she appreciates coming together with the other women. Ofelia, on the other hand, was among the women who do have a partner and a relationship in which both earn money. She generally used to work in ASOMA only once a week and otherwise she worked with her husband in the brick-factory just below Jerusalén. Nonetheless, there were a few occasions when she also worked double for double rations, such as in a period when her husband was ill and they had trouble covering expenses for food and medicine. ASOMA can therefore be important, especially for women without husbands or kin in the city, or in periods when people have low incomes. Similarly for newcomers to the city, this kind of participation is important for accommodating to the city and the neighbourhood as it is a way to get to know people and learn how things work. In this regard, I have previously noted how newcomers in general were often referred to as more innocent due to their inexperience with urban ways, and participation in ASOMA was seen as useful to make people more experienced.

During my first fieldwork in 1997, the women talked about their participation in ASOMA as a way to achieve *progreso*, at the same time as they recognized

[5] That is, potatoes that have been dehydrated through low temperature or cold water.

this participation as a solution first of all for poor people. In many ways, people saw this kind of participation as making them different from middle-class *arequipeños* by actualizing the qualities of hard-working people associated with the Andes. Calderón (1988:225) has noted that social organizations can be viewed as fostering a kind of 'alternative modernity' with respect to how to be both modern and different – or '*como entrar en la modernidad sin dejar de ser indios*' (how to enter modernity without ceasing to be indigenous, my translation). Participation in neighbourhood organizations can in this regard be understood to reflect and reinforce a certain ambiguity in the position of people from the highlands in Peruvian cities. Indeed, these organizations operate in the ambiguous space for citizenship created through the dialectics between citizens' practices and state policies as discussed in Chapter 1. On the one hand, such a recruitment of communal work in the urban context can be seen as reproducing historical relationships of inequality and a form of indirect rule. Many of these arrangements can in this regard be seen to reproduce the position of people from the highlands – as non- or low-paid labourers – in processes of mobility. On the other hand, people are also involved in projects of modernization through this participation, both in the form of infrastructural improvement and the arrangement of courses. Particularly for leaders, the contact with state and NGO agencies may also open up new possibilities and spaces for action.

State Policies and Co-optation

During the government of Belaunde (1963–1968), new urban neighbourhoods in Peru were increasingly seen as an important basis for political support[6] (Blondet 1990:34). The arrangement with *clubes de madre* was for instance institutionalized by the Belaunde government in 1967 in connection to the up-coming elections in 1968, in which participants were expected to give their political support in return for different goods and advantages (ibid:34). During the 1970s and 1980s, there was an expansion also of independent popular, neighbourhood associations and organizations, and the best-known of these organizations is Federación Popular de Mujeres en Villa El Salvador (FEPOMUVES). FEPOMUVES was initiated in 1981 as a women's organization in the shantytown Villa El Salvador in the outskirts of Lima with the aim of improving the situation of inhabitants in general and women and children in particular. Villa el Salvador has later come to represent a success story of urban development. Also in other new urban neighbourhoods, people were mobilizing in the realization of collective work as well as organizing demonstrations in the attempt to improve their situation. Women played a central part in this mobilization in addition to their collective preparation of meals for the participants. This was the

[6] This was motivated by a new municipal law with the implication that mayors should no longer be appointed by the central government but be elected (Collier 1978). According to Blondet (1990:34), this changed the political scene in new urban neighbourhoods.

beginning of the *comedores* that at first got support from religious organizations and was later incorporated in the official programmes of the state in 1982 (Blondet 1990). As similarly illustrated in relation to neighbourhood committees in Chapter 1, some of the initiatives and activities of popular organizations have in this manner been co-opted and incorporated into the projects promoted and run by the state. Similarly, the original idea behind the program for *vaso-de-leche* was first formulated as a demand among women in the organization FEPOMUVES in Villa el Salvador, in their attempt to secure nutrition for poor children in the neighbourhood. This idea was later incorporated into projects of the authorities and realized nearly all over the country.

With the economic crisis that struck Peru and other Latin American countries in the beginning of the 1980s, the necessity for co-ordination and organization of local neighbourhoods to tackle the worsening conditions increased. During the second Belaunde government (1980–1985), the distribution of food as a part of the government's social welfare policy was reinforced to handle the economic crisis, and the authorities thus increasingly encouraged inhabitants in newly occupied and often poor urban areas to work together to improve the situation (Castañeda 1993:219). As today, these food distribution programmes were carried out by private or religious agencies, sometimes based overseas, or by the state apparatus itself, by getting women to perform communal work tasks in return for food (see Blondet 1990:39). In relation to the violent conflict between the guerrilla Sendero Luminoso and the military during the 1980s and beginning of the 1990s, the involvement of the state in local organizational projects gained wider importance. This involvement was expected to represent a buffer against the influence of Sendero in poor urban neighbourhoods in a way that also put the organizations in jeopardy. It was therefore a strained economic situation, along with the violence of the 1980s, which reinforced the state's co-ordination of local initiatives for social organization. Similarly from 1985 and forward, the government of García initiated as well as increased governmental support to several local organizations, among them ASOMA. Alongside the reduction of other parts of the public sector after Fujimori entered the presidency in 1990, the official involvement in new urban neighbourhoods was reinforced and further institutionalized by the initiation of PRONAA in 1992 (see Rousseau 2009). The intention was that PRONAA should co-ordinate the official programmes in new urban neighbourhoods, such as *los comedores* and the school breakfasts.

The political significance of popular urban organizations was made particularly evident in the period of violent conflict between the military and Sendero Luminoso. In this period, Sendero proclaimed their view on popular organizational leaders as traitors, while the authorities regarded them as potential Senderistas. Popular organizational leaders were thus placed in a vulnerable position between the military and Sendero.[7] In Sendero's attempt to establish an

7 This was more so in Lima than in Arequipa. In general, Arequipa was less affected by the violence.

urban base, its antagonistic relationship toward popular organizations also became violent, for example through its aggression towards several popular community leaders and union organizers belonging to rival organizations. The former leader of FEPOMUVES, Maria Elena Moyano was killed in 1992. She had been accused by Sendero of cooperating with the authorities and the democratic left, and for representing a hindrance to the recruitment of new members to Sendero in new urban neighbourhoods (Castañeda 1993:221). Sendero's claim was that the arrangements between state and local organizations represented an exploitation of poor people's workforce and a hindrance to more radical political change. Popular organizations were said to represent 'a pillow for the government to sleep on', by creating what was nothing but an appearance of improvement, since poverty in this way was made less visible, but structurally reproduced. This illustrates the political significance that popular urban organizations and their leaders had come to represent, as reflected in Sendero Luminoso's criticism of the relationship between the state and local, neighbourhood and women's organizations. By thus being important for the political discourses on poverty and development, popular organizations came to be significant in wider political strategies[8] and ideologies.

Through the joint effort of inhabitants who are involved in women's organizations – as well as in neighbourhood associations as previously noted – great improvements can be made in infrastructure as well as living standards at minimal cost to the state. In many ways, it could be seen as a sensible way of making use of the workforce in the midst of unemployment and scarce resources. Local organizations such as ASOMA serve to make this workforce easy to recruit and organize for different kinds of tasks, such as when women in ASOMA were asked to perform work for the local authorities outside their immediate neighbourhood. From a state perspective, this kind of arrangement represents a convenient way to relate to the 'masses', and an opportunity for supervising the growth of new urban areas which is initiated by the settlers themselves and often difficult for the authorities to survey. I have previously noted how the leaders of local organizations play a central role at this interface between state and community (see Arce and Long 1992, Lazar 2002), where contact and communication are made through leaders instead of a non-organized body of actors. Through the involvement with local organizations, the authorities do not need to relate directly to individual citizens, but to the representatives of organizations. This interface at the same time seems to actualize a tension between collectivist and individual interests or values, and is central to the somewhat ambiguous spaces for citizenship created for Andean people in the cities.

---

[8] The terrorist threat served to legitimate state repression and the inclusion of a wide range of popular action. Indeed, the war between Sendero and the military provided a pretext for the suppression of constitutional political life more generally (see Gledhill 2000:177).

The 'Making' of Communal Work

In their realization of projects in new urban neighbourhoods, I have previously mentioned that state and NGO agencies sometimes appeal to the inhabitants with reference to Andean traditions for communal work. On several occasions I heard officials refer to the 'traditions of communal work' among people from the highlands during their visits in Jerusalén as well as in other contexts. On one of the visits I made to the PRONAA office, an official underlined that in PRONAA's projects in new urban neighbourhoods, they seek to adjust to the inhabitants living there, particularly so with respect to their traditions for communal work. As previously mentioned, such a stress on the will and ability to do communal work was also reflected among the participants in ASOMA themselves. At Ana's funeral, for instance, she was continually talked about as a founder (*fundadora*) of the organization and a good *trabajadora*. In other words, it was her ability to work hard and be committed in their joint efforts that was given significance for how she was remembered at her funeral. Also more generally when women in ASOMA spoke positively or negatively about someone, it was often with reference to the person's ability to work, or alternatively a person's notorious laziness. Women in ASOMA often talked about the work they perform in the organization as expressing their qualities as hardworking people from the highlands, and this work thus seemed to be important for the confirmation of their self-image as hard-working people. For instance, they often addressed this participation as marking their difference from *mestizos arequipeños*, and as confirming their ability to work for others, for each other and to gather big work parties.[9] Correspondingly, *arequipeños* were sometimes spoken of with contempt or anger, for not knowing how to work hard, and for only thinking about themselves. People who did not take part in this kind of work were also spoken about as conceited, as thinking of themselves as *gente criolla* or as better than others. Particularly at anniversaries and the like, these issues were highlighted through paroles with the words '*Mujeres trabajadoras, juntas trabajamos por el pueblo*' (Women workers, together we work for the neighbourhood). The significance of working hard and co-operating was also underlined by leaders in their attempts to motivate the participants. Before the opening of the bakery, for instance, the president of ASOMA, Leonarda, reminded the women that they should not work against each other but work together and cooperate, because only by cooperating is it possible to *progresar*. By their participation in communal work then, people seemed to position themselves – and be positioned – as poor and hard-working people from the highlands.

In the literature from the rural Andes, it has been documented how work parties may take different forms such as *ayni*, *minka* and *faena*. In the rural town Huaquirca in the Peruvian Andes, Gose (1994) outlines the significance of different

[9] To be regarded as a good and complete social person also depends on the participation and fulfilment of obligations in festivals and rituals. Indeed, these dimensions are often inter-connected.

work forms with respect to agricultural cycles and the understanding of social relationships, where a move from *ayni* to *minka* distinguishes the seasons, as well as the differences between *runa* and *mistis*.[10] He illustrates how the organization of *minka* involves a group of people coming to work on the land or house of a patron and receiving food and drinks in return. He underlines that the patron in these cases does not, however, do the same kind of work in return, because of his higher social status. Instead, he repays the work in the form of food and drinks. *Minka* thus represents a hierarchical form of exchange, while *ayni* in contrast is based on a more horizontal form of exchange. In *ayni*, work is performed on a rotational basis and interchangeably repaid in the form of similar work, without including the non-reciprocal work that characterizes the work for patrons. One of Gose's points is to demonstrate how these different work forms are constitutive of unequal social relationships, and made significant for people's identification with respect to class belonging. This, he underlines, is made relevant not only in the hierarchical relationship of *minka*, but also in the egalitarian relationship of *ayni*, and illustrates the cultural dynamics of class. It is therefore important to acknowledge that people's participation in communal work projects cannot simply be seen as a cultural practice that confirms a common identification as hardworking people from the highlands, but as a constitutive dimension of class in the Andean context. Indeed, the notions of communal work have further been reconstructed through the discourses of state and NGO agencies, in a reinvention of tradition as previously noted. Communal work practices can on the one hand be considered an egalitarian practice for community construction, and on the other hand as reminiscent of hierarchical relationships and the recruitment of collective work among *indios tributarios* and dependency ties to patrons. In the urban context, it is not primarily a neighbour or landowner who provides the food and drinks in return for work (like in *minka*), but a representative from the state or NGO.

The way in which people in Jerusalén often stressed hard work as a central factor of identification could also be seen to express a kind of counter-identity, or a way in which to express antagonism towards those who dominate. It can be seen as a contemporary expression of Gledhill's (1994) point that colonialism not only produced artificial categories of identification, but also drew people into the process of objectifying their traditions and using them counter-hegemonically (1994:188). However, the notions thus used by the marginalized to express difference or contest the dominant are often the same notions that the dominant use to subjectify citizens as a form of governmentality. In other words, through the reinvention of tradition, elites sometimes manipulate oppositional discourse to their own advantage. It indicates how the significance of work for the conceptualization of personhood is a complex and somewhat contradictory issue. Through the stress on Andean practices of communal work in official projects of

[10] Quechua for *mestizo*, or powerful other.

development, 'cultural traditions' are in many ways essentialized and naturalized as a specific 'cultural condition'.[11]

The perspective on development projects as a form of governance has gained significant ground in developmental studies inspired by Foucault's work on discipline and governmentality (1977, 1991). Important for these perspectives is the view that development projects involve a subjectification of participants and make people govern themselves through the creation of a certain kind of citizen. The relationships that are produced in this manner are what Foucault (1977) refers to as disciplinary power, that is, a modern form of governmentality based on the construction of self-regulating subjects. Power, in this sense, implies the regulation of everyday behaviour and individuals' subjectivities, so that the authorities may regulate the identities of its citizens without the use of force (Schild 1998:97). In this perspective, official programmes in new urban neighbourhoods – such as the *comedores* and *vaso-de-leche* – can be seen to involve a disciplinary form of power based on the creation of subjects as productive and self-helped, market-friendly and credit-worthy (see Alvarez, Dagnino and Escobar 1998, Rose 1999, McNeish 2001, Lazar 2002). This aspect of subjectification is illustrated especially in the notion of *capacitación* (or training) in the projects of state and NGO agencies in Jerusalén. The term *capacitación* can be translated as training or educational formation, and is used to refer to the courses in which the women in ASOMA take part and are trained, that is, in issues ranging from business and production forms to organizational leadership and women's rights. The general recruitment of communal work on which these projects are based can further be seen to involve a subjectification of inhabitants in a way that also entails a creation of *docile bodies* (Foucault 1977) that are accustomed to working hard, together and for little. It can be an example of Foucault's point that, 'Discipline increases the forces of the body (in economic terms of utility) and diminishes these same forces (in political terms of obedience)' (Foucault 1977:138). The emphasis on traditions for communal work is in this regard an important condition for the realization of the state's attempt to improve, modernize or develop new urban neighbourhoods.

Indeed, the realization of these projects generally relies upon a collective, embedded form of economic rationality by drawing on kinship and informal neighbourhood relations to secure the completion of infrastructure or the repayment of loans. This state-provided welfare is therefore possible only because families, kin, neighbours and NGOs take up the slack (see Lazar 2002, Rivera Cusicanqui, Arnold et al. 1996, McNeish 2003). By effectively navigating between 'disembedded' and 'embedded' economic rationalities, Lazar notes that many of these projects are thus built upon people's existing networks of family and friends, and cultural understandings and obligations (2002:230). In Jerusalén, 'embedded' economic rationalities are made important alongside the 'disembedded' not only through the emphasis on communal work as noted above, but also the way in which these projects generally build upon or serve to re-create kinship and neighbourhood

11 A similar point is made by Ramos (1998) in her study from Brazil.

relationships through social obligations and mutual help. This is reflected in the participants' motivations to take part, that is, to improve their situation and enjoy the social relationships that this work involves.

Gender and Modernity

It is important in the continuation of this to ask why so many of these projects of development in new neighbourhoods are directed at women in particular. The background for this focus on women is of course complex, and partly it is a response to the demands of international organizations and donors to give importance to gender or women's issues, and partly an effect of women's own initiatives and struggle to improve their own situation as well as that of their families and neighbourhoods. The integration by the state of these initiatives into official programmes has nonetheless re-confirmed a focus on women, in a way that has made women and gender issues central to the authorities' attempt to modernize and 'civilize' these new urban areas. In this regard, the projects aimed at women seem to be based on specific assumptions about women's role and engagement as primarily connected to the household and the family.

Many of the courses and projects of state and NGO agencies in Jerusalén seem to be aimed at making women into 'urban' or 'modern' citizens, conscious of their rights and economically responsible on the basis of what are regarded as women's tasks. When describing how the women's groups were initiated, Juana said that officials from the local municipality in Mariano Melgar came to encourage women to get together to cooperate more and 'increase their consciousness' about different issues, learn new things and protest against the beatings from men, etc. Indeed, many of the premises for projects and courses in ASOMA have come to be defined by officials from state or NGO agencies, and are thus informed by a predominantly middle-class point of view that often differs from the women's own experience and vocabulary. In the meetings and courses arranged by state or NGO agencies for women in ASOMA, their point of departure was generally a representation of indigenous women as marginalized and oppressed, thus expressing very specific ideas about the lives and needs of these women. The concern in the courses was often health in general and reproductive health and birth control in particular. However, the information given about birth control for instance seemed to be repeated with a seemingly exaggerated frequency. The reason for this appeared to be the facilitators' assumptions of the women's ignorance about these matters, as well as the presumption that Andean women have too many children.[12] In this manner, the officials expressed a somewhat stereotypical point of view on women in the neighbourhood.

Through the involvement of state and NGO agencies, the women are in this manner made the objects of 'expert knowledge' in programmes that involve training

[12] Important to note here is the massive sterilization campaign of indigenous women during the period of Fujimori.

as well as stereotypes, new spaces of action as well as discipline. This indicates how the official involvement in local organizations can be seen to entail the stimulation of specific forms of *gendered* subjectivity. In this regard, the projects aimed at women in new urban neighbourhoods can be understood as an attempt to transform indigenous womanhood – often associated with 'impurity' or seen as radically different and 'dangerous' – into a 'civilized' form of womanhood, through the promotion of qualities related to respectability, home and household. This is in many ways accomplished by the representation of these women as having a particular need of protection and training (or *capacitatión*). In relation to discourses on *mestizaje* and civilization in Bolivia, Stephenson (1999) illustrates how indigenous women and their bodies historically have been ascribed a particular significance. By exploring state projects aimed at indigenous women through a focus on household and fashion, hygiene and nutrition, she demonstrates how these issues are made important in the authorities' attempts to create political, economic and cultural homogenization. She stresses how women are made central in official representations of the 'Indian', and thereby ascribed an important role in the understanding not only of 'cultural origins', but also cultural *change*. Stephenson relates this to a modern imperative that demands a replacement of the Indian woman and mother by a Westernized *mestiza*, and argues that state projects of modernization therefore give the household a central importance as an arena for maintaining a division between a culturally known and 'civilized' inner part and a culturally unknown and 'barbarian' outer part. The responsibility for this maintenance is ascribed to the idealized and acculturated *mestiza*, who is thus given a significant position in reproducing the nation. Such insights can furthermore be related to Ortner's (1996) exploration of how, in stateless societies, women have gone from being represented as dangerous and polluting, to become represented as weak, clean virgins in need of protection in state organized societies. She thus relates what she sees as significant changes in the representations of women and womanhood to the development of states, and particularly to the increased significance of social mobility in state society characterized by a greater degree of social differentiation. According to Ortner, the understanding of women as needing protection is a condition both for patriarchal structures as well as for more individual attempts to achieve social mobility in a society characterized by social differentiation.

Some of the courses arranged in ASOMA also involved the presentation of films, and a common theme in these films is migrant women who suffer because of men who beat them or spend all the money on alcohol. There was thus an emphasis on the ways in which women in Andean neighbourhoods and communities are more marginalized and oppressed than other women in society. In these representations, the counterpart of this marginalized and suffering Andean woman was her violent husband. Although violence in partner relationships is not uncommon in the Andes (see also Harris 1994, Harvey 1994, Lazar 2002), this imagery held by external officials regarding female subordination and male violence among people from the highlands seemed to be about more than gender relationships, since it simultaneously reflected an exaggerated idea about women from the highlands as more subordinated than other women and as suffering more from male dominance and violence. In this manner, the need among women to receive training and protection was legitimized, and their position as marginalized and suffering was ascribed to their relationships with men. However, this way of representing migrant women served to under-communicate the significance of economic differences and social class in the Peruvian society as one of the reasons for their marginalization and suffering. Relating this to Ortner's perspective, it can be seen as an attempt to redefine the image of Andean women – from seeing their position and behaviours as inappropriate, dangerous or polluting to making them into subjects in need of protection or training. Women's already existing or established competence and position, for instance in relation to income-bringing activities or trade, appeared at the same time to be under-communicated. In this manner, some of these projects are designed in a way that does not seem to take into consideration the fact that many women already have years of experience in working to make an income. These representations therefore appear as an attempt also to 'civilize' other ways of being gendered, or other ways of acting out womanhood that are considered 'uncivilized' and 'non-modern'. It illustrates how ethnic stereotypes are made the subject of gendering, and how gender is 'culturalized' or 'racialized'. It also indicates why women are often made key subjects in projects of change and modernization or development.

When it comes to the responses of the women in ASOMA themselves to these courses, many did stress the value and usefulness of some of the things they learned. In particular, they mentioned the courses in human and women's rights, and some said that through these courses, they had been introduced to concepts and ideas that they had applied in their personal life. At the same time, their recognition of and identification with the representation of migrant women as suffering and suppressed by their men was by no means unambiguous. More often they presented themselves as hardworking and economically responsible *trabajadoras* in ways that I have previously illustrated. So while the projects of state and NGO agencies in many ways have made the women in ASOMA into objects of stereotypes and clientification, it is therefore important to note that the women also negotiate dominant notions of gender and the identities they are ascribed. They not only transgress social and spatial categories by performing work in the streets and often work which is physically hard, but also contest social categories and oppositions by playful imitations and exaggerations similar to the joking among traders as previously described. So while Blondet (1990:31) has argued that women's involvement in local organizations serves to reproduce and not challenge any of the ideological precepts that support a division of male and female spheres as the private is extended into the public, these organizations may also involve a potential for negotiating dominant notions about women's roles and expand their spaces of action. It is worth noting a point by Rubin (1998) in this regard, namely that the often hybrid practices of social organizations may serve to blur and defy the dichotomous representations of public and domestic life (1998:254). Through this blurring of dichotomous representations, gender is made significant for the realization of ambiguous spaces for citizenship in new urban neighbourhoods.

New Careers and the Differentiation of Opportunities

Due to her position as the president of ASOMA for many years, Leonarda has acquired significant experience as a leader. She knows how to speak for the group and motivate people, she is familiar with the bureaucrat language and procedures, has experience from meetings with state and NGO agencies and knows how to cultivate financial support. Lately, she has also become involved with leadership in one of the neighbourhood committees as a treasurer, and is also among the few women with a stable job, in a factory. Among the older generation in the neighbourhood is another woman called Justina who used to have an important position as an organizational leader. She started as the president for the mother's groups, a position she had for several years. Probably as a result of this position and the experience it represented, she was later voted in as the president of the central assembly of neighbourhood committees in Jerusalén, thus becoming the first woman to hold this presidency.[13] In this manner, there is a tendency that certain people establish themselves as leaders in local communities by moving between different leadership positions. Leadership in local organizations may even represent a new kind of career[14] for people in new neighbourhoods, a fact that is recognized also by the members more generally.

There were several occasions in which the women in ASOMA stressed what they regarded as more problematic aspects of the organization. Some for instance were dissatisfied with the co-ordination or amount of work obligations, and others complained about the distribution or amount of food rations. In these complaints, it was primarily the leaders of the organization who were made objects of criticism, also with respect to the leaders' ability – or lack of ability – to find external sources of funding. A notion of progress was often applied in these complaints, as people underlined that the organization no longer contributed to progress ('*no hay progreso*'). An increasingly common attitude was also that only the leaders gain the real benefits, for example that they are the ones who have access to resources, work and contacts, and an opportunity to make a career. What was more, the women often talked about their suspicion that the leaders were misusing their positions by taking money or food rations for themselves.

One of the previous treasurers in ASOMA gained particular attention due to the widespread suspicion that she had misused her position. It was said, for instance,

---

13 Lazar (2002) has similarly noted how many leaders in neighbourhood committees in El Alto had previous experience as political leaders, for example in trade unions or mother's clubs. This may be because people with prior experience of organizing will be more politicized or more confident, and more ready to take on leadership positions (ibid:82). There is also an idea that after long enough residence, it becomes your turn. This is very similar to what happens in the countryside, where leadership positions rotate between households (see for instance Abercrombie 1998).

14 Paulina Arpasi, an indigenous woman from Puno and one of Perú Posible's congress members, similarly started her career as a leader in local organizations.

that she had hidden away money and goods from the shop that ASOMA used to run. Since she had been hired by the local authorities in a permanent position as a cleaner, she was also accused of having misused her position to get this job through her contacts and numerous meetings with people in the municipalities while being a leader. As in other cases, it was also in this case difficult to assess the veracity of such accusations. It represents a kind of 'corruption talk' that was in many ways typical of people's suspicions, not only in relation to ASOMA, but also the neighbourhood and merchant associations where people in Jerusalén were involved (see also Lund Skar 1994, Lazar 2002). Similar suspicions came to expression in the period after one of the leaders in ASOMA, Ana, suddenly died during one of my fieldwork trips as previously mentioned. She used to be responsible for distribution for the milk programme, and when she died the women needed someone to take over. At the following meetings many women underlined that they wanted a strong leader who was able to speak well to people – but not necessarily one who could read and write.

Norma, an unmarried woman in her 30s was the one most strongly suggested both by leaders and the other members. Although this was not explicitly mentioned as a requirement, it is important to note that Norma was one of the more fluent in reading and writing. This is interesting to see in relation to a point made by Lazar (2002), that in the city, professional qualifications of whatever kind are highly valued for leadership positions. Indeed, she notes that it is common for Andean communities to choose leaders who show ability to mediate with the '*mestizo*' world (Altamirano 1979), and education is seen to personify that (Lazar 2002:83). This may also be part of the reason why, as I will come back to, leaders in these organizations are often re-elected despite suspicions of corruption. In ASOMA, Norma was not only among the few who were fluent in reading and writing, but also the only one I knew of who was born in Arequipa. She was also generally appreciated for her easy-going ways. Each time she appeared during this period, people asked if she wanted to run as a candidate, while Norma herself appeared to be reluctant. She said she did not want to become like one of the leaders, who she thought tended to hide away money and food that belongs to the whole group. Important to note here is that she said this as a general claim regarding leaders, and not suggesting that Ana herself had necessarily been corrupted. By becoming leader she was afraid she would be pressed into this kind of practice. This is one of several examples of how the participants in ASOMA often suspected leaders of exploiting their positions and misusing the other women's work, trust and engagement to gain advantages for themselves. Angelina similarly said she was certain that the leaders of ASOMA tried to fool or exploit the other members, and that ASOMA in no way had helped her to improve her own situation. She claimed that she did not even get anything proper to eat from the work in ASOMA, and that this kind of work therefore did not help her much. Also other women said that leaders tend to leave the organization and the other women behind as soon as they have acquired something for themselves, like a steady job, a useful contact or resources of some kind, while the rest of them just continue as before and in the same position as always. These suspicions illustrate what I experienced as an increasing tension in the ASOMA organization, as to whether it should function for the progress of the group or for individual participants and especially leaders.

As noted by Lazar (2002), it is important to understand this kind of 'corruption talk' as an idiom for people's attempts to negotiate and control the position of local leaders in their interaction with state institutions and international NGOs. According to her, these rumours and accusations show a struggle between the perception that personal material gain is the most important motivation for leaders, and at the same time a strong conception of communality[15] (ibid:90). She argues that corruption can thus be seen as the most important trope through which rumour and gossip are used to make and resist claims for power or leadership positions,[16] as well as being a way to evaluate community leaders and articulate values about the use of power (ibid:78). As illustrated in the case of ASOMA, this 'corruption talk' seems to fuel and be fuelled by the tension between collectivist and individualist values and interests, and is informed by the ambiguous or hybrid spaces for citizenship created in processes of urbanization. Indeed, these accusations can be seen as a result of the maintenance of a certain level of illegibility in these spaces as previously argued.

The making of *comadres* between leaders and members of the organization was also sometimes criticized as just another example of the problem of corruption. Some leaders were for instance accused of making *comadres* with each other and a whole range of ordinary members in order to secure their loyalty and thus get away with their misuse of position for personal benefit. Indeed, in a previous chapter I have illustrated how some participants reinforced certain relationships in ASOMA by continually creating ties of *compadrazgo*, both among and in relation to leaders, as well as to NGO and state officials. So while relations of *compadrazgo* on the one hand can serve to create trust and confidence in organizational networks, the creation of such relations can on the other hand also cause distrust by accommodating for the corruption of leaders.

---

[15] In this respect, Lazar underlines that the idea that leaders should work for the common benefit of the community rather than for personal interest is a distinction which broadly maps onto the private/public distinction made in Western definitions of corruption (2002:81).

[16] Andean ethnographies tend to view community leadership in rural areas as an obligation that is often very expensive, and that prestige and duty prevail over material interest (see for instance Abercrombie 1998). Also in the city, leaders underline that they spend their own money on all the work that they do, and people do to a certain extent realize that nobody works for nothing and should at least receive some re-compensation. As noted by Lazar, payment for community activity is thus an ambiguous issue, as leaders tread a fine line between being fairly recompensed for their work and spending the zone's money on themselves (ibid:84).

The 'Un-making' of Communal Work? A Decline in Participation

During my fieldwork in 2001, 2004 and 2007, I saw that the number of participants in ASOMA had been declining since my first fieldwork in 1997. There are probably different reasons for this, and the decline can partly be related to changes in financial resources and the reduction in support from official and NGO institutions. There was for instance a reduction of state and municipal support due to the long duration of presidential elections in 2000 and the re-elections in 2001 after the first-round results had been rejected as fraudulent. This long-lasting uncertainty about who would form the government for the next five years affected support for local organizational projects in different ways, since the long-term economic support to continue or start new projects was not decided upon, or the support was delayed. In addition to the effects of this uncertain situation, there has also been a decline during the last decade in external support from international agencies and NGOs to these kinds of projects in Latin America. Indeed, the participants of ASOMA increasingly complained about the lack of activity and interest among NGOs, and said that the Taller still owed them food rations for work they had already done. In correspondence, one of the NGO officials told me that they now planned to move most of their support to rural areas, and focus less on women and more on the initiation of micro-credit projects in general.

The women who decided to quit also related it to their lack of time as well as their need to earn money, and they increasingly spoke about ASOMA as a waste of time. Few meetings were taking place and the work parties that used to be arranged seldom occurred (see also Schild 1998, Lazar 2002). Similarly in the neighbourhood association in Jerusalén, there seemed to have been a marked decline in participation in recent years, and many of those who used to take part did not anymore – or, as illustrated in the first chapter, they had become engaged in work groups in other newer neighbourhoods. What may appear as a general decline of this kind of participation has in this regard been seen – by the officials involved as well as among some scholars – as an indication that the situation of many of these women has improved. In contrast, my impression was that women withdrew because they needed to give preference to other kinds of work that generate an income.

Eugenia was among those who had decided to stop participating in ASOMA in order not to lose time from her work in trade. Similarly Angelina failed to turn up at meetings and work in ASOMA as she increasingly found it difficult to combine it with her business at the market. She also blamed her withdrawal on the corruption of leaders, and that the organization had come to represent a good opportunity for only a few participants, and that there is always someone in the system who ends up becoming corrupt anyway. Her daughter María has never participated in ASOMA as a member herself, but has been involved by sometimes accompanying her mother Angelina to the meetings. She nonetheless had a clear and rather critical opinion about this kind of organizational project, and underlined how glad she was that her mother had retired from participating. One day she was especially critical and exclaimed that most of these projects – like that of PRONAA as well as NGOs – do not really do any good to anyone, but only serve to make the situation look a little better. Indeed, she said that to participate in these programmes is instead the surest way to never achieve any of the progress that they are all looking for. She also claimed that it is better for people to establish a business on their own, so that they can invest what they have, be responsible for their own progress and perhaps earn some money instead of just losing time. Like María, other women were also increasingly critical of the usefulness of such organizational projects financed by local authorities and NGOs, especially so after the corruption scandal in PRONAA following the presidency of Fujimori. The changes of attitude among many women can thus be seen as related to their disillusionment not only with the leaders of the organization but also the external representatives involved. Many women said that instead of participating in ASOMA under the organization of leaders and external officials, people should rather try out a business on their own to earn money and perhaps succeed. Interestingly enough, however, there is a tendency that leaders continue in their positions for several terms, despite the fact that these positions are supposed to rotate. When I arrived for my latest fieldwork in 2007, for instance, I discovered that several of the previous leaders of ASOMA had once again been re-elected.

So, while participation in the organization used to be addressed as essential by the women in ASOMA during my first fieldwork in 1997, they no longer saw it as such during my later fieldworks. Instead, many of them stressed the value of more personal economic initiatives such as trade and business. It indicates how people no longer saw the participation in ASOMA as contributing to progress, and how the significance of collective work in this manner seems to have been 'un-made', at least concerning the participation in ASOMA. It is furthermore interesting to note a new law[17] that was enacted in 2005, saying that all those who make use of the different programmes of the state need to register with name and identification papers. The intention behind this is obviously to get an overview of how many people actually use these programmes, and to make sure that the help gets to people who really need it. Indeed, during the government of Toledo as well as the current government of García, there have been attempts to improve and modernize such programmes in order to make them more effective, or, in other words, more legible. Among participants in many popular organizations, however, these attempts have been met with resistance (see Iversen 2009).

Conclusions

By describing the participation of women in a local organization financed by state, municipal and NGO agencies, this chapter has discussed the relations of power and inequality in which people in this neighbourhood are involved. The

[17] Ley 28540, Lima 2005.

intention has been to outline how the interconnectedness and interface between community and state is negotiated and understood, and the implications of this official involvement for understandings of communal obligation and leadership. In particular, I have been concerned with the tension in ideas about the organization as involving the progress of the individual or that of the group, and how these notions are negotiated. In so doing, I have reflected on the differentiation of possibilities between leaders and participants, and discussed how leadership in local organizations is negotiated as an appreciated and valued contribution to the community on the one hand, and as an opportunity for personal improvement on the other – and an object of distrust and critique.

The recruiting of communal work by official agencies can be seen to reflect and reinforce certain relations of power and inequality in Peruvian society. The training or *capacitación* that these projects entail further seem to involve a hegemonic construction of subjects in the improvement and 'development' of new urban neighbourhoods. I have therefore argued that while the programmes of state and local authorities in these neighbourhoods can be seen as projects of modernization and *mestizaje*, they simultaneously involve a reproduction of difference by relying on a notion of the communally oriented and hard-working people from the highlands. This illustrates how the official policies regarding these new urban neighbourhoods often involve a recreation of somewhat ambiguous or hybrid spaces for citizenship. The decline in participation in the ASOMA organization can be related to the tension between individual and collective values and interests, as well as some of the dilemmas that external involvement seems to produce, especially so with respect to leadership. In this respect, the chapter has illustrated how the relationship between what is conventionally understood as state and civil society has been subject to change during the past decades, due to the co-optation of local practice into official policies in a way that has also served to neutralize local initiatives and efforts. It demonstrates the somewhat contradictory effects of official policies towards new urban neighbourhoods, by serving to individualize the inhabitants on the one hand and working through the stimulation of communal work on the other. The involvement primarily of women in such organizational projects is in many ways central for how the ambiguous spaces for citizenship are (re-)created.

Chapter 7
Trade, *Contrabando* and the Moralities of Markets

In this chapter I will explore how people's involvement in trade and access to markets are negotiated in terms of Andean notions of sociality and exchange. I will do so by referring to trading activities at an outdoor market called La Feria Altiplano, where some people from Jerusalén work. The businesses of these traders are generally realized at the margins of the formal economy, and market participation is often negotiated and formulated in opposition to state bureaucracy. Of particular significance for my discussion will be how traders negotiate questions of formalization and the demands from local authorities, as well as questions of social obligation, competition and trust within the traders' association. My focus is thus on a field of practice where market participation and the access to markets are made objects of negotiation.

In most cultural contexts, the idea of 'markets' has strong moral connotations, often by its association with money and the devil or the destruction of sociality on the one hand, and modernity and consumption, or the participation in society or liberal notions of citizenship on the other. My aim here is to reflect upon how the 'moralization of markets' takes place in a specific cultural context. Economic activity and initiative, or entrepreneurship, seem to be highly valued qualities in the Andean context as elsewhere. While this valuation of entrepreneurship can be interpreted as an expression of a globalized capitalism, it is important to explore the cultural actualization of this valuation, and how it is negotiated in relation to local notions of community and obligation.

In particular, this chapter explores how the involvement in trade entails an intense cultivation of social relationships, and argues that local ideas of market participation and prosperity must be seen as informed by Andean notions of reciprocity and circulation. My focus on the negotiation of social relationships and moralities in this chapter also involves a further exploration of ritual payments and *brujería*, more specifically in relation to the market context. One of my arguments in this regard is that the continued significance of magic and *brujería* should not be seen in terms of resistance as is often asserted in studies from the Andes and elsewhere (for instance Moore and Sanders 2001, Taussig 1989), but in terms of Andean notions of reciprocity and circulation as significant for the establishment and maintenance of prosperity. In this manner, I will illustrate the significance of Andean notions of sociality and fertility to the quest for – and ideas of – economic success and progress related to market participation.

By giving a brief description of the initiation and organization of the association of traders at La Feria Altiplano, I will discuss how trade and the uses of space for trading purposes represent an arena in which the state and official laws and regulations are continually made objects of challenge and contestation. One of my concerns is the practices of *contrabando*[1] across the border with Bolivia, and the way in which they inform the negotiation of social relationships and moralities. I have previously noted that several women in Jerusalén work in trade, some by selling on foot (*ambulante*) and a few from pitches at one of the many outdoor markets in the city, and yet others by travelling to bring contraband goods from Bolivia. The people involved in trade in Jerusalén work in different parts of the city, but I have chosen to focus on one such market context in particular. I begin by describing the trading and contraband activities connected to this market, and then discuss the establishment of the merchant association and the negotiation of moralities among traders in relation to official interferences and questions of informality. Then I turn my attention to the general significance and understanding of social relationships among traders at this market, a section that is followed by an exploration more specifically of practices of reciprocity and ritual payments.

Trade and Negotiations over Space

La Feria Altiplano is a crowded and colourful marketplace located near the avenue of Mariscal Castilla, about ten minutes away from the city centre of Arequipa. The term *Altiplano* (highland) refers to the close association of the Feria with the Andean highlands, and people sometimes said that 'the soul of this market has its origin in the highlands'. This expression reflects the fact that most of the traders at the Feria have migrated from the highlands, or still live in highland communities – mainly around Puno or Juliaca – and regularly travel to Arequipa to sell their merchandise. The present location of the Feria was established after several years during which a group of traders occupied land in a range of different areas of the city for purposes of trade. After they initiated this collective use of land in the early 1980s, the traders had constantly been fined or removed by the police due to their informal/illegal use of space. These difficulties – in establishing stable conditions for trade – resulted in the creation of an association of traders and finally their acquisition of an area that they formally bought in 1999.

Angelina is currently regarded as a quite successful business-woman among her neighbours, friends and colleagues, not only because she is a trader and has managed to make a living out of it, but also because she has established her own pitch where she sells her goods.[2] To establish a permanent place from which to sell is something she would probably not have accomplished without also becoming a member of the merchant association of the Feria. Several times Angelina told

[1] *Contrabando* refers to the smuggling of goods across the borders.

[2] Her pitch is located under the section for clothes and textiles.

me the story of how she, for several years, struggled to establish herself as a trader, selling in the streets as an *ambulante* (walking trader) without a permit or proper pitch. During these years, she sometimes went to the Feria Altiplano and sold her goods from a blanket close to the other more established traders who were members of the merchant association. Angelina recalls that although working more or less informally like herself, some of the more established traders and members of the Feria made a big issue about her not being a member and continually had her thrown out. Other traders told me similar stories about how hard it had been to establish themselves as a trader, and they commonly used terms like *lucha* (struggle) and *sufrimiento* (suffering) when describing their lives as traders.

As Angelina became more experienced within the trade, she established some useful contacts and little by little managed to save some capital. Her aim was to invest on a grander scale and meet the obligations of becoming a member of the association, a membership that involves the buying or renting of an individual pitch from which to sell, as well as regular fees and the participation in work parties. Like Angelina, most traders have to rely on the help and support of family and kin, both to assist at the pitch in busy periods of the day or the year, but also sometimes to get loans to make new investments. In and around the Feria, there are still large numbers of traders who are not members of the association but continue as *ambulantes* and sell while walking with a tray or sitting on the ground. These walking traders do not usually have a permit, nor do they pay taxes to the local authorities, and are repeatedly thrown out of the place, mainly by the police or the guards hired in by the association, only to return a few minutes later. All over Arequipa one can see traders walking around selling like this, at all times of the day and night. The responses of the urban authorities to these more or less informal economic activities vary from tacit acceptance to occasional moves or campaigns to abolish them. In many ways, the authorities' variable and somewhat inconsistent approaches illustrate how a certain level of illegibility in relation to these economic activities is often maintained.

As demonstrated in a previous chapter, the access to space represents an important and much contested factor in processes of mobility and settlement, and similarly so for earning a living through trade. There are a variety of ways in which spaces in the urban context are used, occupied or informally claimed in people's attempts to earn a living. For instance at the Banco Nacionál that is located in the centre of Arequipa, there are a couple of women who have made the often long queues in this bank into a source of income by selling places in the queue to impatient customers. A whole range of official fees and taxes must be paid in this bank, and the line is generally extremely long and tiresome. One of these women, Manuela, comes from Jerusalén each morning to spend the whole day queuing up and selling her place in one of the long lines in front of the bank desks. Approximately ten soles a day are gained through this kind of work, and it thus takes long hours to earn very little. But as one of the women underlined, it is nonetheless worth the effort as long as there are no other jobs to be had. In answer to my question as to whether the guards in the bank gave them any trouble, she said that they actually tended to treat them quite nicely. They mostly let them continue their business without interfering, because they are aware that there is a scarcity of jobs. This indicates instances in which the acknowledgement among public officials of high unemployment – in this case among guards – can create a basis for more or less stable, while informal, work conditions, for instance through this kind of mutual agreement.

In addition to many people's self-employment in the mines where they extract stones for stone-washed jeans, another widespread practice in the area above Jerusalén is the utilization of garbage and garbage dumps as an income source. There are a few people from Jerusalén who come to this garbage dump to find objects that may be useful for re-sale or recycling. Certain objects are thus carefully selected, gathered, sorted and then sold to the Parque Industrial or other enterprises. Most of the people who work like this seem to struggle to define a certain area of the garbage dump as 'their own', so that nobody can just come by and take the most valuable objects away. Some even try to restrict the area by bringing dogs along to accompany them and drive intruders away. They also leave some of the dogs behind during night hours, in order to guard the place and the valuable objects that they sometimes leave behind for the next day. In this manner, space in the urban context is continuously put to new use and commercialized in new ways, not only through occupations and the privatization of new plots of land as previously discussed, but also through commercial activities. There are in this regard constant negotiations about the use and (re-)definition of space in the urban context, not only between traders and authorities, but also between traders or other citizens who try to make a living. This negotiation particularly concerns the how, when and by whom certain localities are to be used or not. What is interesting about the Feria is how traders have managed to get access to land by organizing as a group of traders, and thus making way for communal work arrangements and finally the establishment of a permanent market.

The Merchant Association

The merchant association of the Feria currently consists of about 1500 members, and collectively they own the land close to Mariscal Castilla where the market currently functions. Communal work has been organized to prepare the area for use, including the installation of water, electricity, toilets and a parking lot, and the materials have been financed through the collection of money from members. Money has also been collected among members to buy the land and to cover the expense of formalizing ownership. As a result of the merchant organization then, the activities of the traders are increasingly becoming formalized and cannot simply or unambiguously be addressed as 'informal'.

The goods offered at the Feria are mainly agricultural products like fruits, vegetables, herbs, meat or milk-products, as well as textiles and artisan crafts. In addition, there are also electrical supplies and a wide range of industrial products that are either imported or smuggled (*contrabando*) into Peru from Bolivia, where prices tend to be much lower. In addition to the *contrabando* merchandise from Bolivia, there are also other goods that are illegally produced in Peru, often pirated-CDs and illegal computer software. At the Feria, people can buy or sell all kinds of goods at cheaper prices than in other, more formalized retail outlets in the city, and poor as well as wealthy people come to the Feria to do their shopping. More formalized enterprises also tend to rely on the Feria as a supplier of crucial services and goods.

The merchant association is divided into different sections for different kinds of merchandise, and in addition to the leadership positions in the general committee, each section has a separate committee of leaders who are elected for two years. Leadership is supposed to rotate, and membership involves the acquisition of an individual pitch, the participation in work parties, and regular fees for maintenance, salaries to the guards, etc. While most members of the Feria initially began as small-scale traders and *ambulantes*, many of them currently run well-established businesses from their permanent – sometimes multiple – pitches. However, as the case of Angelina demonstrates, becoming a member has not necessarily been easy. In order to be accepted into the association, Angelina had to perform a great number of tasks requested by the leaders, such as taking part in *faenas* (communal work) for the construction of infrastructure, cooking and cleaning during festivals, and all before she had even joined the association. Angelina was thus accepted only after proving her commitment through her hard (and non-reciprocal) labour, as well as accepting the often humiliating manner in which she was spoken to. This illustrates the significance of the ability to endure (*aguantar*) among people from the highlands, not only as a cultural value in the way illustrated in a previous chapter, but also for inclusion in social networks and cooperative groups. After she became a full-time member, she has several times been asked to stand as a candidate for leadership positions in the association. Until recently she has chosen to decline these requests because of what she regards as her own lack of competence, especially in reading and writing. However, recognizing that these positions are supposed to be taken on a rotary basis, she finally agreed to accept the position of treasurer (*tesorera*).

The last time I was in Arequipa in April-May 2007, the issue of land ownership was still in question. Although the association had acquired the title of ownership for the area as a whole, they had not yet managed to acquire the final titles of ownership for individual members. One of the reasons for the delay was that all the demands made by the municipality for sanitation and parking had not been met, and the money collected for the purpose had apparently disappeared. According to rumours, this was due to the corruption of the leaders, who had apparently stolen it. Other rumours suggested that the municipalities were reluctant to give them the final titles anyway because of their plans to use the area for other purposes. This illustrates how the tension between collective and individual organization of and entitlements to land is often maintained, thus reflecting the somewhat ambiguous spaces of citizenship in the city for people from the highlands. Indeed, it may illustrate how a certain level of 'illegibility' is maintained also through the authorities' approaches to these matters.

Smuggling from Bolivia

Some of the merchandise offered at the Feria is brought by *contrabandistas* (smugglers) who regularly travel to Bolivia to bring back different goods, mainly electronic articles and industrial products of all kinds, such as soaps, cigarettes, clothes, technical artefacts, toys and sweets, as well as coca leaves and some agricultural products. The incentive for this smuggling is that wages and prices are generally lower in Bolivia than in Peru, so that people can buy cheaply in Bolivia and sell at a profit across the border. This price difference is the result of a variety of factors, such as the lower industrial production and poorer economy in Bolivia, and that Bolivia's borders with its neighbours are long and difficult to control. Some of these contraband goods have first been smuggled into Bolivia from Brazil, Ecuador and Argentina, and from Bolivia the goods continue into Peru. These practices should be seen in light of Seligman's (2004) point that people in the Andes have long traditions of learning to use space and regional differences to their advantage. People have not only used altitudinal differences actively by growing and controlling different kinds of crops and livestock, but have also used these differences to develop cross-regional practices of trade and barter. Seligman notes how these practices have demanded an intense cultivation of social relationships, a cultivation that in many ways are transferred to the worlds of urban markets (2004:29–30).

Some *contrabandistas* sell their products at the Feria themselves, but many of them rely on selling their goods to other traders or bigger shops *por mayor* (in big quantities). This traffic in smuggled goods represents an important supply of products for traders at the market, and although both the police and customs officials are aware of the traffic, controls and confiscations were for a long time rather irregular. This said, during my fieldwork in 2001, the custom controls had started an intensive search for illegally imported products at all the markets in Arequipa. At the Feria, warnings reached the traders from colleagues at other markets before the customs officials arrived, so that people had time to hide their goods. Among them was Angelina, who came home at night in a taxi with all the industrial products she had bought from *contrabandistas* to hide. Since that time, however, there has been an intensification of controls and confiscations of the traffic in contraband goods. This intensification is especially related to the import of energy resources such as gas and petrol, the illegal traffic of which has increased in recent years.

Most of the smugglers are women from Puno (*puneñas*) wearing long braids and *polleras* (several layers of skirts). Although some of them live in Arequipa, many *contrabandistas* live in rural or urbanized parts of the Andean highlands, often close to the border with Bolivia. Many of these *contrabadistas* travel continuously, since they often have agricultural land and animals in the highlands, the products of which they sometimes bring to sell at the market in Arequipa along with the contraband goods. Angelina's *comadre* Paulina is one of the *contrabandistas* at the Feria who travels regularly between Arequipa and Bolivia. She lives in one of the villages[3] around Desaguadero, which is a small city located on the border, half in Bolivia and half in Peru, and therefore is a central location for trade. Paulina travels with her husband Victor and their two children, and has worked as a *contrabandista* for several years. Sometimes they go by bus, but generally they travel the distance between Desaguadero and Arequipa in the lorry of their *compadres* from home. Paulina started working as a *contrabandista* when she was a little girl, accompanying and learning from her mother who is also a *contrabandista.* She soon learned to save, invest and earn money on her own. Indeed, Paulina works with a group of *contrabandistas* who are all related to each other as kin or affines, among them her husband's sister who is also a *contrabandista.* While Paulina's father stays at home to work the land and watch the animals, Paulina travels each week between Bolivia and Arequipa with her mother, two of her sisters, a cousin and her husband and his sister. Although they make investments and take out their incomes more or less independently of each other, they travel together and develop their market strategies in co-operation. This illustrates the often kin-based and relational character of this trade, and particularly so as there is a tendency for young people to learn the trade from their parents, most often girls from their mothers or older sisters. Some of the agricultural products produced from these traders' fields are also sold at the Feria in Arequipa, but most of their merchandise is *contrabando* from Bolivia. Paulina's husband Victor had no experience with *contrabando* before they met, but has learned by accompanying Paulina on her travels. For some time, Paulina and Victor have been planning to invest in a bus, since they see this as a way of making some extra income. Back home, Paulina and Victor are regarded as a very successful couple. They have a prosperous business, own both land and animals, and have already constructed several houses in their village as well as in Arequipa. In this regard, Angelina several times commented that her *comadre* Paulina is '*bien progresada*' (has had significant progress).

It is not uncommon for *contrabandistas* to earn enough to invest on a grander scale like this. Some manage to invest in trucks for trafficking across the border as a service for other *contrabandistas* and earn extra income by charging a fee for carrying the goods. To be working as a *contrabandista* demands knowledge of regional differences in price, supply and demand, as well as the maintenance of social relationships and contacts at different places in order to secure the support of kin or fellow-traders, as well as the access to goods and customers. At the Feria, the *contrabandistas* are generally much respected for their often tough and

---

3 Due to the informal or illegal character of these activities I have omitted the name of the village.

clever ways of earning a living, which are recognized as illegal but not regarded as immoral. It is worth noting in this regard that the term *contrabandista* has different connotations than those of the English translation 'smuggler', which tends to be understood in an unambiguously negative way. At the Feria, *contrabandistas* enjoy positive respect for their hard work and what is regarded as an honest way of making a living. *Contrabandistas* are also seen as important suppliers of merchandise for the other traders, thus, as I will come back to, performing a valuable social service by regularly travelling to bring goods for the other traders to sell. Even amongst people who have come to Arequipa primarily to study and have earned a professional title, there are those who choose to start up as traders or *contrabandistas* instead of performing the profession they once struggled so hard to acquire. This choice is the result of difficulties in finding jobs, as well as the often low salaries within more formal forms of employment. These factors make trading – and *contrabando* in particular – the only or even most prosperous alternative for many.

As this chapter is intended to illustrate, the participation of Andean people in the market cannot simply be understood as a break with their rural past. This is an important point since money and markets have often been highlighted by scholars as a key signifier of European domination and the rupture with the Andean past (Murra 1980). Arguing against such claims, Harris (1995b:301–2) and others have more recently noted how the early decades of European colonial rule did witness a rapid, massive and above all successful intervention of Andean peoples in the expanding market economy. Prior to the arrival of the Spaniards, there were no markets in the Andes in a conventional sense, but there was substantial exchange involving relations between kin and neighbours as well as between regions (Murra 1980, Larson and Harris 1995). So although money and markets were previously not developed in the Inca economy, Harris argues that it is mistaken to conclude that indigenous people in the early colonial period only engaged in commercial activity under pressure, or that they resisted the introduction of money. A series of publications have provided evidence that supports her line of argument (Nash 1979, Bradby 1982, Stern 1987, Harris and Larson 1995, Saignes 1995). According to Saignes (1995), the market can be seen as the catalyst for many of the transformations that took place in the Andean context during the colonial period – that is, not the market of abstract mercantilist theories, but rural and urban markets as real places where producers, consumers and intermediaries encountered each other (ibid:191). One of my points in this respect is that today the trading activity of Andean people continues to be significant not only as a vehicle of change and an important way for people to make a living, but also as a context in which the Andean background of many traders is revitalized and acquires new importance.

In Peru, the trade in *contrabando* has expanded significantly during the last decade, and represents an important part of the total national economy, although un-documented. The failure of the authorities to control this traffic is increasingly given attention in the Peruvian as well as the Bolivian media, and the authorities have become more concerned as the operations of *contrabandistas* are seen to increasingly take on mafia-like proportions through well-organized networks (see for instance La Razón/digital 16.06.2003). There are also networks of cooperatiom among people who reside close to the borders, some of whom try to help the *contrabandistas* avoid being caught. This kind of local support is reinforced by the fact that customs officials are often disliked and their interventions criticized by people in local communities (La Razón/digital 16.06.2003, see also McNeish 2001). This local support given to *contrabandistas* is a reflection of a general questioning of official laws and interventions, and an emphasis on the right to make a living that I address below.

According to my conversations with Paulina and Victor in 2004 and during my most recent fieldwork in 2007, many *contrabandistas* experience their work as becoming increasingly difficult and have seen their incomes decline. In their view, this is the result of increasing restrictions and control at the same time as competition between traders is becoming tougher. For the *contrabandistas* in particular, confiscations had become more regular and some of them told me they had been caught several times in just the last few months. In this manner, *contrabandistas* sometimes lose the capital they have invested, occasionally with the result that they have to start working on a smaller scale again, or borrow money from relatives or colleagues in order to invest anew. After García became president in 2006, attempts to restrict the trade in *contrabando* have intensified, and trucks are more frequently stopped by customs, especially in search of illegally imported energy resources from Bolivia and Ecuador. Many *contrabandistas* were critical of this development, but only a few had started considering alternative sources of income.

Extra-legality and the Moralization of Markets

Notions of the 'informal economy' have represented a key issue in discussions about the extent and implications of small-scale trade in Latin America. The term was first coined by Hart (1973) in a study from Ghana, and the terms formal/informal soon were adopted in international discourses, for example by the International Labour Office (ILO). One of the most widely used definitions from ILO describes the informal sector as characterized by 'its ease of entry, reliance on indigenous resources, family ownership of enterprises, small scale operations, labour-intensive and adapted technology, skills acquired outside the formal school system and unregulated and competitive markets' (Hansen and Vaa 2004:10). Given the increasing heterogeneity of informal economic activities, however, many scholars prefer the term 'informal economy' rather than the 'informal sector', since it is the extra-legality rather than the type or size of the enterprise or the incomes earned there that most significantly characterizes informal economic activities (ibid:11). Indeed, another approach to that of ILO has argued that informal economic activities should be characterized primarily by their extra-legality (Castells and Portes 1989:12). In one of his later works, however, Hart has argued that given the fact that so much of the economy is *informal*, we should ask whether these terms have actually outgrown their usefulness (2001:155).

While Hart has a point, I would argue for a continued exploration of the relationship between formalized/non-formalized businesses as long as we acknowledge the often hybrid nature of their interrelationship. This is especially because the degree of formalization is of vital importance for the daily lives of traders, primarily in relation to the level of risk and insecurity connected to this kind of work. Although much of the activity at the Feria can be understood as informal, unregulated or illegal, there has also been a degree of formalization in recent years, as certain parts of this trade have increasingly been registered and legalized. Members of the Feria have finally acquired titles of land ownership (although yet incomplete), they pay the local authorities for a licence and their economic activities are generally quite visible and more or less recognized by the local authorities.[4] Nonetheless, the activities of these traders cannot be considered completely formalized either, not only because the traders do not pay taxes, but also because the merchandise they offer often consists of illegally imported products – or *contrabando*. This market is also still conceptualized among customers, authorities and police as a black market, while at the same time representing an important supplier of goods and services to more formalized enterprises in the city. It would therefore be more accurate perhaps to refer to the Feria as semi-formal, or as being realized at the margins of the formal economy and only partly documented. Indeed, the Feria is an example of the strong symbiotic links between so-called formal and informal economies, illustrated by the way in which individuals constantly move between the two, and how formalized businesses often depend on informal economic activities (see also Preston-Whyte and Rogerson 1991:2, Lazar 2002:215, Tandberg and Vaa 2004). It is similarly difficult to be precise when differentiating between informal and illegal economic activities. While informality refers to economic practices and business operations that are not registered and do not generate taxes, illegality refers to acts that break the law. In this respect, the smuggling of goods involves an illegal import that transgresses the law, *as well as* an undocumented trading of goods. What is simply an undocumented trading of goods is therefore often considered somewhat *less* problematic than the import of contraband. The Peruvian authorities also appear to be more concerned with abolishing the illegal import of goods than the forms of trade that are simply not registered or taxed.

When it comes to small enterprises in general, it is interesting to see how the authorities, in Peru as elsewhere, work to restrict economic activities that are not registered or taxed on the one hand and encourage the general involvement in small enterprises on the other. Concerning the official promotion of small enterprises in the form of micro-credit and the arrangement of training, Lazar (2002:215) argues that the authorities seek to measure and formalize what is already there in the

4 This is at the same time as the traders continue to have disputes with the local authorities about the way in which the market should function and the definition of its boundaries.

informal economy, making it 'legible' in Scott's terms (1998), and harnessing its benefits to the formal sector. While this is indeed a significant dimension, it is at the same time important to acknowledge that the interventions of the authorities are also somewhat random and thus contribute to the maintenance of a certain level of illegibility.

Since the Velasco administration in Peru sought to coordinate and institutionalize the group efforts of marginalized inhabitants in the late 1960s, similar policies were later created to accommodate collective efforts and to facilitate the formalization of informal use of land and economic activity. As previously noted, one of Fujimori's initiatives was the creation of Comisión de Formalización de la Propiedad Informal (COFOPRI), a state institution meant to assist the formalization of businesses as well as the ownership of illegally occupied land and construction of housing. These were processes that used to be especially difficult and time-consuming for people from rural areas, and de Soto (1989) has illustrated how it previously could take over 14 years for a group of traders to finalize the authorization of a market. Now, as a result of state initiatives – and to a certain extent in response to the arguments forwarded by de Soto – it has become easier to go through with processes of formalization. Nonetheless, processes of formalization may still require significant efforts in terms of time and money, and, as illustrated in the case of the Feria, an uncertain legal status is often maintained.

While being presented as the way out of poverty by de Soto, the official promotion of small enterprises has increasingly come in for criticism. For example, the official promotion of this kind of economic activity is criticized for introducing new forms of governmentality (Foucault 1991), and for involving the production of more credit-worthy and market-friendly subjects (McNeish 2003). In other words, the official promotion of small enterprise can be viewed as a way to legitimatize the abandonment of social services by the state, making people turn to the market and not the state when making their demands, with the result that people's reliance on the use of kin and neighbourhood networks, commitments and strengths is reinforced (see Lazar 2002, McNeish 2003). In this regard it is worth noting an important point made by economic anthropologists in the 1970s, namely that apparently traditional forms of economy are in fact often aspects of the way capitalist accumulation is secured (see Meillassoux 1975). More recently, Gudeman (2001:12) has argued that over the long run, the relationship between market and community is dialectical – using the term in an open-ended sense – since many activities can appear under either guise, and each is constituted in relation to the other. As I will demonstrate in the following, traders often celebrate the idea of 'the market' with reference to liberal notions of citizenship as well as Andean notions of sociality and exchange. So while their celebration of market participation could be seen as a response to global discourses of self-help and market participation, it must also be understood in relation to the traders' understandings of sociality and their own position in Peruvian society.

After Toledo became president in 2001, he expressed his concern that the traffic in *contrabando* would undermine the sale of national products and weaken both Peruvian industry and agricultural production. At the Feria, neither *contrabandistas* nor other market-traders showed any particular concurrence with this kind of argument. They commented that there are no jobs anyway, and that the authorities, police and customs officers make it impossible for people with initiative to work and earn a living. There is, for instance, a common phrase among traders expressed with great contempt in cases when someone gets caught, that '*no dejan trabajar*' (they do not let people work). They thus ascribe more significance to the value of work and the possibility of being self-supporting, than to the degree of formalization.

Traders generally do not regard the informal or illegal aspects of their economic activities as necessarily problematic, that is, unless they get caught, or are blamed for fooling their own *compañeras*. These attitudes towards informality and illegality reflect an understanding of morality that competes with official understandings and laws. It is an example of the sometimes contradictory claims made by state laws and local morality, since laws may forbid actions that in a local moral codex are completely acceptable (Harris 1996:2). What is more, it can be seen as an expression of a lack of belief and confidence in the good intentions and 'morality of the state' (see also Goldstein 2004). In this respect, the Feria is a context in which state laws are differentiated from local morality, and it represents a moral community in which laws are not only broken but also challenged. This is legitimized by the traders' reference to poverty and unemployment, in relation to which the state's attempts to control their trade are criticized and sometimes considered to be immoral in their own right. The attitude among traders to their semi-formal economic activities thus seems to be informed by their ideas of difference and separateness from the official community and the state (see also McNeish 2001). In this respect, the non-registered nature of people's work is legitimized not only through reference to poverty and unemployment, but also cultural stigma and racial discrimination. Through their celebration of 'market participation', traders in many ways seem to share the opinion of liberal theorists such as de Soto (1989) by seeing state bureaucracy as systematically impeding entrepreneurship.

Dangerousness or Invisibility

I have previously indicated how the trading activities of people from the highlands – and especially those of women – involve an unsettlement of dominant social and spatial categories. This is partly because these market activities are often performed by people from the rural Andes – who are sometimes represented as 'outside' modernity in local discourses, but who in fact often act as the most innovative and flexible entrepreneurs. Considering that most of the traders at the Feria are women, it is important to note how the work of these women is sometimes regarded as improper and not suited for '*gente decente*'. Hence, at the same time as women's work and gaining of income is both valued and seen as necessary, there is also an idea that the work of women at markets and in the streets is not proper for those who want to be regarded as '*gente decente*'. Indeed, the imageries connected to female traders is manifold and somewhat ambiguous, since they are appreciated as tough and strong on the one hand, but also seen as somewhat rude, dirty and dangerous on the other. In this respect, it is worth noting that one of the main issues of negotiation between the Feria association and municipalities is that of hygiene, an issue that also entails symbolic dimensions in the sense that it reflects how the market activities of women are seen to involve a destabilization of social categories and boundaries.

De la Cadena (1996) has similarly observed that as early as the 1940s and 1950s, the educated classes in Cuzco regarded market women as 'vulgar' and 'grotesque', and that their very presence in the city was written about as a public scandal (ibid:131). In another study from rural Chitapampa outside the city of Cuzco (de la Cadena 1995), she has also argued that due to their work within trade, women are considered more Indian than men. In Cuenca, Ecuador, Weismantel (2001:45) has illustrated how the *cholas* at the markets are seen as *groserías* (images of dirtiness), and often in contrast with the *cholas* who work as servants. She thus underlines that unlike the peasant girls who stay at home in the countryside or work as servants, submitting to their employers' wishes, women who sell in the market undergo a disturbing transformation. Similarly, with reference to the *cholas* at the market places of Cuzco, Seligman (2004) has argued that the boundaries of this social category are ill-defined in terms of race, class, ethnicity or geographic locus. Despite being such a familiar sight in Andean cities then, it has been noted that market women are still seen as 'matter out of place' within dominant gender ideologies (Weismantel 2001:46). Following Douglas (1966), Weismantel argues that we can read a kind of moral hygienics in these responses, as ideas about 'dirt' can be seen as 'the by-product of a systematic ordering and classification of matter, in so far as ordering involves rejecting inappropriate elements' (1966:35). The association of markets with dirt is thus not necessarily related to their actual dirtiness, since the perception of un-cleanliness involves symbolic as well as practical judgements. To the elites, the insalubrious conditions in which market women work appear as signs of dirtiness – a *grosería* – in a way that is seen to violate 'the ideal order of society' (Weismantel 2001:45–6). According to Weismantel, the 'offense against order' committed by market women is related to sex just as much as to 'race', by violating a cultural order in which the public sphere is masculine, and feminine realms are enclosed and hidden away from the eyes of strangers. The market woman is thus seen as an indecent figure, arousing rumours of sexual anomaly as well as unsettled racial meanings (ibid:47). As illustrated in Chapter 5, these somewhat ambiguous images of indigenous women can be further illustrated by the way in which they are sometimes referred to as *machistas*, a term that otherwise mainly refers to men.

The ambiguity in these images of market women is also related to their ways with money and possible prosperity. For instance, women who work with trade – and the *contrabandistas* in particular – are often said to be clever at managing money (*saben manejar dolares*) and that they carry dollars under their skirts. In this regard, the images of these women are also characterized by the way in which they are seen as powerful and possibly prosperous. Although market women in different ways thus unsettle dominant discourses on womanhood – and sometimes quite explicitly and deliberately so – this does not preclude the fact that market women themselves may also integrate some of the ideas about indecency and inappropriateness with respect to their working in the streets. This is illustrated in their attitudes for instance towards food in the streets and eating while at work. Although most of them eat their daily meals in the streets or at the market (either brought or bought), there nonetheless seems to be an agreement that it is somewhat inappropriate and bad for the health to do so, because it puts one in danger of diseases and other negative (or magic) influences.

Considering the significant extent of trading activities at the margins of the formal economy, it is interesting to note that the official interferences at these markets appear to be rare or at least un-systematic. What is more, it seems as if the un-documented trading activities – of women in particular – are to a great extent accepted and permitted by the authorities as well as the public. This may be because the (un-documented) work of women appears to be considered less economically harmful – or 'dangerous' in economic terms – than the work of men (although also sometimes un-documented) and thus considered less informal/illegal. In relation to similar markets in Bolivia for instance, Lazar (2002) notes that men's activities are often more regulated than women's, partly because the authorities understand them to be more permanent and more important. This reflects the idea that it should be the man who is ultimately responsible for earning an income, and that women's economic activities are seen as extra. It reflects a point made in Chapter 5, namely that women's economic activities are often considered an extension of their domestic duties, and are therefore frequently associated with the household. Indeed, this is also a way of under-communicating the work of women, as well as the existence of un-documented trade itself. The un-documented nature of women's work is perhaps often accepted due to the obvious necessity of this kind of work due to unemployment, as well as what may even be the significance of such economic activities for the national economy and for preserving distributive capacity in the country.

Managing as a Trader

Previously I have stressed how many people actually succeed in their un-documented or semi-formal businesses, although it is important to bear in mind that this work also may involve mechanisms for further exclusion of those already excluded. This is especially so for those who never manage to become included in a network of traders such as in the traders' associations, and who are thus less likely to acquire a permanent space from which to sell their goods. Indeed, many traders have difficulties in expanding their businesses and continue working by foot all their careers. For those involved, however, this kind of work may be their only opportunity to gain any income at all.

In the business of *contrabando* as well as in regular trade, there are often large differences between those who fail and those who succeed, between those who continue to sell leftover potatoes or chocolates in the streets and those who end up investing in buses and trucks or start a factory. According to the experiences of many traders, it seems as if the successful trader is the one who manages to keep a certain balance between activities that are sufficiently formalized/legalized so as not to get caught too often, and enough informal/illegal to actually earn money. The successful trader is also experienced with the management of urban *mestizo* codes, such as the Spanish language and the bureaucratic system, the management of loans and treatment of customers. In order to be successful, it is necessary to be *vivo* (smart, creative, energetic) it is said, and to know how to avoid theft or being cheated.

I several times heard traders refer to situations in which they had been cheated, either by customers or other traders or retailers. Shortly after she had started her own business at another market in town, Angelina's daughter María had such an experience when she was travelling to buy merchandise. She had started travelling to Desaguadero and Bolivia each month to buy certain artefacts like rolls of film and cigarettes at a cheap price to sell from her pitch in addition to pirated CD copies. In Desaguadero, she could get things significantly cheaper than in Peru, and on some units she could earn about 20 centavos per piece, which is much more than she otherwise would have gained. On one of these trips, she went to Cuzco on the way back from Desaguadero in order to bring some artisan crafts and simultaneously let her son see the ruins at Saqsaywamán. She found some nice clothes at one of the markets in Cuzco, but just after she had paid, she was startled as the trader suddenly turned back and accused her of having given her false money. She knew that the money was not false, since she is careful always to check, and suspected that the trader had switched her money with some other false money. Despite her protests, however, the trader called the police and she was taken to the police station. At the station, the police checked the rest of her money and said that all of it was false, and she had to pay the policemen 50 dollars to be allowed to leave. When returning to Arequipa, she said she was sure that she had been victim of a trap set up by the trader in co-operation with the police.

This and similar cases serve to illustrate how people in the business of trading must always be prepared to not let themselves be fooled. There is a need to be tough and self-reliant in order to be successful, and among traders, these qualities are greatly admired. As similarly noted by Mintz (1971), trading is not a business for the stupid and soft-hearted, but for the smart and strong. Each time Angelina discovered that her husband Juan had been cheated, for instance by receiving too little money or accepting counterfeit money without noticing, she scolded him and called him a *sonso* (stupid). Also in other cases I got the impression that if somebody gets fooled in business – and even if they get robbed – people often regard it as their own fault, in the sense that they must have acted stupidly and carelessly, and if they were alert or smart enough they could have prevented it. After being cheated or robbed, I often heard people say that they felt stupid, and in some cases they were also made fun of by other traders. Traders are generally easy targets for thieves since they work in the streets and have to carry their money on them. Most of the traders I know have several times experienced getting robbed, but I have never heard of anyone who has reported it to the police, partly because theft or robbery will only be investigated and therefore worth reporting if it exceeds a certain sum (which used to be set at 2000 soles). People may thus have all their valuables stolen without the possibility of police assistance.

The risk of being cheated or robbed reinforces the necessity for cultivating certain relationships of trust and support among traders. So at the same time as prosperity and success in this business necessitates that people act in an autonomous fashion, it also depends on the quality of social relationships. It depends on the ability not to be fooled or too soft-hearted, but at the same time sufficiently soft-hearted and generous so that one maintains a network of cooperation and mutual support and trust. In addition to the reliance on kin and *comadres*, the ability to establish a network of stable customers, suppliers and fellow-traders is important in the general management of business and to be informed with respect to prices, supply and demand. Through their relationships to kin, *comadres* and colleagues, some traders also accumulate capital by the arrangements of *redondillos* (money-go-rounds), as groups of people collect a weekly contribution of cash for a lottery. Loans are generally acquired from kin or colleagues as well as the bank, and the established traders at the Feria are often used to managing a range of different loans (see also de Soto 1989, 2000, Harris 1995, Lazar 2002). As similarly noted by Lazar, the mechanisms of a 'credit culture' are thus nothing new among Andean traders. She notes that this is illustrated by the central significance among traders of the relationships to particular customers or suppliers of goods referred to as *caseras* (home-maker) (2002:231). Similarly at the Feria, the relationship to *caseras* is important because it is supposed to involve a stable business relationship of security and trust. A trader must make her *casera* feel special in order for her to be loyal, and people often use the terms *casera* or *caserita* to stress this. These terms are also used when traders try to attract customers or appeal to each other in a situation of negotiation, or otherwise to initiate an exchange. Indeed, it has been suggested that the *casera* relationship illustrates what is often the traders' attempt to bridge kinship and the market (Rivera Cusicanqui 1996, with Arnold). While it has thus been argued that this cultivation of social relationships is one of the ways in which traders combat the fragmentation of social networks, my point is that such an intense cultivation of social relationships is also expression of a fundamentally different understanding of sociality in market participation, that is, as understood on *relational* terms. Social relationships and reciprocity are fundamental to this understanding of market participation, and the quality of social relationships is therefore of central importance for people's success in business.

While transactions at the Feria generally take place with the main goal of increasing capital and making capital gains for individual traders, their realization would be difficult without a joint effort. The dynamics of communal work and organization in this market context can in this regard be seen to resemble practices of agricultural work in the rural Andes, where sowing is collectively organized and harvest performed by individual households (Gose 1994). Through joint efforts and a great degree of communal work organized by the Feria association, traders have acquired a permanent location and stable conditions for trading in a business that used to be characterized by a greater degree of instability and 'informality'. Compared to the significance of communal work in agriculture, however, co-operation between traders at the Feria seems to be constantly debated and their relationships characterized by intense competition. So while the values of communal work and collective obligation continue to be important, there is a high level of competition between traders that seems to increase the tension between communal and individual interests. Arrangements concerning communal effort as well as leadership are for instance constantly debated.

At the Feria, there are several ways in which the risk involved in un-documented or illegal trade is made into a collective concern and not just a concern for individual traders. There have been cases when the police or local customs officers have come to confiscate illegal goods or ban traders who have no papers, in response to which the traders have joined forces and physically denied the police access to the area. In some of these cases, the officers have had to give up and let the traders continue as before. There are also cases in which official interferences may cause tension and conflict between the traders, however, and this is central to how questions of morality and social relationships are often negotiated. For instance, some traders seek to remove competition by informing the police about illegal aspects in the businesses of other traders. Although still relatively new in the business of trade, María has already experienced such situations a couple of times, as competing traders who sell illegally copied material similar to hers, apparently have told the police about her business. After one of these incidents María started to consider doing something legal instead, and a few months later she had bought herself a photocopier in what is now a formalized business for which she pays all the required taxes, etc.

The tension between communal and individual values and arrangements comes to expression especially through the ways in which leadership in the market association is negotiated. Members recall that from the outset, they have been preoccupied with disputes with respect to economic co-ordination, the lack of confidence in leaders, and continual accusations of corruption. At one point, such accusations even caused a previous leader to leave his house for several weeks, since he was suspected of having bought a house and bus with money from the association.

It is furthermore worth noting that while the bureaucratic rationality of the state in many ways conflicts with the work and sociality ethics of traders, there also appears to be an interesting relationship here between traders who do business through social relationships and bureaucrats who are supposed to control their economic activities. Formally employed officials may sometimes have interests in common with the more or less informally working traders, and some officials may cooperate with traders or accept payments for closing their eyes to the traders' sometimes extra-legal arrangements. In this manner, the *relational* character of trade even seems to constitute a means by which state officials at different levels of the hierarchy are able to make money from the extra-legal activities of traders. This illustrates how the level of illegibility in these practices is often maintained through the approaches of officials. Some *contrabandistas* try to stop these circuits of goods in which officials are sometimes involved, however, by destroying their goods when getting caught at the borders. For instance, I have heard that some *contrabandistas* put petrol on their goods when getting caught, so that their goods will be without value for the customs officers.

There is a range of communal obligations that constantly compete with the strategies for – and the values ascribed to – accumulation for the individual trader (Arrosquipa Quispe 2002). In this regard, it seems to be through the intersection between values of communality and personal achievement that *progreso* or success in this business is sought and sometimes achieved – but also possibly jeopardized through mechanisms of distrust and exclusion in the management of informality, instability and competition. Indeed, the relationships between partners, kin and colleagues at the Feria are also vulnerable to envy and the use of *brujería* (magic acts to do harm), in the sense that a person's ability to earn money may be destroyed. So although based upon networks of cooperation with other traders, competition and quarrels continually rise to the surface not only in the form of accusations of corruption, but also through suspicions and accusations about the (mis-) use of *brujería*. Before I discuss this, however, I want to explore how ritual payments in the market context is seen to improve success in business.

Success and Ritual Payments

Work is regarded as an important characteristic of the moral person also among traders at the Feria. Great value is ascribed to hard work and industriousness, at the same time as money is seen to be generated in other ways than merely through work or regular investments, such as through ritual contracts, payments or 'investments'. Indeed, the significance of this work ethos is closely connected with the value of reciprocity and collective consumption, thus reflecting Harris's point (2000) that people's work ethos in the Andes is informed by Andean notions of community and the fertility of exchange.

I have previously illustrated how the shared consumption of alcohol represents an important way in which people seek to maintain their relationships with each other as well as the powers of the surroundings, and similarly so among traders. Alcohol is important for the initiation and maintenance of different kinds of relationships among traders at the Feria, and before drinking, people usually pour some of it on the ground in the name of *pachamama* or the *apus*. During the celebration of the Day of the Mother at La Feria in 2007, groups of close colleagues, friends, kin or *comadres* got together, and after the official programme was over, people took turns inviting each other to drink beer. One woman started for instance by buying some bottles of beer to put in front of one of the other women as a gesture of friendship and respect. These bottles were then shared within the group, and then another woman went to buy some new bottles of beer to share. In the group I joined along with Angelina, one of the leaders of the association, Olinda, also took part. Olinda is known to be a particularly successful business woman who owns several pitches. Each time someone put some bottles in front of her, she took the foam from the bottle to put under her arms, because this is said to '*traer plata*' (bring money) she explained. Since the foam came from alcohol that was shared, she thus regarded the foam as 'fertile', or to bring money.

Many traders try to secure their success in business through the daily offerings to *pachamama*[5] and the *apus*[6] of coca, drinks or cigarettes as I have previously mentioned. In this manner, ritual knowledge and powers are considered important for the strengthening of business, and can in many ways be seen as a ritual investment. Although these ritual investments may become rather expensive and sometimes compete with concerns related to the accumulation of capital and investment in goods, most traders regard such payments as important. Among *contrabandistas* and grand-scale entrepreneurs in particular, it is common also to make a pilgrimage to specific luck- or wealth-bringing places. This is meant to secure success for large investments and risky businesses. Best known is Copacabana in the highlands of Bolivia, a pilgrimage goal for merchant people from all over the Andean region. The virgin of Copacabana – Candelaria – is supposed to be extremely prosperous, and many *contrabandistas* and traders gather there each year to celebrate her and make offerings to secure their economic success. Success in business can also be sought through payments to other saints or virgins, especially by serving as a sponsor for religious festivals or parties.

As previously mentioned, Paulina and Victor are among the more experienced and successful *contrabandistas* at the Feria, and from their business they earn enough to continuously re-invest their income. They are also committed to different social, ritual and religious obligations, and are among the many traders who travel each year to attend the festival of the Virgin of Copacabana. They go to make payments to the Virgin, and expect this to benefit their business. In 2003, however, they celebrated the patron saint of their village of origin instead. They had been appointed as *padrinos* for this festival, and were financially responsible for the occasion and for covering the expenses for costumes, food and drink. Compared to the prosperous Virgin of Copacabana, the saint of their home village is poor, and they did not really expect their input to strengthen their economic success. Instead, they accepted the appointment in order not to get punished by the saint and risk the failure of their business. They stressed that this is only one of their many other commitments to kin, neighbours and colleagues, that they try to meet regardless of the expense, even if they have to borrow the money. As a quite successful couple,

---

5 *Pachamama* is the mother earth.

6 *Apus* are the mountain Gods.

their involvement as ritual sponsors illustrates the responsibility of the wealthy to secure the prosperity of others by sponsoring parties or festivals and maintaining a good relationship with the source of their prosperity, in this case referring to the Virgin or patron saint. If they had shirked their responsibilities, they said, they would have risked exclusion and the loss of work help and gift giving that these relationships provide. This would ruin not only their own prosperity, but perhaps also the prosperity of others in their network.

In order to succeed as a trader and contribute with the regular payments to the merchant association, Angelina has borrowed money from some of her friends as well as the bank. Although she still has to struggle to return some of these loans, she now has access to capital in a way she never had before. In order to have a secure and prosperous business, she also prays to God and pays the *pachamama* or *apus* with coca leaves. Unlike many of the other more successful traders, however, Angelina has never been to the Virgin of Copacabana or visited any other saints able to confer prosperity, because of the high costs entailed by travel, food and ritual gifts. In contrast, coca leaves represent no great expense, and when she feels that a bigger payment is needed, she sometimes hires a *curandero* to make a more expensive offering (for example of liquor or an animal). However, because of the way in which her situation has improved, she has increasingly come to fear the envy of other traders as illustrated in a previous chapter. She felt that people were constantly watching her to see how well she eats, she said, because they envy her for the money she earns.

These practices of 'ritual investment' in the market context seem to vary according to the kind and scale of people's businesses. *Contrabandistas* are for instance more likely to make journeys to Copacabana and payments to *pachamama* or the *apus* than other traders who work on a smaller scale or are less likely to get caught and lose their investments. On the one hand, the higher ritual expenditure among grand-scale traders compared to that of small-scale traders may illustrate the particular responsibility of grand-scale traders as ritual sponsors. On the other hand, the higher level and expense of ritual investment among grand-scale traders also seems to depend on the risk that is implied, be that in economic or other ways. The more a person risks economically or personally then, the more necessary it is for that person to spend money on festive celebrations or ritual payments in order to compensate for the economic or other risks that are taken. Concerns related to market engagement, investment and accumulation are in this manner closely connected to ritual practices as well as social obligations. What is interesting here is the way in which these apparently differing logics are not necessarily seen to compete with respect to how money should be invested – economically, ritually or socially – but at times also to reinforce each other with regard to the ways in which ritual investment or communal obligation may increase the capital to invest in goods.

Successful business people may provoke envy among colleagues, relatives or neighbours, however, and tempt them to direct *brujería* at such a trader through the services of a *curandero*. The person who is thus made the object of *brujería* may fall ill and be unable to work or make money. When someone experiences bad luck in business therefore, it is often commented that '*la plata no para en sus manos*' (the money does not stop or stay in their hands). This condition may be interpreted as the result of *brujería.* Once *brujería* is established as the reason for a person's misfortune,[7] efforts to counter it are usually initiated. This may involve the use of herbs or a curse, the sacrifice of an animal, or other kinds of payment to *pachamama* and the *apus*. In other words, the attempts to undo an act of *brujería* often involve a reestablishment of reciprocity that includes the powerful surroundings.

Although uncommon, people said that some traders also make payments to the devil to improve their access to money. Among most traders, this kind of relationship was generally disapproved of, and it was said that one should stay away from people who '*hablan con el diablo*' (speak with the devil). After having her house robbed, María needed to replace the old entrance door that was destroyed in the burglary. She went to make an agreement with one of the saleswomen offering doors and furniture at the Feria, but when she came back she was in a bad mood. She complained that the woman had made her agree to accept an unreasonably high price. Even though she recognized this while negotiating with the woman, María said that she for some reason felt unable to do anything but accept the deal. Quite dissatisfied with herself for having been cheated, she said that the powers of the woman had been too strong for her to protest. When she told her mother, Angelina, about the incident, Angelina responded that she too had had a similar kind of experience with the very same woman. She referred to an occasion when she similarly had been tricked into buying something from this woman at too high a price herself. This, Angelina said, was probably a result of her becoming spell-bound by the woman, who she regarded as having an evil power acquired through contact with the devil.

Notions of Prosperity and the Fertility of Exchange

Discussing the symbolism of money and ritual payments in the Andean context, Taussig (1980) has argued that devil contracts should be seen as a question of resistance and not just a way to accumulate capital. According to him, it reflects the way in which money has come to be associated with the devil among wage earners and miners in the region. He claims that the association between money and the devil should be seen as an expression of the resistance and alienation of peasants in processes of integration into the money economy, and as related to the problems of proletarianism and the distortion of the 'natural economy'. Various scholars have underlined, however, that this kind of argument reflects a dualistic and oppositional thinking in anthropology that simply divides 'traditional' from

7 Generally by a *curandero* who consults the coca-leaves, or *mirar la suerte* (read the luck).

'modern' capitalist economies. Harris (1995b) has for instance stressed that the appearance of money in an economy where circulation was previously organized on some other basis has often been assumed to initiate a teleological sequence of changes in which the values attached to collective interests and socialities are destroyed and replaced by accumulation for individual gain. This, however, is not a clear-cut or unambiguous form of change, and, as Harris notes, is often conceptualized in a way that reflects European thought[8] where money itself came to be seen as evil and unnatural (ibid:302). It is important to emphasize that in the Andes, ritual payments are made not only to the devil, for example as owner of the mines (Nash 1979, Taussig 1980), but also to *pachamama* and the *apus*,[9] and are important in a range of different social relationships and *rites de passage* as previously illustrated.[10] This can serve to illustrate Harris's (1995b) argument that ritual payments in the Andean context are informed by more general notions of fertility that are associated not only with production and reproduction, but also fertility as created and maintained through a logic of reciprocity, circulation and exchange. Money for festive expenditure is seen to reproduce collective prosperity,[11] and is therefore not seen as alien or threatening *per se* (ibid:307–8), but is rather associated with fertility. Instead of being treated as antithetical to the sources of fertility then, Harris underlines that money is closely identified with them, and comes from the same sources that ensure the harvest or reproduction of flocks. By offering food, humans enter into communication with this source (ibid:315–16). Thus underlining what she sees as the general notion of fertility in the Andes, Harris notes that profits are seen to 'give birth', arguing that circulation and production is part of a single process and that we should be wary of separating them. For instance, the uses to which money among her Bolivian informants are put – the purchase of ritual materials and the acquisition of livestock – counteract any outward flow since they are both productive and 'reproductive' (ibid:310).[12]

[8] As noted by Harris (1995b:302), such a contrast, particularly in the form of self-sufficiency versus exchange, has long historical antecedents in European thought. Money often signifies the interest of individuals as opposed to that of the community, and has thus come to represent the antithesis of the holy, and a potent symbol of the evils of capitalism.

[9] Like the devils, the *apus* and the *pachamama* are unpredictable and the sources both of fertility and wealth, of sickness, misfortune and death.

[10] Harris notes that there is also an association between the devil who owns the mineral, the metal that becomes money, and the Virgin who is the Christian patron of the mine. While these spheres are symbolically contrasted in many contexts, they sometimes merge (1995b:311). The same duality is evident in Nash's (1979) description of the worship of the Virgin alongside the cult of the devils in the mining city of Oruro.

[11] According to Harris, when Laymi pour libations for the local mines, they are celebrating and ensuring fertility not just for themselves, but the whole universe. The offerings are for all the sources of wealth in whose circuits they are implicitly or explicitly involved, whether or not they personally have direct links with them. Prosperity thus seems not to be a competitive state, a 'limited good', but is desired for everybody (1995:314).

[12] *Tío* or *tía* is associated with the devil.

Those who engage in trading and make money give birth are thus thought to perform a valuable social service. This is because money, when it returns in the form of profit, is fertile, not through the process of planting and maturation, but through exchange (1995:309). In this regard, *pachamama* and the mountains are understood as guardians not only for the fertility of fields and stocks as stressed by Harris, but also, as in my study, for the fertility or prosperity of business.

Traders at the Feria hold different opinions with respect to money which illustrate the multiple and somewhat contradictory values attributed to it. Some argue that money makes people evil, and that rich people are consequently greedy and selfish, while those who are poor and humble are kinder and better people. It is not necessarily the ability to earn money that makes people dislike traders with particular success in business, however, since this kind of criticism or envy rather seems to be related to the lack of generosity. As long as they are generous, people generally appreciate and respect hard-working and successful traders. This reflects not only the significance of gift-giving in the Andean context, but also how circulation and exchange is appreciated as important values in themselves, by representing a fertilizing dynamic associated with prosperity. This appreciation of circulation and exchange can also be seen as one of the reasons why trade, in general, is valued as a good and important way to earn an income, despite its un-documented or sometimes illegal character. It is thus in the light of the Andean understandings of fertility as outlined above – or prosperity understood in relational terms – that we must explore further the reasons why practices of *contrabando* and informal trade are not regarded as problematic or immoral among traders at the Feria. It is not only a question of resistance, or of traders contesting the legitimacy of state restrictions and formalization demands, but also of the values ascribed to circulation and exchange in themselves.

This logic of circulation and exchange also has implications for how to understand the question of *brujería* in this context. Indeed, my point in this regard is that such acts must similarly be understood in terms of a *relational* logic of sociality and the understanding of prosperity, in the sense that *brujería* reflect people's attempts to reorganize prosperity through relational means. In the same way as practices of reciprocity and ritual are inherently relational, the continued significance of *brujería* is therefore also due to its relational character, although representing the *failure* of reciprocity or social relationships. So while it is often asserted that the continued significance of witchcraft and magic in modern societies should be seen as a response to the competition, individualism and alienation initiated by processes of modernization and economic globalization (for example Moore and Sanders 2001, Taussig 1980), my point is that the contemporary significance of ritual payments and *brujería* in the Andean context ought to be understood in the light of their *relational* character, in the sense that they involve the attempt to control a specific situation through relational means. Practices of reciprocity, ritual payments *and* witchcraft (or in this case *brujería*, or harmful acts) are all made relevant in the quest for success in business, and indicate the *relational* dimension in people's understandings of prosperity. Indeed, it illustrates how understandings of prosperity in the Andean context are associated with notions of fertility (Harris 1995b), that is, a general notion of fertility that is associated not only with production and reproduction, but fertility seen as created and maintained through a logic of reciprocity, circulation and exchange. This logic works to reinforce the significance of ritual payments as well as *brujería* in market participation, rather than representing a response to modernization and the globalization of the economy as is often assumed. Indeed, it illustrates the significance of Andean notions of prosperity to people's participation in markets.

Conclusions

My concern in this chapter has been how trading activities in the urban context involve an intense cultivation of social relationships, and how the participation in 'markets' is negotiated in terms of local notions of morality. Independent of its more or less informal or illegal dimensions, entrepreneurship and market participation are made objects of celebration, and can be seen as connected to how trade involves a level of autonomy that is contrasted to people's previous experiences and relations of dependency. Of particular importance to people's involvement in and understandings of markets are also Andean ethics of work, sociality and exchange. The chapter has therefore continued the analysis of relational and ritual practices from previous chapters by outlining the significance of ritual payments more specifically in the market context. The understanding of reciprocity, exchange and circulation in the Andean context as 'fertile', and as reproducing collective prosperity (for example making money 'give birth', Harris 1995b) is significantly re-created in market participation, where the quest for money and success is seen to depend on ritual payments and the fertilizing force of exchange and circulation as such. Accumulation and prosperity is therefore perceived to depend on monetary as well as ritual investments. Indeed, this understanding of exchange and circulation as in itself a force of prosperity can also represent one of the reasons why *contrabando* and informal forms of trade are not seen as immoral – despite their informal or illegal dimensions – but appreciated as a morally accepted and important way to make an income. In this regard, traders in this context do not make claims, for instance to land, with reference to 'indigenous identities' as similarly noted with respect to settlements, but with reference to their right to participate in markets.

The celebration of market participation and cultivation of social relationships is actualized within ambiguous spaces for citizenship that appear to be recreated through official approaches and the co-existence of collective and individual arrangements concerning land and labour. Indeed, the uncertain legal status of these kinds of market and trading activities is often maintained. I have therefore tried to illuminate how local ideas of market participation, reciprocity and circulation must be seen in relation to the approach also of the authorities, varying between silent acceptance and occasional moves to abolish these practices. It reflects a point made in Chapter 1, namely how a certain level of illegibility in relation to land ownership and economic activities is often re-created.

The significance of reciprocity among traders does not mean, of course, that these markets are realized through harmonious relationships without conflict and exploitation. At the same time as trade in this context is based upon an intense cultivation of social relationships, it is important to note how distrust and contestations over power are significant and reflected in accusations of corruption against leaders, as well as the use of *brujería*. The continued significance of ritual payments and *brujería* should not be conceptualized as a response to economic globalization and competition as is often asserted, however, but in terms of Andean notions of reciprocity and circulation as significant for the establishment and maintenance of prosperity. In the same way as practices of reciprocity and ritual are inherently relational, the continued significance of *brujería* is also due to the relational character of sociality. In this regard, the intense cultivation of social relationships in market participation illustrates how understandings of prosperity in the Andean context are associated with notions of fertility (Harris 1995b), or prosperity seen as created and maintained through logics of reciprocity, circulation and exchange. These logics work to reinforce the significance of ritual payments as well as *brujería* in market participation.

My point is that we therefore need to go beyond the question of resistance in the understanding of 'occult economies', ritual payments and witchcraft in processes of economic globalization, and explore rather the nature of the socialities involved. To understand these practices simply as questions of resistance is to simplify a complex dynamic of sociality and assume an artificial opposition, for example between dominant and dominated, power and resistance, modernity and tradition. Indeed, if we go beyond the question of resistance and see these practices in terms of the values ascribed to circulation and exchange as such, we can acknowledge the extent to which certain levels of the bureaucracy may also have a certain interest in maintaining the uncertain legal status of these circuits of exchange.

Conclusions

The processes of mobility described in this book have been explored in relation to people's quest for progress and social mobility and involve a negotiation of social as well as spatial categories. This search for mobility and progress can be considered in light of the ideology of *mestizaje* in the Peruvian context, and as involving people's search not only for an urban way of living but often also a quest for *mestizo*-ness. The search and demand for work represent decisive factors in these processes of mobility, but I nonetheless argue that migration in this context must be understood in more general terms, as being the result of people's attempt to redefine the conditions of their lives. Indeed, these processes of mobility can be understood as an effect of what is often an exclusion from citizenship among people in the highlands on the one hand, and the ideology of *mestizaje* on the other.

One of my points in this regard is that people's movement from the highlands to the cities can be viewed as an effect of state processes, that is, as a consequence of state processes and policies although unintended by the state. Already during the colonial period, people were not only forced to move due to the labour tribute to the state, but some also chose to move – for instance to the cities – in an attempt to manipulate or change their position in relation to fiscal categories (Silverblatt 1990, Saignes 1995, Larson and Harris 1995). The migration to Peruvian cities from the rural highlands already during the colonial period can in this respect be understood as an effect of the bifurcation of the state, a bifurcation that in different ways has been reproduced after independence. In the light of this, migration can be seen as intimately connected to the position of people in the highlands as 'second-class' citizens at the margins of a modernity defined as primarily associated with the urban *mestizo*. As part of the nation-building projects after independence, the ideology of *mestizaje* seems to have increased the orientation toward the cities among people in the highlands, a movement that was further encouraged by changes in the agricultural economy and industrializing endeavours in the 1940s and 1950s. The ideology of *mestizaje* apparently involved a possibility for social mobility among people in the rural Andes as long as they decided to leave their Andean background and identity behind. Thus the efforts for homogenization and modernization captured in the notion of *mestizaje* have served to reinforce certain centralizing effects and to stimulate the need, as well as the urge, among people to migrate. Similarly today, migration can be understood as a response to certain state processes and the production of social and spatial categories, as people seek to redefine their position in relation to categories of identity produced through the definition of spatial hierarchies. In this respect, the significance of migration and increasing urbanization serves to highlight the many contradictions connected to state processes since they can be seen as effects of the modernizing (and homogenizing) efforts of the authorities, but an effect that in many ways works contrary to its aims (to site de Certeau 1984). This is not to say that there was no migration before the formation of statehood, but that migration is connected to modern nation-states through the significance of territoriality – and spatialization as a significant state effect (Trouillot 2001) that can serve both to inhibit *and* to stimulate migration.

Among the effects of an ideology of *mestizaje* has been a de-legitimatization of indigenous people's demands for cultural and territorial rights. This is illustrated also by the way in which people who have migrated to the city from the Andean highlands generally do not organize or claim rights, such as in relation to land, by referring to an indigenous identity. This is probably a result of the ideology of *mestizaje* as noted above, and people's realization that in the city, such a claim would not be recognized. Instead, people increasingly seem to make demands in terms of the 'market'.

Urban Spaces and the Maintenance of Illegibility

Processes of migration have at the same time created a foundation for the adjustment of state arrangements and motivated the initiation of new state policies and institutions through the incorporation and appropriation of popular practices. In response for instance to the popular practices of land occupation and collective construction of neighbourhoods, the authorities have created different policies and institutions to facilitate the formalization of land ownership and to coordinate popular organizational efforts. An example of this is how the collective organization of inhabitants into neighbourhood committees has been made a requirement by the authorities in order to formalize people's land ownership. This illustrates how processes of migration and mobility often lead to new forms of state regulation and control, creating an interesting dialectics between popular practices and official arrangements. It shows how a society's margins play a significant and necessary role in state processes (Das and Poole 2004), and how people's practices at the margins of society may also be added to the state's repertoire of governance. My point in this respect is that the dynamics of state-society interaction illustrate how the re-creation of the state – in the midst of globalizing processes – is specifically due to its capacity to appropriate and include the responses of inhabitants (or civil society) by the (re-)creation and adjustment of official policies. Indeed, it illustrates state-society interaction as a hegemonic field for the exercise, contestation and concealment of power in a Gramscian sense. Practices of communal work are referred to among inhabitants in Jerusalén as reflecting an important cultural value and source of identity that define them as different from people born in the city. This significance of communal work is underlined not only by the inhabitants themselves, but also by state and NGO agencies involved in the area. In this manner, collective work seems to have been made the object of an invention or re-invention of tradition (Hobsbawn and Rangers 1983, McNeish 2002). It indicates how the significance of work for the conceptualization of personhood is a complex and somewhat contradictory issue, and how notions of communal work are being 'made' and 'un-made' in state-society interaction and relations of power and inequality.

At the same time as there is a de-structuring of urban spaces through the practices of occupation and collective construction, there is also a re-structuring of such spaces due to the appropriation of popular practices into policy. These spaces seem to revolve around a dialectics between 'city as concept' and 'city as practice' (De Certeau 1984), in the sense that 'city as concept' is continually reformulated through the integration in official policies of citizens' practices. The making of what are considered 'Andean traditions of collective work' into a means of administration is an example of this dialectic. While the claims to land among Andean migrants are not made with reference to their 'indigenous' background, the arrangements created in response to these new urban practices are nonetheless specific to migrant or indigenous groups, although not limited to them. Another category for the use of urban space (and citizenship) is thus created, based on a partly collective and partly individualized use and organization of land as well as workforce. In these spaces, a co-existence between collective and individual organization of, entitlements to and responsibility for land is (re-)constructed. Such co-existence is (re-)produced and maintained for instance through the official obligation or recruitment of collective work alongside programmes that also promote individualization and accommodate the formalization and commodification of land. The ambiguous spaces for citizenship that are thus created may open up new possibilities for marginalized urban citizens on the one hand, but may on the other hand fuel practices of clientelism and problems of distrust, speculation and misuse. In this respect, I have discussed whether these policies do actually serve to make popular practices 'legible', or whether they serve to maintain a certain level of 'illegibility'. Indeed, I have indicated how the ambiguously defined, hybrid spaces for citizenship – created through the co-existence between collective and individual organization of land and labour in new urban neighbourhoods – may leave room for manoeuvre both for authorities and inhabitants in a way that often serves to reproduce informal arrangements.

The Negotiation of Identities and Social Categories

In general, people's search for mobility and progress in the urban context is often characterized by attempts to redefine their position in relation to social categories, and involves a fundamental ambiguity in the relationship to an Andean background and identity. In some contexts, people's quest for progress and mobility seems to involve and be defined by a search for *mestizo*-ness, thus illustrating how these categories of identity are to a certain extent re-created – at the same time as they are continually questioned and destabilized. People do not unambiguously seek to become *mestizos*, nor do they necessarily seek to confirm their Andean identity, and these categories continue to be blurred, contested *and* reproduced in a highly complex and contradictory way. This co-existence reveals the persistence of social categories as well as their ultimate blurriness by being continually done and undone. On some occasions, people seem to internalize the stigma and negativity associated with the Andean by under-communicating their background, whilst on other occasions they celebrate their Andean background as positive in contrast to the urban or *mestizo* way of life. These ambiguities are further illustrated by the way in which notions about 'race' and 'culture' are made relevant and negotiated also in kin and social relationships, and how the relationship to family and kin is made an object of rejection as well as extension in the transition from highland to city. The effects of an ideology of *mestizaje* are in many ways contradictory in this regard, and despite the possibility of unsettling and redefining the boundaries of social categories, there is still a polarization and essentialization in this context of the 'indigenous' and 'Hispanic', and a reproduction of inequality based on class as well as ethnicity. I have therefore argued that the dynamics of this unsettlement may even serve to disguise the existence of inequality and racism, in the sense that the processes of mobility and *mestizaje* involve an unsettlement of social categories that actually serve to reproduce the very same categories, along with consent to the principles of inequality (see de la Cadena 2000). The fundamental ambiguities that these processes involve are illustrated by the switching between speaking positions as people often change the viewpoints from which they speak depending on situation and relationship.

People's experiences with respect to language and their management of a position as bilinguals in a Spanish-dominated context have been given particular attention in this regard. I have explored the process from exclusion to inclusion in relation to the Spanish language, and the way in which people's relationship to Quechua is altered and imprinted with ambiguity in the process. Through a focus on language, I have thus explored people's relationship to an Andean stigma, and illustrated the interchange between Quechua and Spanish in different situations. Hence the Quechua language is not necessarily under-communicated in the urban context, but also made use of in an often playful interchange between languages and viewpoints that works to comment upon and make fun of dominant categories and forms. In this respect, I have drawn on Gramsci and Bakhtin in order to stress the ways in which the interchange between different viewpoints may involve accommodation to dominant forms on one level and a reflective juxtaposition of different ways of viewing the world on another.

Indigenous Socialities and the Powerful Surroundings

The stigma of the Andean and the negotiation of social identities do not necessarily entail that the significance of indigenous socialities is un-made in the process. On the contrary, the cosmological and ontological underpinnings of personhood and social relationships are in different ways reproduced. Andean notions of the powerful surroundings continue to be made important in processes of migration and mobility, and a reciprocal relationship to the landscape is in different ways re-created in the urban context. While spaces are made objects of commodification in a variety of new and different ways as people move to the cities, that is, for purposes of investment, sale or income-generating work, the spatial surroundings are at the same time ascribed a spiritual significance. People's accommodation to the city therefore does not entail a one-sided process of, for example, a bureaucratization or commercialization of spatial categories, since space is simultaneously understood as animated and powerful. Indeed, the powerful surroundings are made important for people's quest for belonging and progress in the urban context, for example through ritual payments to secure their goodwill and to seek protection and success in work or business.

Movement and mobility can also appear to actualize the significance of spatial powers, in the sense that the surroundings are seen to affect people positively or negatively in the process of moving. This ontological continuity with rural life can serve to make places out of spaces, in the sense that the powerful surroundings are appealed to as mediators in the attempt to make hostile spaces into meaningful places, or places of identification and possible prosperity. By seeing themselves as influenced by their surroundings, people seek to recreate these influences in processes of mobility, and re-conceptualize the surroundings as mediators in their quest for belonging. The continued significance of these practices thus illustrates how people actively relate to their new surroundings and engaging in processes of place making. In processes of mobility therefore, people involve themselves in a process of re-creating places and creating new ones, and making mobility into a process of place-making.

As illustrated in the notion of *ánimo*, people's ideas about soul and well-being are understood as connected to their relationship with the surroundings, and demonstrate how places are seen as an integral part of people's formation. These understandings of place are intimately connected to ideas about kin and community, and the dangers related to movement thus throw an interesting light on personal experiences of movement in relation to collective structures. My contribution in this regard has been to explore how the reciprocal relationship to kin, land and the animated surroundings in the Andes is important for understandings of movement and mobility as such. Movement in space can be considered potentially dangerous at the same time as it involves the potential for communication with new sources of prosperity, and movement can itself be seen to create or threaten people's well-being or prosperity. I have therefore explored how the powers of the surroundings are associated with prosperity, and how movement may actualize different sources of prosperity and power. Prosperity and power are perceived as differently distributed in space as well as time, thus informing the movement in space as related to different spatial (and time-based) configurations and directions. Places are imagined as locations for different visions of and aspirations for the future as well as the past, such as hopeful visions for the city or expectations of the powerful ancestors. Also in the urban context, different sources of powers and prosperity are seen to co-exist, that is, in urban, modern, as well as ancient forms. In this respect, notions of progress and modernity are also given new meanings through local ideas about prosperity and the animated surroundings.

These understandings of the powerful surroundings do at the same time become objects of change and negotiation, and some people regard these practices as a tradition belonging to their rural past, insignificant for their lives and prospects in the city. Others see them as a necessary means of protecting themselves and ensuring the possibility of progress through the engagement with the surroundings as sources of prosperity as well as danger. These differences illustrate how different logics are made relevant in relation to people's prospects in the city, and therefore how progress may be ascribed with different and contested meanings. Such different meanings often seem to depend upon the nature of people's work involvement, and people employed as wage labourers seem to ascribe a different meaning to their quest for progress than people who are self-employed, for instance in market work where the cultivation of social relationships and the powerful surroundings are made particularly important in people's everyday lives.

Gift giving and practices of reciprocity are of general significance among people in Jerusalén, and the ability to give is seen as an important value. By focusing on *compadrazgo* in particular, I have therefore described the meanings of reciprocity in the urban context, both in everyday lives and on festive occasions. These practices involve gift giving and forms of consumption that serve to confirm social relationships and a sense of community on the one hand, and to express or create prestige and an image of personal successfulness on the other. My argument in this respect is that people's quest for mobility and progress can articulate and even reinforce certain practices of reciprocity, because of the relational understanding of personhood as well as the necessity to be involved in social relations of mutual help, trust and support. In processes of migration, practices of reciprocity – such as those related to *compadrazgo* – may also work as vehicles of change and social mobility, by representing a flexible institution that is made important in the confirmation and initiation of social relationships with people from the neighbourhood as well as people from the city at large. A central argument is therefore that ritual exchange represents a practice through which people seek to re-position themselves in their accommodation to the city, through the initiation and cultivation of social relationships as a way to negotiate the manners and means of belonging.

The social relationships and positions that are negotiated through practices of *compadrazgo* must also be seen as constructed within and on the basis of relations of power and inequality. I have therefore tried to reveal the subtle forms of power that are being reproduced as well as negotiated through relations of reciprocity. These subtle forms of power are related to the actualization of questions related to respect, equality and autonomy in practices of reciprocity, in a way that makes *compadrazgo* involve also a reproduction of certain inequalities. Although possibly involving a source of prestige and re-creation of social networks, people enter these relationships in a way that at the same time may reflect and reproduce their positioning in the social hierarchy.

Some of the festive forms of reciprocity and consumption that I have described are also made objects of criticism, however, not only by people from the city but also by leaders of the Evangelical churches in the neighbourhood, for representing an irresponsible way to spend resources and as unsuitable for Christians. This attitude also seems to gain certain credence among some of the inhabitants themselves. While most people in the neighbourhood understand the involvement in these practices as a social obligation, there are also people who regard the evangelical critique of such practices as a legitimate way to escape this kind of expense. As similarly noted above, these differences illustrate how different logics are made relevant in people's negotiation of their lives and prospects in the city, and how progress may be ascribed with different and contested meanings.

Mobility, State and Gender

In my exploration of the ways in which processes of urbanization involve an unsettlement of dominant social and spatial categories and boundaries, I have paid particular attention to the way in which there is also a fundamental gendered aspect to this unsettlement. Building on my discussions about the significance of work in processes of mobility and people's self-understandings, I have been especially concerned with the work practices of women and how they serve to actualize different imageries of gender.

Migration encompasses two partly contrasting discourses on gender, that is, Andean notions of gender complementarity and the working couple on the one hand, and the middle class gender ideals connected to *machismo* on the other. I have therefore discussed the negotiation of gender relationships and ideals in processes of mobility, by focusing on same- and opposite-sex relationships in the household, between the generations and among colleagues. In people's search for mobility and progress, gender ideals associated with the middle-class are increasingly made significant, at the same time as these ideals are also unsettled and challenged, for instance through the work practices of migrant women and their destabilization of dominant social categories such as *casa* and *calle*, or the private and the public. This is reflected in the highly ambiguous imageries of migrant women and especially women who trade, and indicates the importance of gender for ethnicity and processes of 'othering'. While I have illustrated how the understanding of women's trade as an extension of household work is at the same time partly reproduced also by the women themselves, I have stressed how this work simultaneously involves a blending of activities and functions conventionally understood in terms of private/public, reproduction/production. People's involvement in trade at the margins of the formal economy can generally be seen as a (de-centralized) response to urban conditions of marginalization in a globalized economy. The risk and insecurity involved in this work is minimized through the reliance on social networks and kin – in which women play a central role.

Gender is also important to understanding the relationship between community and state in the development of new urban neighbourhoods, as illustrated by the involvement primarily of women in official programmes and local organizational work. I have therefore related the significance of communal work to questions of gender, and illustrated how the workforce of women in particular is made important through the efforts made to develop and improve these new urban neighbourhoods. Indeed, women have not only played an active role in the work organized by the neighbourhood committees, but have also been involved in women's organizations working to improve the conditions in the neighbourhood, through projects of state, municipal and NGO agencies. By describing the participation of women in a local organization financed by the authorities as well as NGOs, I have discussed the relations of power and inequality in which people in this neighbourhood are involved. The intention has been to outline how the interconnectedness and interface between the community and authorities is negotiated and understood, and the implications of this official involvement for understandings of communal obligation and leadership. I have outlined the way in which participation in organizations like ASOMA is viewed as a way to improve the neighbourhood as well as the situation of individual participants, and in this regard how the organization is related to notions of progress. In particular, I have been concerned with the tension that appears to exist in perspectives on the organization as involving the progress of the individual or that of the group, and how these tensions are conceptualized and managed among the members. Leadership in local organizations is for instance negotiated as an appreciated and valued contribution to the community on the one hand, and as an opportunity for personal improvement and object of distrust and critique on the other. In this respect, the rumours of corruption in the ASOMA organization can be related to the negotiation of personal effort and gain *vis-à-vis* the obligations toward the group.

The focus on women in projects of development and modernization in new urban neighbourhoods also entails the subjectification and clientification of women according to dominant ideals of womanhood and *mestizaje*. In this respect, I have illustrated how the imageries of gender relationships projected by middle-class professionals are informed by middle-class ideas about gender while they are also informed by ethnic stereotypes. By exploring the background and implications of the focus on women and gender issues in these projects, I have therefore discussed the significance of gender for discourses of and about *mestizaje* and modernity. I have drawn on Ortner's (1996) discussion of the dynamics between the state and patriarchy's need to protect women – and the women's increasing mobility which challenges these perceptions – and argued that the focus on women involves an attempt to redefine indigenous women into 'civilized' *mestizas*. Indeed, these projects can be regarded as a way of making a 'dangerous' kind of womanhood into a more 'civilized' one, one that is in need of protection, therefore revealing how indigenous women are sometimes defined and re-defined within projects of modernization. Ironically, while these projects seek to redefine participants according to dominant, middle-class ideals of womanhood, they are at the same time based on the often hard, physical work of the same women.

The recruiting of communal work by state and local authorities reflects and reproduces certain relations of power and inequality in Peruvian society. The arrangement also of training or *capacitación* through local organizations can be seen to involve a hegemonic construction of subjects in the attempt to modernize and 'develop' the new urban neighbourhoods. While the official programmes offered to these inhabitants thus represent projects of modernization and *mestizaje*, they simultaneously involve a reproduction of difference by relying on a notion of the communally oriented and hard-working people from the highlands. The official policies towards new urban neighbourhoods may indeed have some rather contradictory effects, by serving to individualize the habitants on the one hand while working through the stimulation of communal work on the other. This illustrates how the official policies regarding these new urban neighbourhoods often involve a recreation of somewhat ambiguous spaces for citizenship. Participation in social organizations may furthermore serve to blur and defy the dichotomous representations of public and domestic life (Rubin 1998:254). In this blurring of dichotomous representations, gender is made significant for the re-creation of ambiguous spaces for citizenship in new urban neighbourhoods. Indeed, the involvement primarily of women in these organizational projects is in many ways central for the maintenance of such vague spaces for citizenship, and illustrates the significance of gender not only for governance in development projects but also for the maintenance of a certain level of illegibility.

The gradual decline in people's participation in the ASOMA organization may be partly related to Fujimori's exit from the presidency and the uncertain period that followed concerning the continued official support for this kind of organization. According to what people told me, I got the impression that the decline was also related to an increasing scepticism towards leaders, as well as the dilemmas that external involvement seemed to produce, for instance with respect to local leadership. In this regard, I have related the changing significance of this local organization to a discussion of the changing relationship between 'state' and 'civil society' during the past decades, that is, in relation to the co-optation of local practice into official policies in a way that has also served to neutralize local efforts and initiatives. While there appeared to have been an agreement among members during my first fieldwork that this kind of organizational work is important for the progress of the community as well as individual members, there seemed to be an increasing disagreement about this during my later fieldwork. Instead of associating the involvement in the women's organization with progress and improvement, several women had started to see this work as problematic and increasingly prioritized other kinds of work, such as trade or other income-generating activities. Again, this illustrates how ideas about progress are ascribed different and sometimes contested meanings. What is more, it indicates how the women involved do not simply accommodate to the imageries and ideas presented to them through state and NGO involvement, but that they simultaneously engage in processes of creating new identities and spaces of action for themselves. The women also contest and unsettle the social and spatial categories of dominant *mestizo* discourse, through their involvement in trade and social networks that are importantly unregulated by the mechanisms and limits of the state.

The Moralities of Markets

People's involvement in trade in the urban context entails an often intense cultivation of social relationships, and one of my concerns has been the way in which market participation is negotiated in terms of moralities in a context where trade is of a more or less informal kind. Independent of its un-registered or illegal dimensions, market participation is highly valued and celebrated as an important and good way to make a living. Central to my argument in this regard is that people's involvement in and understandings of markets must be understood in terms of an Andean ethos of work, sociality and exchange. Traders often criticize the authorities for their interference in the business, and the celebration of trade can in this regard be seen as connected to how trade involves a level of autonomy that is contrasted to previous experiences and relations of dependency. The celebration of market participation and cultivation of social relationships is in many ways a response to the ambiguous spaces for citizenship that are recreated through official approaches and the co-existence of collective and individual arrangements concerning land and labour in the urban context. As similarly noted with respect to settlements, traders do not make claims, for example to land, by referring to an indigenous identity, however, but with reference to their right to participate in markets.

An Andean understanding of reciprocity, exchange and circulation as 'fertile' and as reproducing collective prosperity (Harris 1995b) is in different ways re-created in the urban context. Such an understanding is made particularly important among traders, where the quest for money and success are seen to depend on ritual payments and the fertilizing force of exchange and circulation as such. Accumulation and prosperity is therefore understood as dependent on monetary as well as ritual investments. Indeed, this understanding of exchange and circulation as in itself a force of prosperity can also represent one of the reasons why *contrabando* and undocumented forms of trade are not considered immoral – despite their informal or illegal dimensions – but appreciated as a morally acceptable and important way to make an income. In this regard, I have illuminated how local ideas of market participation, reciprocity and circulation can be viewed in relation to the approach taken by the authorities, varying between tacit acceptance and occasional moves to abolish these practices. Despite the authorities' occasional interferences as well as policies of formalization, the uncertain legal status of this kind of trade and market activity is often maintained. In this manner, a certain level of illegibility in relation to land ownership and economic activities is often re-created, partly due to what appears to be the acceptance of urban authorities. This confirms the importance of going beyond the question of resistance in relation to these so-called 'occult' economic practices. Instead, if we see these practices in terms of the values ascribed to circulation and exchange as such, we can account for the extent to which certain levels of the bureaucracy may also have a certain interest in maintaining the uncertain legal status of these circuits of exchange. Rather than seeing these 'occult' exchanges in terms of resistance therefore, or alternatively as compliance to dominant ideologies, these practices can be understood as constructed through the dialectics between bureaucratic rationality and local notions of progress, sociality and ritual.

These values ascribed to circulation and exchange do not infer that people's involvement in markets is realized through harmonious relationships devoid of conflict and exploitation. At the same time as trade in this context is based upon an intense cultivation of social relationships and ritual payments, the question of distrust and contestations over power is also significant. This is reflected in the accusations of corruption against leaders, as well as the suspicion of *brujería*. While it has often been argued that the continued importance of witchcraft and magic should be considered a response to the competition, individualism and alienation initiated by processes of modernization and economic globalization (see Moore and Sanders 2001, Taussig 1980), I have stressed that practices of ritual payments and *brujería* in the Andean context ought to be understood in the light of their *relational* character. Instead of seeing such practices as attempts to stop or counter the flow of globalization therefore (Geschiere 1997), I see them as a way in which people seek to influence or redirect such flows. Indeed, these practices involve the attempt to control a specific situation through relational means. In this manner, I have explored how the flow of money and commodities is negotiated in terms of local understandings of sociality, and as thus being informed by people's ideas about reciprocity and exchange. In the same way as practices of reciprocity and ritual are inherently relational, the continued significance of *brujería* is also due to a relational understanding of sociality, although representing the *failure* of reciprocity or social relationships. The importance of these practices especially in the context of trade can be seen to illustrate also the *relational* character of people's involvement in and understanding of markets. It is an example of how understandings of prosperity in the Andean context are associated with general notions of fertility (Harris 1995b), or prosperity seen as created and maintained through a logic of reciprocity, circulation and exchange. This logic works to reinforce the significance of ritual payments as well as *brujería* in market participation.

My argument is therefore that we need to go beyond the question of resistance in the understanding of 'occult economies', ritual payments and witchcraft in processes of economic globalization, and stress rather the nature of the socialities involved. To understand these practices simply as questions of resistance is to simplify complex dynamics of sociality and assume an artificial opposition, for example between dominant and dominated, power and resistance, modernity and tradition. Instead of separating these practices of 'occult' economic activity and *brujería* from the general understanding of social relationships in processes of change therefore, I have tried to regard them as interconnected. In this manner, I have tried to avoid the reduction of complex processes of sociality to simple notions of 'the occult' or 'the resistance to globalization'. Despite such continuity in the significance of indigenous socialities, however, this does not mean that they unambiguously represent a form of endo-sociality as discussed by Friedman and Ekholm (2008:141), that is, as a sociality that transforms all that enters from the outside world into the local logic.[1] This is related to the ways in which the ideology of *mestizaje* and the stigma of the Andean have created a fundamental ambiguity in people's social and cultural identifications, as well as the different and often contested understandings connected to what *progreso* is supposed to entail. Due to the ideology of *mestizaje*, important sources of prestige and power are also significantly disassociated from these indigenous logics of sociality, resulting in a continual negotiation of the values related to personhood and identity. Importantly implicated in this negotiation are different understandings connected to mobility and progress.

1 As mentioned in the introduction, this kind of endo-sociality is defined in contrast to exo-sociality, the latter being understood as a strategy of appropriation of the world which is strongly other-directed and consisting of the identification of the foreign as life-force to be appropriated (Friedman and Ekholm 2008:141).

Bibliography

Abercrombie, Thomas, *Pathways of Memory and Power: Ethnography and History among an Andean People* (Madison: University of Wisconsin Press, 1998).

Albó, Xavier, *La Paradoja Aymara* (La Paz: CIPCA, 1975).

Albó, Xavier, Tomas Greaves and Godofredo Sandoval, *Chukiyawu. La Cara Aymara de La Paz. vol 3. Cabalgando Entre dos Mundos* (La Paz: CIPCA, 1983).

Allen, Catherine, *The Hold Life Has: Coca and Cultural Identity in an Andean Community* (Washington, DC: Smithsonian Institution Press, 1988).

Altamirano, Teófilo, *Regional Commitment and Political Involvement Amongst Migrants in Lima: The Case of Regional Associations*, PhD thesis (Durham: Durham University, 1979).

Altamirano, Teófilo, *Cultura Andina y Pobreza Urbana Aymaras en Lima Metropolitiana* (Lima: Pontificia Universidad Catolica del Perú, 1988).

Altamirano, Teófilo, *Migración. El Fenomeno del Siglo. Peruanos en Europa, Japon, Australia* (Lima: Pontificia Universidad Catolica del Peru, 1996).

Altamirano, Teófilo and Lane Ryo Hirabayashi (eds), *Migrants, Regional Identities and Latin American Cities*, Society for Latin American Anthropology Publication Series (Washington, DC: 1997).

Alvarez, Sonia, 'Latin American Feminisms "Go Global": Trends of the 1990s and Challenges for the New Millennium', in Sonia Alvarez, Evelina Dagnino and Arturo Escobar (eds), *Cultures of Politics, Politics of Cultures: Re-visioning Latin American Social Movements* (Boulder, Colorado and Oxford: Westview Press, 1998, pp. 293–324).

Alvarez, Sonia, Evelina Dagnino, and Arturo Escobar (eds), *Cultures of Politics, Politics of Cultures: Re-visioning Latin American Social Movements* (Boulder, Colorado and Oxford: Westview Press, 1998).

Arce, Alberto and Norman Long, 'The Dynamics of Knowledge: Interfaces between Bureaucrats and Peasants, in Norman Long and Alberto Arce (eds), *Battlefield of Knowledge: The Interlocking of Theory and Practice in Social Research and Development* (London: Routledge, 1992), pp. 211–47.

Archetti, Eduardo, *Masculinities: Football, Polo and the Tango in Argentina* (Oxford: Berg, 1999).

Archetti, Eduardo, *Guinea-pigs: Food, Symbol and Conflict of Knowledge in Ecuador* (Oxford: Berg, 1997).

Ardener, Shirley (ed.), *Perceiving Women* (London: Dent and New York: Halsted, 1975).

Arguedas, José Maria, *Todas las Sangres* (Lima: Peisa, 1964 [2001]).

Arrosquipa Quispe, Percy, *Cultura empresarial: una visión antropológica desde las PYMEs*, Bachelor thesis, Universidad Nacional de San Agustín, Arequipa (2002).

Ashworth, G.J. and B. Graham, *Senses of Place: Senses of Time* (Aldershot: Ashgate, 2005).

Babb, Florence, 'Market/places as Gendered Spaces: Market/women's Studies Over Two Decades', in Linda Seligman (ed.), *Women Traders in Cross-cultural Perspective: Mediating Identities, Marketing Wares* (Stanford, California: Stanford University Press, 2001), pp. 229–40.

Bakhtin, Mikhail, *The Dialogic Imagination: Four Essays by Mikhail Bakhtin*, in M. Holquist (ed.) (Austin: University of Texas Press, 1981 [1996]).

Bakhtin, Mikhail, *Rabelais and His World* (Bloomington: Indiana University Press, 1984).

Bastién, Joseph, 'Shaman Versus Nurse in an Aymara Village: Traditional and Modern Medicine in Conflict', in Robert Dover, Katharine Seibold and John McDowell (eds), *Andean Cosmologies Through Time: Persistence and Emergence* (Bloomington and Indianapolis: Indiana University Press, 1992), pp. 137–66.

Bateson, Gregory, *Steps to an Ecology of Mind: Collected Essays in Anthropology, Psychiatry, Evolution and Epistemology* (Frogmore: Paladin, 1973).

Berger, M. and M. Buvinic (eds), *Women's Ventures: Assistance to the Informal Sector in Latin America* (West Hartford, Connecticut: Kumarian Press, 1989).

Blondet, Cecilia, 'Establishing an Identity: Women Settlers in a Poor Lima Neighbourhood', in Elizabeth Jelin (ed.), *Women and Social Change in Latin America*, UNRISD/United Nations Research Institute for Social Development (London and New Jersey: Zed Book Ltd. 1990), pp. 12–46.

Bradby, Barbara, 'Resistance to Capitalism in the Peruvian Andes', in David Lehman (ed.), *Ecology and Exchange in the Andes* (Cambridge, New York and Sydney: Cambridge University Press, 1982).

Bunster, Ximena and Elsa M. Chaney (eds), *Sellers and Servants: Working Women in Lima, Peru* (Granby, Massachusetts: Bergin and Garvey Publishers, 1989.

Burt, Jo-Marie, 'Contesting the Terrain of Politics: State-Society Relations in Urban Peru', in Paul W. Drake and Eric Herschberg (eds), *State and Society in Conflict: Comparative Perspectives on Andean Crises* (Pittsburgh: University of Pittsburgh Press, 2006), pp. 220–56.

Calderón, Fernando (ed.), *Imagenes Desconocidas: La Modernidad en la Encrucijada Postmoderna* (Buenos Aires: CLACSO, 1988).

Calderón, Fernando and Alicia Szmukler, *La Política en las Calles: Política, Urbanización y Desarrollo* (La Paz: CERES, Plural, UASB, 2000).

Canclini, Nestor, *Hybrid Cultures, Strategies for Entering and Leaving Modernity* (Minneapolis and London: University of Minnesota Press, 1995).

Canessa, Andrew, 'Procreation, Personhood and Ethnic Difference in Highland Bolivia', *Ethnos*, vol. 63, no 2 (1998): pp. 227–47.

Carsten, Janet and Stephen Hugh-Jones (eds), *About the House: Levi-Strauss and Beyond* (Cambridge: Cambridge University Press, 1995).

Castañeda, Jorge, *Utopia Unarmed: The Latin American Left After the Cold War* (New York: Vintage Books, 1994).

Castells, Manuel and Alejandro Portes, 'World Underneath: The Origins, Dynamics and Effects of the Informal Economy', in Alejandro Portes, Manuel Castells and Lauren Benton (eds), *The Informal Economy: Studies in Advanced and Less Developed Countries* (Baltimore, MD: Johns Hopkins University Press, 1989), pp. 11–40.

Castro, Daniel, 'War is Our Daily Life: Women's Participation in Sendero Luminoso', in Gertrude Yeager (ed.), *Confronting Change, Challenging Tradition: Women in Latin American History* (Wilmington, Delaware: SR Books, 1994), pp. 219–25.

Collier, David, *Squatters and Oligarchs: Authoritarian Rule and Policy Change in Peru* (London: Johns Hopkins University Press, 1976).

Comaroff, Jean and John Comaroff, *Of Revelation and Revolution: Christianity, Colonialism and Consciousness in South Africa* (Chicago and London: The University of Chicago Press, 1991).

Comaroff, Jean and John Comaroff, *Legality, Modernity and Ethnicity in Colonial South Africa: An Excursion in the Historical Anthropology of Law* (London: LSE Centenary Lecture in Law and Society, 1995).

Comaroff, Jean and John Comaroff, 'Millenial Capitalism and the Culture of Neoliberalism', in Marc Edelman and Angelique Haugerud (eds), *The Anthropology of Development and Globalization: From Classical Political Economy to Contemporary Neoliberalism* (Malden, Oxford and Victoria: Blackwell Publishing, 2005), pp. 177–88.

Comaroff, Jean and John Comaroff, *Ethnicity, Inc.* (Chicago and London: University of Chicago Press, 2009).

Coronil, Fernando, *The Magical State: Nature, Money and Modernity in Venezuela* (Chicago and London: The University of Chicago Press, 1997).

Crain, Mary, 'The Gendering of Ethnicity in the Ecuadorian Andes: Native Women's Self-fashioning in the Urban Marketplace', in Marit Melhuus and Kristi Anne Stølen (eds), *Machos, Mistresses and Madonnas: Contesting the Power of Latin American Gender Imagery* (London and New York: Verso, 1996), pp. 134–58.

Das, Verena and Deborah Poole, *Anthropology in the Margins of the State* (Santa Fe: School of American Research Press, 2004).

de Certeau, Michel, *The Practice of Everyday Life* (Berkeley, Los Angeles and London: University of California Press, 1984).

de la Cadena, Marisol, 'Women Are More Indian: Ethnicity, Gender in a Community Near Cusco', in Brooke Larson and Olivia Harris (with Enrique Tandeter), *Ethnicity, Markets and Migration in the Andes: At the Crossroads of History and Anthropology* (Durham and London: Duke University Press, 1995), pp. 329–48.

de la Cadena, Marisol, 'The Political Tensions of Representations and Misrepresentations: Intellectuals and Mestizas in Cuzco (1919–1990)', *Journal of Latin American Anthropology*, vol. 2(1) (1996): pp. 112–47.

de la Cadena, Marisol, *Indigenous Mestizos: The Politics of Race and Culture in Cuzco, Peru, 1919–1991* (Durham and London: Duke University Press, 2000).

de Soto, Hernando, *The Other Path: The Invisible Revolution in the Third World* (London: I.B. Tauris and Co., 1989).

De Grandis, Rita and Zila Bernd (eds), *Unforeseeable Americas: Questioning Cultural Hybridity in the Americas*, vol. 13 (Amsterdam and Atlanta: Critical Studies, 2000).

Díaz-Barriga, Miguel, 'Beyond the Domestic and the Public: *Colonas* Participation in Urban Movements in Mexico City', in Sonia Alvarez, Evelina Dagnino and Arturo Escobar (eds), *Cultures of Politics, Politics of Cultures: Re-visioning Latin American Social Movements* (Boulder, Colorado: Westview Press, 1998), pp. 252–77.

Dore, Elizabeth and Maxine Molyneux, *Hidden Histories of Gender and the State in Latin America* (Durham and London: Duke University Press, 2000).

Doughty, Paul, 'Behind the Back of the City: Provincial Life in Lima, Peru', in William Mangin (ed), *Peasants in Cities* (Boston: Houghton Mifflin, 1970), pp. 30–46.

Doughty, Paul, 'Life Goes On: Revisiting Lima's Migrant Associations', in Teófilo Altamirano and Lane Ryo Hirabayashi (eds), *Migrants, Regional Identities and Latin American Cities*, Society for Latin American Anthropology Publication Series (Washington, DC: 1997).

Douglas, Mary, *Purity and Danger* (London: Routledge and Kegan Paul, 1966).

Dover, Robert, Katharine Seibold and John McDowell (eds), *Andean Cosmologies Through Time: Persistence and Emergence* (Bloomington and Indianapolis: Indiana University Press, 1992), pp. 137–66.

Dumont, Louis, *Homo Hierarchicus: The Caste System and its Implications* (Chicago: University of Chicago Press, 1980).

Escobar, Arturo, 'Imagining a Post-Development Era', in Marc Edelman and Angelique Haugerud (eds), *The Anthropology of Development and Globalization: From Classical Political Economy to Contemporary Neoliberalism* (Malden, Oxford and Victoria: Blackwell Publishing, 2005), pp. 341–51.

Evans-Pritchard, Edward E., *Witchcraft, oracles and magic among the Azande* (Oxford: Clarendon Press, 1937).

Feld, S. and K. Basso (eds), *Senses of Place* (Santa Fe: School of American Research Press, 1996).

Femenías, Blenda, *Gender and the Boundaries of Dress in Contemporary Peru* (Austin: University of Texas Press, 2005).

Ferguson, James, *Expectations of Modernity: Myths and Meanings of Urban Life in the Zambian Copperbelt* (Berkeley, Los Angeles, London: University of California Press, 1999).

Foucault, Michel, *Discipline and Punish: The Birth of the Prison* (New York: Penguin Books, 1977 [1991]).
Foucault, Michel, 'Governmentality', in Hubert Dreyfus and Paul Rabinow (eds), *Michel Foucault. Beyond Structuralism and Hermeneutics* (Chicago: University of Chicago Press, 1991), pp. 87–104.
Friedman, Jonathan and Kajsa Ekholm, *Modernities, Class, and the Contradictions of Globalization: The Anthropology of Global Systems* (London: AltaMira Press, 2008).
Frykman, Maya, 'Transnational Travel and the Sense of Place', Paper presented at the University of Bergen: The 14th Nordic Migration Researchers' Conference, 14/11-2007.
Gandolfo, Daniella, *The City at its Limits: Taboo, Transgression, and Urban Renewal in Lima* (Chicago and London: The University of Chicago Press, 2009).
Geschiere, Peter, *The Modernity of Witchcraft: Politics and the Occult in Postcolonial Africa* (Charlottesville: University of Virginia Press, 1997).
Giddens, Anthony, *The Constitution of Society* (Cambridge and Oxford: Polity Press, 1984).
Giddens, Anthony, *The Consequences of Modernity* (Stanford, Cambridge and Oxford: Polity Press, 1990).
Giddens, Anthony, *Modernity and Self-identity* (Cambridge: Polity Press, 1991).
Gill, Lesley, 'Like a Veil to Cover Them: Women and the Pentecostal Movement in La Paz', *American Ethnologist*, vol. 17, no. 4 (1990): pp. 708–21.
Gill, Lesley, 'Relocating Class: Ex-miners and Neoliberalism in Bolivia', *Critique of Anthropology*, 17(3) (1997): pp. 293–312.
Glass-Coffin, Bonnie, *The Gift of Life: Female Spirituality and Healing in Northern Peru* (Albuquerque: University of New Mexico Press, 1998).
Gledhill, John, *Power and its Disguises: Anthropological Perspectives on Politics* (London and Sterling, Virginia: Pluto Press, 1994 [2000]).
Goddard, V.A., *Gender, Family and Work in Naples* (Oxford: Berg, 1996).
Goldstein, Daniel, *The Spectacular City. Violence and Performance in Urban Bolivia* (Durham and London: Duke University Press, 2004).
Gose, Peter, *Deathly Waters and Hungry Mountains: Agrarian Ritual and Class Formation in an Andean Town* (Toronto, Buffalo and London: University of Toronto Press, 1994).
Gramsci, Anthony, *Selections from the Prison Notebooks*, ed. and tr. by Q. Hoare and G. Nowell Smith (New York: International Publishers, 1987 [1971]).
Grønhaug, Reidar, 'Scale and Social Organization: Scale as a Variable in the Analysis', Warner-Green Foundation for Anthropological Research, no. 55 (New York: 1972).
Gudeman, Stephen, 'The Compadrazgo as a Reflection of the Natural and Spiritual Person', *Proceedings of the Royal Anthropological Institute of Great Britain and Ireland for 1971* (1972): pp. 45–71.

Gudeman, Stephen, 'Spiritual Relationships and Selecting a Godparent', *Man*, vol. 10 (1975): pp. 221–37.

Gudeman, Stephen and Alberto Rivera, *Conversations in Colombia: The Domestic Economy in Life and Text* (Cambridge: Cambridge University Press, 1990).

Gudeman, Stephen, *The Anthropology of Economy: Community, Market and Culture* (Malden, Oxford and Victoria: Blackwell Publishing, 2001).

Gudeman, Stephen and Stuart B. Schwartz, 'Compadrio e batismo de escravos na Bahia no século XVIII', in José Reis (ed), *Escravidao e invencao da liberdade* (Sao Paulo: Ed. Brasiliense, 1988), pp. 33–59.

Gumperz, John (ed.), *Language and Social Identity*, Studies in Interactional Sociolinguistics, 2 (Cambridge: Cambridge University Press, 1982).

Gupta, Akhil and James Ferguson, *Anthropological Locations: Boundaries and Grounds of a Field Science* (Berkeley: University of California Press, 1997).

Gutmann, Michael, *The Meanings of Macho: Being a Man in Mexico City* (Berkeley, Los Angeles, London: University of California Press, 1996).

Hale, Charles R., 'Travel Warning: Elite Appropriations of Hybridity, Mestizaje, Antiracism, Equality, and Other Progressive-Sounding Discourses in Highland Guatemala', *The Journal of American Folklore*, vol. 112, no. 445 (1999): pp. 297–315.

Hansen, Karen Tranberg and Mariken Vaa, *Reconsidering Informality: Perspectives from Urban Africa* (Stockholm: Nordiska Afrikainstitutet, 2004).

Harris, Olivia, *To Make the Earth Bear Fruit: Ethnographic Essays on Fertility, Work and Gender in Highland Bolivia* (London: Institute of Latin American Studies, 2000 [1978]).

Harris, Olivia, 'The Dead and the Devils among the Bolivian Laymi', in Maurice Bloch and Johnny Parry (eds), *Death and the Regeneration of Life* (Cambridge: Cambridge University Press, 1982), pp. 45–73.

Harris, Olivia, 'Condor and Bull: The ambiguities of Masculinity in Northern Potosí', in Penelope Harvey and Peter Gow (eds), *Sex and Violence: Issues in Representation and Experience* (London and New York: Routledge, 1994), pp. 40–65.

Harris, Olivia, 'Ethnic Identity and Market Relations: Indians and Mestizos in the Andes', in Brooke Larson and Olivia Harris (eds), *Ethnicity, Markets and Migration in the Andes: At the Crossroads of History and Anthropology* (Durham and London: Duke University Press, 1995a), pp. 351–90.

Harris, Olivia, 'The Sources and Meanings of Money: Beyond the Market Paradigm in an Ayllu of Northern Potosi', in Brooke Larson and Olivia Harris (eds), *Ethnicity, Markets and Migration in the Andes: At the Crossroads of History and Anthropology* (Durham and London: Duke University Press, 1995b), pp. 297–328.

Harris, Olivia, *Inside and Outside the Law: Anthropological Studies of Authority and Ambiguity* (London and New York: Routledge, 1996).

Harris, Marvin, *Patterns of Race in the Americas* (New York: Walker, 1964).

Hart, Keith, 'Informal Income Opportunities and Urban Employment in Ghana', *Journal of Modern African Studies*, 11/1 (1973): pp. 61–89.

Hart, Keith, *Money in an Unequal World: Keith Hart and His Memory Bank* (New York: Texere, 2001).

Harvey, Penny, 'Domestic Violence in the Peruvian Andes', in *Sex and Violence: Issues in Representation and Experience* (London: Routledge, 1994), pp. 66–89.

Harvey, Penny, 'Peruvian Independence Day: Ritual, Memory and the Erasure of Narrative', in Rosaleen Howard-Malverde (ed.), *Creating Context in Andean Cultures* (Oxford: Oxford University Press, 1997), pp. 21–44.

Harvey, Penny and Peter Gow, *Sex and Violence: Issues in Representation and Experience* (London: Routledge, 1994).

Harvey, Penny, 'Landscape and Commerce: Creating Contexts for the Exercise of Power', in Barbara Bender and Margot Winer (eds), *Contested Landscapes: Movement, Exile and Place* (Oxford: Berg, 2001), pp. 197–210.

Harvey, Penny, 'Road Building in Peru: Corruption Stories and the Politics of Knowledge', Paper at the Department of Social Anthropology, University of Bergen, May, 2006.

Harvey, Penny, *Language, Power and Betrayal*, Forthcoming.

Hirsch, Eric and Micael O'Hanlon (eds), *The Anthropology of Landscape: Perspectives on Place and Space* (Clarendon: Oxford University Press, 1995).

Hirschon, Renee, *Heirs of the Greek Catastrophe: The Social Life of Asia Minor Refugees in Piraeus* (Oxford: Berghahn, 1998).

Hobsbawm, E.J. and T. Ranger (eds), *The Invention of Tradition* (Cambridge: Cambridge University Press, 1983).

Hollis, Martin, *The Philosophy of Social Science: An Introduction* (Cambridge University Press, 1994).

Hondagneu-Sotelo, Pierrette, 'Working "Without Papers" in the United States: Towards the Integration of Legal Status in Frameworks of Race, Class and Gender', in Elizabeth Higginbotham and Mary Romero (eds), *Women and Work: Exploring Race, Ethnicity and Class*, vol. 6 (Thousand Oaks, London and New Delhi: Sage Publications, 1997), pp. 101–26.

Howell, Signe (ed.), *The Ethnography of Moralities* (London: Routledge and European Association of Social Anthropologists, 1997).

Human Rights Watch, *Untold Terror: Violence Against Women in Peru's Armed Conflict* (New York: Americas Watch and the Women's Rights Project. Divisions of Human Rights Watch, 1992).

Ingold, Tim, 'The Temporality of the Landscape', *World Archaeology*, vol. 25, no. 2 (1993): 152–74.

Isbell, Billie Jean, *To Defend Ourselves: Ecology and Ritual in an Andean Village*, University of Texas, Institute of Latin American Studies, Latin American Monographs no. 47 (Austin: 1978).

Iversen, Marianne Sandstad, *Desarrollo, Progreso y Modernidad: Sosiale drama ogønsker om social mobilitet blant kvinner tilknyttet et stalig utviklingsprogram i Lima, Peru*, Master's thesis, University of Bergen (2009).

Jelin, Elizabeth, *Women and Social Change in Latin America*, UNRISD/United Nations Research Institute for Social Development (London and New Jersey: Zed Books Ltd., 1990).

Jelin, Elizabeth (ed.), *Family, Household and Gender Relations in Latin America* (London: Kegan Paul International, 1991).

Jongkind, Fred, 'A Reappraisal of the Role of the Regional Associations in Lima, Peru', *Comparative Studies in Society and History*, vol. 16 (1974): pp. 471–82.

Kaarhus, Randi, '*Organiserende Prinsipper i Tid og Rom: Historie, Språk og Kultur Hos Quechua-indianere*', Department of Social Anthropology, Oslo: Occasional Paper No. 15 (1988).

Kapferer, Bruce, *Beyond Rationalism: Rethinking Magic, Witchcraft and Sorcery* (New York: Berghahn Books, 2002).

Larson, Brooke, 'Andean Communities, Political Cultures, and Markets: The Changing Contours of a Field', in Brooke Larson and Olivia Harris (with Enrique Tandeter), *Ethnicity, Markets and Migration in the Andes: At the Crossroads of History and Anthropology* (Durham: Duke University Press, 1995), pp. 5–54.

Larson, Brooke and Olivia Harris (eds), *Ethnicity, Markets and Migration in the Andes: At the Crossroads of History and Anthropology* (Durham: Duke University Press, 1995).

Latour, Bruno, *Vi Har Aldri Vært Moderne: Essays in Symmetrisk Antropologi* (Oslo: Spartacus Forlag, 1996).

Lazar, Sian, *Cholo Citizens: Negotiating Personhood and Building Communities in El Alto, Bolivia*, PhD thesis, Goldsmiths College, University of London (2002).

Lazar, Sian, *El Alto, Rebel City: Self and Citizenship in Andean Bolivia* (Durham and London: Duke University Press, 2008).

Leacock, Eleanor and Helen Safa, *Women's Work and the Division of Labour by Gender* (South Hadley, Massachusetts: Bergin and Garvey Publishers, 1986).

Levi-Strauss, Claude, *Totemism* (London: Merlin Press, 1964).

Li, Tania Murray, 'Masyarakat Adat, Difference, and the Limits of Recognition in Indonesia's Forest Zone', *Modern Asian Studies*, vol. 35, no. 3 (July 2001): pp. 645–76.

Llanos Layme, David, *Diaspora Comunal y Sistema Productivo Altoandino: Una Aproximacion al Impacto de la Migracion y Participacion Popular en la Organizacion Social y Productiva de la Comunidad Chari* (La Paz: Universidad Mayor de San Andres, 1998).

Lloyd, Peter, *The 'Young Towns' of Lima: Aspects of Urbanization in Peru* (Cambridge University Press, 1980).

Lobo, Susan, *A House of My Own: Social Organization in the Squatter Settlements of Lima, Peru* (Tucson: University of Arizona Press, 1982).

Lund Skar, Sarah, *Worlds Together, Lives Apart: Quechua Colonization in Jungle and City* (Oslo: Scandinavian University Press, 1994).

Lund, Sarah, 'Andean Women and the Concept of Space/time', in Shirley Ardener (ed.), *Women and Space: Ground Rules and Social Maps* (Oxford and New York: Berg, 1997), pp. 35–49.

Lund, Sarah, 'Bequeathing and Quest: Processing Personal Identification. Papers in Bureaucratic Spaces (Cuzco, Peru)', *Social Anthropology: The Journal of the European Association of Social Anthropologists* (Cambridge: Cambridge University Press, 2001): pp. 3–24.

Lund, Sarah, 'Education and Biography in Peru's Southern Highlands: Changes in an Urbanizing Landscape', paper at NOLAN conference, Bergen: September 2008.

McDowell, John, 'Exemplary Ancestors and Pernicious Spirits: Sibundoy Concepts of Culture Evolution', in Robert Dover, Katharine Seibold and John McDowell (eds), *Andean Cosmologies Through Time: Persistence and Emergence* (Bloomington and Indianapolis: Indiana University Press, 1992), pp. 95–114.

Machaca, Marianne Eriksen, *'Es Costumbre de Mi Tierra': En Studie av Helse og Landskap i Nye Omgivelser, Arequipa, Peru*, Master's thesis, University of Oslo, 2005.

McNeish, John, *Pueblo Chico, Infierno Grande: Globalisation and the Politics of Participation in Highland Bolivia*, PhD thesis, Goldsmiths College, University of London, 2001.

McNeish, John, 'Globalization and the Reinvention of Tradition: The Politics of Community and Ethnicity in Highland Bolivia', *The Journal of Peasant Studies*, vol. 29, 3/4 (2002): pp. 228–69.

McNeish, John, 'Citizenship and Poverty in Latin America', paper at CROP workshop, NFU conference, Oslo: October 2004.

Mamdani, Mahmood, *Citizen and Subject: Contemporary Africa and the Legacy of Late Colonialism* (Princeton: Princeton University Press, 1996).

Mannheim, Bruce, *The Language of the Inca Since the European Invasion* (Austin: University of Texas Press, 1991).

Massey, Doreen, *Space, Place and Gender* (Cambridge and Oxford: Polity Press, 1994).

Matos Mar, José, *Las Barriadas de Lima 1957* (Lima: Instituto de Estudios Peruanos, 1977).

Matos Mar, José, *Desborde Popular y Crisis del Estado. El Nuevo Rostro del Perú en la Decada de 1980* (Lima: Instituto de Estudios Peruanos, 1985).

Mauss, Marcel, *The Gift: The Form and Reason for Exchange in Archaic Societies* (London: Routledge, 1954 [1990]).

Mayer, Enrique, 'Beyond the Nuclear Family', in Ralph Bolton and Enrique Mayer (eds), *Andean Kinship and Marriage* (Washington, DC: American Anthropological Association, 1977), pp. 60–80.

Meillassoux, Claude, *Maidens, Meal, and Money: Capitalism and the Domestic Economy* (Cambridge: Cambridge University Press, 1975).

Melhuus, Marit, 'The Troubles of Virtue: Values of Violence and Suffering in a Mexican Context', in Signe Howell (ed.), *The Ethnographies of Moralities* (London: Routledge, 1997), pp. 83–94.

Melhuus, Marit, 'Power, Value and Ambiguous Meanings of Gender', in Marit Melhuus and Kristi Anne Stølen (eds), *Machos, Mistresses and Madonnas: Contesting the Power of Latin American Gender Imagery* (London and New York: Verso, 1996), pp. 230–59.

Melhuus, Marit and Kristi Anne Stølen (eds), *Machos, Mistresses and Madonnas: Contesting the Power of Latin American Gender Imagery* (London and New York: Verso, 1996).

Mendoza, Zoila, *Shaping Society through Dance: Mestizo Ritual Performance in the Peruvian Andes* (Chicago: University of Chicago Press, 2000).

Mintz, Sidney, 'Men, Women and Trade', *Comparative Studies in Society and History: An International Quarterly*, vol. 13, no. 3 (1971), Cambridge University Press: pp. 247–69.

Mitchell, Timothy, 'Society, Economy and the State-Effect', in George Steinmetz (ed.), *State/Culture: State Formation After the Cultural Turn* (Ithaca and London: Cornell University Press, 1999), pp. 76–98.

Mitchell, Timothy, *Rule of Experts: Egypt, Techno-Politics, Modernity* (Berkeley: University of California Press, 2002).

Moore, Henrietta, *A Passion for Difference: Essays in Anthropology and Gender* (Cambridge: Polity Press, 1994a).

Moore, Henrietta, 'The Problem of Explaining Violence in the Social Sciences', in Penny Harvey and Peter Gow (eds), *Sex and Violence: Issues in Representation and Experience* (London and New York: Routledge, 1994b), pp. 138–57.

Moore, Henrietta and Todd Sanders, *Magical Interpretations, Material Realities: Modernity, Witchcraft and the Occult in Postcolonial Africa* (London: Routledge, 2001).

Morphy, Howard, 'Landscape and the Reproduction of the Ancestral Past', in Eric Hirsch and Michael O'Hanlon (eds), *The Anthropology of Landscape: Perspectives on Place and Space* (Clarendon: Oxford University Press, 1995), pp. 184–209.

Murra, John Victor, *The Economic Organization of the Inca State* (Greenwich, Connecticut: Jai Press, 1980).

Narotzky, Susana, *New Directions in Economic Anthropology* (London and Chicago: Pluto Press, 1997).

Nash, June (ed.), *We Eat the Mines and the Mines Eat Us: Dependency and Exploitation in Bolivian Tin Mines* (New York: Columbia University Press, 1979).

Nash, June (ed.), *Social Movements: An Anthropological Reader* (Malden, Massachusetts: Blackwell Publishing, 2005).

Nash, June and Helen Icken Safa (eds), *Sex and Class in Latin America: Women's Perspectives on Politics, Economics and the Family in the Third World* (South Hadley, Massachusetts: J.F. Bergin Publishers, 1980).

Nugent, David, 'The Morality of Modernity and the Travails of Tradition', in *Critique of Anthropology*, no. 18 [1] (1998): pp. 7–33.

Nugent, David, 'Before History and Prior to Politics: Time, Space, and Territory in the Modern Peruvian Nation-State', in Thomas Blom Hansen and Finn Stepputat (eds), *States of Imagination: Ethnographic Explorations of the Postcolonial State* (Durham and London: Duke University Press, 2001), pp. 257–83.

Ødegaard, Cecilie V., 'Symbolske Substanser – Om Matens Betydning for Andinsk Subjektivitet', *Replikk*, University of Bergen, no. 8 (5), (1999): pp. 59–68.

Ødegaard, Cecilie V., *A Quest for Progress: Migration, Work and Gender in the Peruvian Andes*, Doctoral dissertation (University of Bergen, 2006).

Ødegaard, Cecilie V., 'From Stigma to Celebration: The (Re-)Generation of Dilemmas in Discourses on Cultural Hybridity', in Alireza Asgharzadeh, Erica Lawson, Kayleen U. Oka and Amar Wahan (eds), *Diasporic Ruptures: Globality, Migrancy, and Expressions of Identity*, vol. 2 (Rotterdam and Taipei: Sense Publishers, 2007), pp. 3–20.

Ødegaard, Cecilie V., 'Informal Trade, Contrabando and Prosperous Socialities in Arequipa, Peru', *Ethnos Journal of Anthropology*, vol.73:2 (June, 2008): pp. 241–66.

Ødegaard, Cecilie V., 'Land and Labour in Processes of Urbanization: The Dialectics between Popular Practices and State Policies in Peru', forthcoming.

Ortner, Sherry, 'Resistance and the Problem of Ethnographic Refusal', *Comparative Studies in Society and History*, Cambridge University Press, no. 37 (1), 1995: pp. 173–93.

Ortner, Sherry, *Making Gender: The Politics and Erotics of Culture* (Boston: Beacon Press, 1996).

Ossio, Juan, *Locality, Kinship and Ceremonial Kinship: A Study of Social Organization of the Communidad de Andamarca, Ayacucho – Peru*, Doctor of Philosophy thesis, Oxford University, 1978.

Ossio, Juan, 'Cultural Continuity, Structure and Context: Some Peculiarities of the Andean Compadrazgo', in Raymond Smith (ed.), *Kinship Ideology and Practice in Latin America* (Chapel Hill and London: The University of North Carolina Press, 1984), pp. 118–46.

Paerregaard, Karstein, *Linking Separate Worlds: Urban Migrants and Rural Lives in Peru* (Oxford: Berg, 1997a).

Paerregaard, Karstein, 'Imagining a Place in the Andes: In the Borderland of Lived, Invented and Analyzed Culture', in Karen Olwig and Kirsten Hastrup (eds). *Siting Culture: The Shifting Anthropological Object* (London: Routledge, 1997b), pp. 39–57.

Parry, J. and M. Bloch (eds), *Money and the Morality of Exchange* (Cambridge: Cambridge University Press, 1989).

Peet, Richard and Michael Watts (eds), *Liberation Ecologies: Environment, Development, Social Movements* (London: Routledge, 1996).

Perlman, J. *The Myth of Marginality: Urban Poverty and Politics in Rio de Janeiro* (Berkeley: University of California Press, 1976).

Pérus, Francoise, 'Dialogism and Historical Bakhtinian Poetics from the Perspective of Cultural Heterogenity and Narrative Transculturation in Latin America', in Rita de Grandis and Zila Bernd (eds), *Unforeseeable Americas: Questioning Cultural Hybridity in the Americas*, vol. 13 (Amsterdam and Atlanta: Critical Studies, 2000), pp. 124–42.

Platt, Tristan, *Espejos y Maís: Temas de la Estructura Simbólica Andina* (La Paz: CIPCA, 1976).

Polanyi, Karl, *The Livelihood of Man* (New York: Academic Books: 1977).

Polar, Antonio Cornejo, 'A Non-Dialectic Heterogenity: The Subject and Discourse of Urban Migration in Modern Peru', in Rita de Grandis and Zila Bernd (eds), *Unforeseeable Americas: Questioning Cultural Hybridity in the Americas*, vol. 13 (Amsterdam and Atlanta: Critical Studies, 2000), pp. 112–23.

Poupeney-Hart, Catherine, 'Mestizaje: "I Understand the Reality, I Just Do Not Like the Word": Perspectives on an Option', in Rita de Grandis and Z. Bernd (eds), *Unforeseeable Americas: Questioning Cultural Hybridity in the Americas*, vol. 13 (Amsterdam and Atlanta: Critical Studies, 2000), pp. 34–55.

Preston-Whyte, Eleanor and Christian Rogerson (eds), *South Africa's Informal Economy* (Cape Town: Oxford University Press, 1991).

Radcliffe, Sarah, 'Ethnicity, Patriarchy and Incorporation into the Nation: female migrants as domestic servants in Peru', *Environment and Planning D: Society and Space*, vol. 8, (1990): pp. 379–93.

Radcliffe, Sarah, 'Imagining the State as a Space: Territoriality and the Formation of the State in Ecuador', in Thomas Blom Hansen and Finn Stepputat (eds), *States of Imagination: Ethnographic Explorations of the Postcolonial State* (Durham and London: Duke University Press, 2001), pp. 123–48.

Ramos, Alcida Rita, *Indigenism: Ethnic Politics in Brazil* (Madison, Wisconsin and London: The University of Wisconsin Press, 1998).

Randall, Robert, 'Qoyllur Rit'I, an Inca Fiesta of the Pleiades: Reflections on Time and Space in the Andean World', *Boletín del Instituto Francés de Estudios Andinos*, vol. 11 (1982): pp. 37–81.

Riofrío, Gustavo, 'Notas Sobre el Problema Habitacional en 'El Otro Sendero', *Bulletin DESCO*, vol. 17, no. 1 (Lima: Centro de Estudios y Promoción del Desarrollo, 1988): pp. 13–17.

Rivera Cusicanqui, Silvia, Denise Arnold, Zulema Lehm, Susan Paulson and Juan de Dios Yapita, *Ser Mujer Indigena, Chola y Birlocha en la Bolivia Postcolonial de los Años 90* (La Paz: Ministerio de Desarrollo Humano, 1996).

Roberts, B.R., *The Making of Citizens: Cities of Peasants Revisited* (London: Arnold, 1995).

Rosaldo, Michelle, 'The Use and Abuse of Anthropology: Reflections on Feminism and Cross-cultural Understanding', *Signs* 5 (3) (Spring 1980): pp. 389–417.

Rose, Nicholas, *Powers of Freedom. Reframing Political Thought* (Cambridge: Cambridge University Press, 1999).

Roseberry, William, 'Hegemony and the Language of Contention', in Joseph Gilbert and Daniel Nugent (eds), *Everyday Forms of State Formation: Revolution and the Negotiation of Rule in Modern Mexico* (Durham: Duke University Press, 1994), pp. 355–66.

Rousseau, Stéphanie, *Women's Citizenship in Peru. The Paradoxes of Neopopulism in Latin America* (New York: Palgrave Macmillan, 2009).

Rubin, Jeffrey, 'Ambiguity and Contradiction in a Radical Popular Movement', in Sonia Alvarez, Evelina Dagnino and Arturo Escobar (eds), *Cultures of Politics, Politics of Cultures: Re-visioning Latin American Social Movements* (Boulder, Colorado and Oxford: Westview Press, 1998), pp. 141–64.

Rudolph, James, *Peru – The Evolution of a Crisis* (Westport: Praeger, 1992).

Safa, Helen Icke, 'Race and National Identity in the Americas', *Latin American Perpectives*, vol. 25, no.3, (1998): pp. 3–20.

Sahlins, Marshall, *Stone Age Economics* (Chicago: Aldine-Atherton, 1972).

Said, Edvard, *Orientalism* (New York: Vintage, 1979).

Saignes, Thierry, 'Indian Migration and Social Change in Seventeenth-century Charcas', in Brooke Larson and Olivia Harris (eds), *Ethnicity, Markets and Migration in the Andes: At the Crossroads of History and Anthropology* (Durham: Duke University Press, 1995), pp. 167–95.

Sallnow, Michael, *Pilgrims of the Andes: Regional Cults in Cuzco* (Washington, DC: Smithsonian Institution, 1987).

Salman, Ton and Anneliez Zoomers (eds), *Imaging the Andes: Shifting Margins of a Marginal World* (Amsterdam: Aksant/CEDLA Latin America studies series, 2003).

Sandoval, Godofredo and Fernanda Sostres, *La Ciudad Prometida: Pobladores y Organizaciones Sociales en el Alto* (La Paz: ILDIS-SYSTEMA, 1989).

Sapir, Edward, *Language: An Introduction to the Study of Speech* (New York: Harcourt, Brace and Company, 1921).

Schild, Veronica, 'New Subjects of Rights: Women's Movements and the Construction of Citizenship in the New Democracies', in Sonia Alvarez, Evelina Dagnino and Arturo Escobar (eds), *Cultures of Politics, Politics of Cultures: Re-visioning Latin American Social Movements* (Boulder, Colorado and Oxford: Westview Press, 1998), pp. 93–117.

Scott, James, *Domination and the Arts of Resistance: Hidden Transcripts* (New Haven: Yale University Press, 1990).

Scott, James, *Seeing Like a State: How Certain Schemes to Improve the Human Condition Have Failed* (New Haven: Yale University Press, 1998).

Seligman, Linda (ed.), *Women Traders in Cross-cultural Perspective: Mediating Identities, Marketing Wares* (Stanford, California: Stanford University Press, 2001).

Seligman, Linda (ed.), *Peruvian Street Lives: Culture, Power, and Economy among Market Women of Cuzco* (Urbana and Chicago: University of Illinois Press, 2004).

Sharma, Aradhana and Akhil Gupta, *The Anthropology of the State: A Reader* (Malden, Massachusetts: Blackwell, 2006).

Sherbondy, Jeanette, 'Water Ideology in Inca Ethnogenesis', in Robert Dover, Katharine Seibold and McDowell (eds), *Andean Cosmologies Through Time: Persistence and Emergence* (Bloomington and Indianapolis: Indiana University Press, 1992), pp. 46–66.

Sieder, Rachel, 'Rethinking Citizenship: Reforming the Law in Post-war Guatemala', in Thomas Blom Hansen and Finn Stepputat (eds), *States of Imagination. Ethnographic Explorations of the Postcolonial State* (Durham and London: Duke University Press, 2001), pp. 203–20.

Signorelli, Amalia, *Antropología Urbana* (Barcelona: Universidad Autonoma Metropolitana, 1999).

Silverblatt, Irene, *Moon, Sun and Witches: Gender Ideologies and Class in Inca and Colonial Peru* (Princeton: Princeton University Press, 1987).

Silverblatt, Irene, 'Mujeres del campesinado en el alto Peru', in Verena Stolcke (ed.), *Mujeres Invadidas: La Sangre de la Conquista de América*, Cuadernos inacabados (Madrid, Horas y Horas, 1990), pp. 47–66.

Simmel, Georg, *The Philosophy of Money* (London: Routledge and Kegan Paul, 1978).

Skar, Harald, *The Warm Valley People: Duality and Land Reform Among the Quechua Indians of Highland Peru* (Oslo: Universitetsforlaget, 1982).

Slaattelid, Rasmus, *Bakhtin's Vitenskapsteori i et Hermeneutisk Perspektiv*. Master's thesis in philosophy, University of Bergen, 1993.

Solomon, Thomas, *Mountains of Song: Musical Constructions of Ecology, Place and Identity in the Bolivian Andes*, PhD thesis, University of Texas at Austin, 1997.

Starn, Orin, *Nightwatch: The Politics of Protest in the Andes* (Durham and London: Duke University Press, 1999).

Starn, Orin, Carlos Iván Degregori and Robin Kirk (eds), *The Peru Reader: History, Culture, Politics* (Durham and London: Duke University Press, 1995).

Steinmetz, G. (ed.), *State/Culture: State-Formation After the Cultural Turn* (Ithaca and London: Cornell University Press, 1999).

Stephen, Lynn, 'Gender, Citizenship and the Politics of Identity', in June Nash (ed.), *Social Movements: An Anthropological Reader* (Malden, Oxford and Victoria: Blackwell Publishing, 2005), pp. 54–69.

Stephenson, Marcia, *Gender and Modernity in Andean Bolivia* (Austin: University of Texas Press, 1999).

Stepputat, Finn, 'Violence, Sovereignty, and Citizenship in Postcolonial Peru', in Thomas Blom Hansen and Finn Stepputat (eds), *Sovereign Bodies: Citizens, Migrants and States in the Postcolonial World* (New Jersey and Oxfordshire: Princeton University Press, 2005), pp. 61–81.

Stern, Steve (ed.), *Resistance, Rebellion, and Consciousness in the Andean Peasant World, 18th–20th Century* (Madison: University of Wisconsin Press, 1987).

Stevens, Evelyn, 'Marianismo: The Other Face of Machismo', in Ann Pescatello (ed.), *Female and Male in Latin America: Essays* (Pittsburgh: University of Pittsburgh Press, 1979), pp. 51–74.

Stolcke, Verena (ed.), *Mujeres Invadidas: La Sangre de la Conquista de América*. Cuadernos inacabados, Horas y Horas, Tan Ceti: Madrid, 1990.

Strathern, Marilyn, *The Gender of the Gift* (Berkeley and Los Angeles: California University Press, 1988).

Stølen, Kristi Anne, *The Decency of Inequality: Gender, Power and Social Change on the Argentine Prairie* (Oslo: Scandinavian University Press, 1996).

Taussig, Michael, *The Devil and Commodity Fetishism in South America* (Chapel Hill: The University of North Carolina Press, 1980).

Thurner, Mark, *From Two Republics to One Divided: Contradictions of Postcolonial Nationmaking in Andean Peru* (Durham: Duke University Press, 1997).

Trouillot, Michael R., 'The Anthropology of the State in the Age of Globalization: Close Encounters of the Descriptive Kind', *Current Anthropology*, 42 (1) (2001): pp. 125–39.

Turner, Victor, *The Forest of Symbols: Aspects of Ndembu Ritual* (Ithaca: Cornell University Press, 1967).

Urciuoli, B., 'Language and Borders', *Annual Review of Anthropology*, vol. 24, (1995).

Urton, Gary, 'Communalism and Differentiation in an Andean Community', in Robert Dover, Katharine Seibold and McDowell (eds), *Andean Cosmologies Through Time: Persistence and Emergence* (Bloomington and Indianapolis: Indiana University Press, 1992), pp. 229–66.

Van den Berghe, Pierre (ed.), *Class and Ethnicity in Peru* (Leiden: E.J. Brill, 1974).

Wagley, Charles, *Minorities in the New World: Six Case Studies* (New York: Columbia University Press, 1958).

Warren, Kay, 'Indigenous Movements as a Challenge to the Unified Social Movement Paradigm for Guatemala', in Sonia Alvarez, Evelina Dagnino and Arturo Escobar (eds), *Cultures of Politics, Politics of Cultures. Re-visioning Latin American Social Movements* (Boulder, Colorado and Oxford: Westview Press, 1998), pp. 165–95.

Weber, Max, *The Protestant Ethic and the Spirit of Capitalism* (London and New York: Routledge, 1930 [1993]).

Weismantel, Mary, *Food, Gender and Poverty in the Ecuadorian Andes* (Philadelphia: University of Pennsylvania Press, 1988).

Weismantel, Mary, *Cholas and Pishtacos: Stories of Race and Sex in the Andes* (Chicago and London: University of Chicago Press, 2001).

Werbner, Pnina and Tariq Modood (eds), *Debating Cultural Hybridity: Multi-cultural Identities and the Politics of Anti-Racism* (London and New Jersey: Zed Books, 1997).

Widmark, Charlotta, *To Make Do in the City: Social Identities and Cultural Transformations among Aymara Speakers in La Paz*, Uppsala Studies in Cultural Anthropology, no.36 (Uppsala: 2003).

Yeager, G. (ed.), *Confronting Change, Challenging Tradition: Women in Latin American History* (Wilmington, Delaware: SR Books, 1994).

Young, Robert J.C., *Colonial Desire: Hybridity in Theory, Culture and Race* (London and New York: Routledge, 1995).

Yudice, Georg, 'The Globalization of Culture and the New Civil Society', in Sonia Alvarez, Evelina Dagnino and Arturo Escobar (eds), *Cultures of Politics, Politics of Cultures: Re-visioning Latin American Social Movements* (Boulder, Colorado and Oxford: Westview Press, 1998), pp. 353–79.

Zavala, Iris M., *Colonialism and Culture: Hispanic Modernisms and the Social Imaginary* (Bloomington and Indianapolis: Indiana University Press, 1992).

Zigon, Jarrett, 'Moral Breakdown and the Ethical Demand: A Theoretical Framework for an Anthropology of Moralities', *Anthropological Theory*, vol. 7(2) (2007): pp. 131–50.

Zulawski, Ann, 'Mujeres Indígenas y la Economía de Mercado en la Bolivia Colonial', in Verena Stolcke (ed.), *Mujeres Invadidas: La Sangre de la Conquista de América*, Cuadernos inacabados (Madrid, Horas y Horas, 1990), pp. 67–92.

Newspapers/Web Sites/Official Sources

Comisión de Formalización de la Propriedad Informal, N 009-99-MTC, Lima 1999.

INEI (Instituto Nacional de Estadística e Informática del Peru), *Censos nacionales*, (1994).

INEI (Instituto Nacional de Estadística e Informática del Peru), *Información Socio Demográfico, Población e indicadores demográficos*, (2002).

INEI (Instituto Nacional de Estadística e Informática del Peru), *Peru en cifras – indicadores demográficos Peru: Población Urbana y Rural 1940–2005*.

La Razón/digital, national newspaper in Bolivia, Monday 16 June.2003-10-08.

La Republica, national newspaper published in Lima, 1/8-2006.

La Republica, national newspaper published in Lima, 1/5-2006.

Ley 13517, Lima 1961.

Ley 28540, Lima 2005.

RED-ADA, December 1998: *Migración y genero*. La Paz.

Index

For Product Safety Concerns and Information please contact our EU representative GPSR@taylorandfrancis.com
Taylor & Francis Verlag GmbH, Kaufingerstraße 24, 80331 München, Germany

www.ingramcontent.com/pod-product-compliance
Ingram Content Group UK Ltd.
Pitfield, Milton Keynes, MK11 3LW, UK
UKHW011002180926
475701UK00004B/512
9781032099323